BACH'S FUGAL WORKS

The First Page of the Keyboard Fugue in E flat from Book 2 of the
"Forty-Eight"

Reproduced from the autograph copy, British Museum

(G.438)

Bach's Fugal Works

With an Account of Fugue Before and After Bach

BY

A. E. F. Dickinson

Lecturer in Music, University of Durham
Author of "The Art of J. S. Bach"

LONDON
SIR ISAAC PITMAN & SONS, LTD.

First published 1956

SIR ISAAC PITMAN & SONS, LTD.
PITMAN HOUSE, PARKER STREET, KINGSWAY, LONDON, W.C.2
THE PITMAN PRESS, BATH
PITMAN HOUSE, BOUVERIE STREET, CARLTON, MELBOURNE
27 BECKETTS BUILDINGS, PRESIDENT STREET, JOHANNESBURG

ASSOCIATED COMPANIES
PITMAN MEDICAL PUBLISHING COMPANY, LTD.
45 NEW OXFORD STREET, LONDON, W.C.I
PITMAN PUBLISHING CORPORATION
2 WEST 45TH STREET, NEW YORK
SIR ISAAC PITMAN & SONS (CANADA), LTD.
(INCORPORATING THE COMMERCIAL TEXT BOOK COMPANY)
PITMAN HOUSE, 381-383 CHURCH STREET, TORONTO

MADE IN GREAT BRITAIN AT THE PITMAN PRESS, BATH
E6—(G.438)

PREFACE

BEFORE I plunge into my subject-matter, some explanation of my
purpose may be in season. After a nodding acquaintance with
Bach's work as a whole, a fresh study of "The Art of Fugue" and,
in the light of it, of the organ fugues and the "Forty-eight," as
fugue *per se*, suggested that here was a piece of historical evolution
worth defining, in its various stages and as the fruit of a coherent
craftsmanship. From there I sought the origins of eighteenth century fugue, and followed the trail from Bach down to the present
day. These travels are recorded, with some conclusions, here.

It may be asked, why go to the trouble? The neglect of the subject as a literary whole is explained in the first chapter, but the
reader may still question the extent of the field surveyed. The
broad answer is, first, that, as the evolution of Bach's technique
becomes clear in the major successive collections, the impetus to
cover his fugal work as completely as possible grows stronger in
any observer of spirit and nice perceptions. Similarly, as the
twisted course of fugue before Bach and its uncertain survival
after his time are assimilated, with their respective problems of too
little or too scattered and then too voluminous evidence, the
desire to impose a pattern of spontaneous or arrested development
or decline, and to enrich it with cumulative instance, becomes
irresistible, without any particular obsession with abstruse know-
ledge or recondite technique. The discovery of a widening background of structural precedent, and of the textural invention
equally necessary to keyboard fugue, has a perpetual fascination,
and the later struggles to keep fugue alive, while different in
quality of appeal, have their critical interest. The incidental
sifting of scanty or elusive evidence (the neglected Bull fantasias
in letter-notation at Vienna, for example) is also a stimulating
challenge to any investigator, once the general unfamiliarity of
terrain and customs is overcome. The main problem is to keep
the subject within bounds, and I have had, indeed, to compress
the first draft considerably, chapter by chapter. This book will

have failed in its intention if it does not send the reader chasing
for fresh evidence or re-examining the recognized examples. It
will not have failed because its net is constantly widening.

Yet it may also be asked, what is the use of remarking that a
comparatively inaccessible piece, printed only in a *Collected Works*
or *Denkmäler* edition or perhaps not even that, is a double fugue
with chromatic tendencies, since for any reader who consults the
reference this information is superfluous, while any one who does
not take that trouble is no wiser. The answer to this is that
"double fugue with chromatic tendencies" (without further
comment) is the most compact way of indicating that here, as
elsewhere, processes made creative by Bach and others were
tried or revived by other composers with varying musicianship,
sometimes surprisingly long before or after his time. Musical
thought is not invalidated by being out of print. If the comment
is purely technical, the correct impression is left of a period or
composer obsessed—in fugue, at least—with nice or ingenious
rhetoric or the mechanically strained expression of semitonal
texture. An aesthetic thrill cannot be claimed for every example
given, even in the most imaginative ears. Nor have I shrunk
from rejecting, in part or whole, many of the fugues of Bach
and other great composers. Books on a composer are commonly
expected to be acts of promotion or nothing. Yet I cannot admit
to a charge of having broken faith with the reader because I have
presumed to point to some substantial failures and crudities in
the hundred and fifty Bach fugues mentioned, and have been
candid about the surrounding music.

But this temper of analysis at the first encounter is not to under-
value the wonderful convergence of creative purpose and technical mastery in Bach's fugues, and in more random, scattered and
spasmodic fashion in the earlier period, with some inspiring
revivals later. On the contrary, the observation of fugue in the
raw, before and after Bach, enhances our appreciation of the
creative force at work in the pieces of exuberant virtuosity, exquisite miniature, structural expansion, or altogether overwhelming expression. Of the outer features and inner motives of these
great or rare works we cannot know too much, in the preliminary

approach. Together they put beyond question the evolution of fugue, up to and including Bach, as a live critical topic, capable of expansion by any inquisitive reader. I have made Bach's own development the main subject and focus, but this does not imply that the other periods and personalities of fugue are of purely historical interest, the concern only of the professional student.

From another point of view, the book may be found lacking in "roundness," owing to superficial or perfunctory treatment at obvious points. This is not to be denied, and there are various reasons for it. As I have hinted, it is expedient to keep this *Companion* to fugue within certain limits, and to preserve a balance between demonstration and allusion. This is a book, not a thesis. If detail is lost, something also is gained by bringing into one orbit of comparison an amazing diversity of periods and passions. Scholars confined to "their" period are not necessarily ideal listeners. Even great composers, each renowned for the cultivation of a particular style, meet more in fugue than in almost any other field. I am satisfied on musical grounds that, apart from the gaps in early records of keyboard music, a larger account would not add much more than personal idiosyncrasy and corroboration in principle. And I frankly do not intend to spend another six years in the byways of fugue, even if it is J. S. Bach's, having already pushed aside juster claims on my time in order to complete this sketch. On that understanding I offer the reader this survey to fill the present gap in historical studies. If he classes it eventually as a Prolegomenon, I shall be flattered. It will mean that the subject is established, and its vital place in musical history provisionally documented and appraised.

Finally, in a wide field with a rich play of ideas and patterns of appreciation and sheer "reading," it is not always easy to register the personal origins of an interpretation or discovery long since taken for granted, but if I have here and there advanced original concepts or information without acknowledgment I hereby express in advance my regrets to the individual concerned. Oddly enough, it seems more compliment to adopt a given view, as being a true and legitimate one, than to father it on a particular brain, and, when in the past I have "suffered" in this way, I have made the most of this consolation. In general, apart from titles, dates and provenance, I draw my conclusions from personal hearing, yesterday, today and (where certitude is complete) while life shall last.

A. E. F. DICKINSON

DURHAM
March, 1955

CONTENTS

Chapter I

INTRODUCTORY

THE art of music has grown from ritual and the dramatic rehearsal of legends and other symbolic experience, but it has expanded increasingly on its own. In the process certain types of sound-relationship have crystallized and formed a deposit of experience, fluid in detail but firm in pattern, for a considerable period. From time to time, under the control of a strong and decisive artistic personality, not only principles of composition but details of personal custom have acquired a peculiar authenticity. In this manner music has presented its own dialectic and its own judgments of value. Most audiences of today, in city hall and on the domestic hearth, accept symphonic expression as the prime concern of composers since the time of J. S. Bach, along with the less calculable trends of opera and music-drama on and off the stage. From organized classes to individual enterprise, a growing minority of listeners are setting out to listen and learn, and amongst other things to assimilate the changing patterns of expression which have marked the development of the symphony from one composer to another, and in signal instances from one work to another.

That flight of theme which musicians call fugue has made a much vaguer impression. Limited in most cases to a single mood and movement, and having been developed waywardly and circumstantially before and after Bach, in spite of number-less attempts, it has made an uncertain impact on listening experience. Even in the case of Bach's fugues, the salient developments and recurrences of type from the earlier to the later periods have yet to become common experience. Nor has much discrimination of quality been established between the competent and the compelling, between serious and light-hearted pieces. Beethoven's piano sonatas still enjoy comprehensive recital, and in many homes their varied humours and structural surprises are

I

common household knowledge. Bach's deliverances remain isolated, unrelated and widely unrecognized. His technical procedure has in part been studiously tabulated and debated, chiefly as demonstrations of craftsmanship for the notice of students, but most writers are so much concerned with correct and fluent treatment on the canonic side (answer and *stretto*) that they have little space for anything else. The contrapuntal and episodic invention, the amazing structural versatility, and many other characteristic features which strike the ear of an observant listener who is not interested in grammatical niceties or technical display, have received scant notice.

Above all, justice has not been done to the growth of Bach's mind in fugue from the breezy competence of the mature organ works to the exquisite craftsmanship of the "Forty-eight," from the richly episodic quality of the Chromatic and kindred fugues to the serene concentration of the second E major and B flat minor fugues, and from the unfaltering but fortuitous resource of the "Forty-eight" to the logical sequence of "The Art of Fugue," a historical demonstration of fugue *per se*. There are some useful books on the various collections, from Harvey Grace's still pertinent survey of the organ fugues in *The Organ Works of Bach* to Tovey's *Companion to "The Art of Fugue*," but none to define the underlying unity of these broad stages of Bach's creative evolution. Even Parry is perfunctory on this point, and he is oddly unsympathetic to the sheer musical appeal of "The Art of Fugue." Foreign studies have been equally specialized.

The adventurous listener who has a piano and a capable pianist or two at his command may make up his mind, none the less, to settle his account with Bach's fugues as a whole. He finds himself confronted with a body of creative and concentrated experience in a style he rarely meets elsewhere. Some working knowledge of the forms these fugues commonly take becomes an immediate necessity, and, since there is almost no indication of order, beyond the known dates of completion of the three main keyboard collections, an order of survey must be sought which distinguishes the styles in each collection in turn, as Bach did in his last set.

The present volume is an attempt to provide such an explorer with a comprehensive study of Bach's fugues, as a body of practical composition which happens to constitute the chief, perhaps the sole, landmark of fugal expression. As the listener becomes more aware of the complexity of the subject, he will find it more and more troublesome to be vague on salient points. First, then, will come a broad definition of what fugue meant to Bach as a recurring title. Next, the main stages of Bach's progress will be followed in convenient subdivisions, according to method or scale of composition. The gradual survey of the organ and keyboard works will be supplemented by a chapter on the choral fugues. The main ground covered, we may go on to consider Bach's art in its general technical aspects. Here the comparative analysis of texture and structure may even be of use to fugue-examination students, whose aim is not likely to go far beyond writing "what Bach would have done," as a coach once modestly described to a pupil his solution of a fugal problem. This chapter may also jog creative minds to a more realistic conception of fugal possibilities in fresh contexts. But it is primarily addressed, as always, to the critical *listener* who, not content with personal reactions to successive fugues, wishes to know why the forms are (or are not) fair, and by what common pursuits of rhetorical device and musical invention Bach achieves a characteristic and coherent appeal in fulfilment of the initial statement. Such investigation may reveal standards by which the methods and experiments of other fugal composers may be assessed. After this, I shall try to place Bach's fugues in the context of the long and often tortuous growth of fugue up to his time, with special reference to the development of its precursor, fantasia, in English and other hands. I shall then summarize the progress of fugue after Bach, partly as a measure of the permanence of Bach's principles of craftsmanship. From that aftermath the impact of fugue upon musical experience, of which Bach gave so historical a demonstration, may be estimated in the light of present know-ledge, and the future of fugue (if any) judged accordingly. In the process, the reader will encounter, incidentally, Byrd and Orlando Gibbons, Mozart and Haydn, Beethoven and Brahms, Vaughan Williams and Hindemith, and other distinguished names. In surveying and passing judgments on so wide a field I may seem sometimes, to authorities on special periods, to display an amateur non-conformity with accepted estimates, not least in the omission of names, but this risk of showing unreasonable apathy must be taken for the sake of the larger perspective that may be gained by considering fugal potentialities and standards through the ages. Moreover, a more realistic attention to the fugues of the classical and romantic periods is overdue, and the fantasias of the Renaissance are rarely considered for their musical worth.

What is more, a general pattern of expression will have been observed in its early growth from a hazardous and provisional method of beginning a piece to a more uniform process, and from its masterly exploitation and refinement in the hands of Bach to its insouciant revival by Mozart, its vital incorporation by Beethoven in wider structures, and the breezy and complacent reflections of *l'ancien régime* which distinguished the worthies and unworthies of Victorian oratorio and caused Wagner infinite mirth. So to the last period of questionable revival, or of application so metaphorical as to be no more than a matter of texture. Basically there can be no further "Art of Fugue" series, as there may be another Choral Symphony. The original deposit of experience is burnt out, for the making of a whole piece on or around one subject, let alone eighteen pieces. A phoenix may arise from the ashes, but it will not be fugue as so far understood. Fugal practice will doubtless continue to exercise the island race behind academic walls, but it will be derivative, unnecessary construction, educationally justifiable but no disturbance of a history that is past and done with.

It may be asked, why concentrate on Bach's *fugues*? The answer is, first, that they represent the most methodical type of composition Bach attempted, and its elaborations are far more substantive than the arbitrary variants, for example, of so elastic a form as the *ritornello* plan of aria and concerto-movement. Further, as a single key to the working of Bach's mind, fugue opens nearly all the main doors. It played congregations out of church from his first appointment onwards, it took keyboard students on numberless swift or extended journeys of the imagination, and it led the devout from the exultant committal of "God's Time is the Best" to the deeper verities of "Kyrie eleison," "Confiteor in unum Baptisma" and "Dona nobis pacem." If there is to be a cross-sectional approach to Bach's art, fugue is the obvious choice. Moreover, where a fugue derives its full force of expression from its context, that context will receive due consideration. The companion preludes will thus come under frequent notice.

For later composers fugue has been a special resort or an unusual obsession. Nevertheless, a comparison of the great masters and others on this nominally common ground has its peculiar interest. Similarly, the preliminary use of fugue, as a method of opening or continuing rather than as a whole pattern of development, remains with Variation the chief line of early instrumental music on an extended scale. The confusion of the two, from Sweelinck onwards, has, indeed, been fugue's evil spirit, for the purist, and for broader ears at least fugue's most redoubtable imp.

On the straight Bachian route a certain monotony, of routine concentration on one *Affekt*, must be faced; and there are over a hundred playable fugues by Bach alone. A pianist (with a second player for the pedal part of the organ fugues) has a considerable advantage. The fugues were written for performance, not to illustrate Prout, as one might suppose from that worthy's *Fugue* and *Fugal Analysis*. For a composer to whom music was chiefly a family or church activity, the address to a listener did not enter his consciousness as it did Handel's. The modern listener must bridge the gap by listening in a performing spirit, which includes as accurate a perception as possible of what is to be played. For anything beyond a general understanding of Bach's intentions, access to the written music is well-nigh essential, and inevitably many details will be identified here by reference to the printed page. (The minimum outlay is not exorbitant in proportion to the output. One guinea should secure the "Forty-eight" and "The Art of Fugue." Another guinea will fill many gaps. The only waste for a slender purse will be in the organ works, owing to the absurd jumble of mature and immature works in most volumes of any edition available.)

The journey is long, if it is to be reasonably comprehensive and remembered in the heart, not by a mere entry in a diary in tourist fashion. The listener must at his own pace make Bach's often advanced contrapuntal thinking his own, and that pace cannot be forced. Bach's freedom of expression is astounding, and, when the listener becomes aware of it, he will know he is going where Bach went—and not merely when he can identify the canonic and contrapuntal *tours de force* on which Bach occasionally drew. The actual time of total performance, however, is quite measurable. Eighteen hours (three hours daily for a week) would cover two hearings of most of the fugues. From a selection of these the alert listener can take his bearings, decide which groups have most interest for him, and broaden acquaintance at his leisure. An approximation to Bach's general order of composition is, however, essential in the long run, and in this survey the outline of each stage will naturally take the previous steps for granted.

Some readers, and some reviewers I could name, will find it irksome to follow the contrapuntal and harmonic analysis of the texture given here. Nevertheless, this book is intended for the curious, rather than for the would-be learned, listener. If there is perceptible elaboration or refinement in the music, it will not be concealed either in cloudy metaphor or obscure under-statement. Technical terms cannot be avoided. Some will appear in the next chapter, and the glossary at the end of the book may fill in gaps. But these terms will be used for economy, not to display the superiority of the more closely informed. Key-changes, for example, are a constant feature of fugal punctuation, and an obvious pointer to midway reference for the ear. They will generally be named by their relation to the tonic or main key (subdominant, etc.), not by their nominal pitch (e.g. D minor), because this is what matters to the ear. Every major and every minor key admits, respectively, an accession to common relative keys and, if called for, uncommon and remote ones. The established literary terms for the seven degrees of the scale, which define the range of such modulations from the central key, only involve four root words (tonic, mediant, dominant, leading-note), and as a recurring key-base is observed in successive instances in different fugues, the name will increasingly suggest the sound relation and its stimulating or relaxing associations. Repeated references to one such relative key will naturally indicate (far more immediately than the name of the key) Bach's set habits of thought, and perhaps a lapse into routine. Constant references to such abiding corners of fugue are inevitable, just as no account of a number of Gothic cathedrals could avoid innumerable references to nave and transept and the rest. Fugue is more variable in shape and size than the cruciform pattern of a cathedral, but it is regular in its pursuit of one main symbol along central and side aisles of key.

Apart from key, there is a great deal of pertinent detail, by the observation of which one becomes most aware of the kind of decisions that make a collection of fugues historical or not. Today this island is full of noises that delight and hurt not, of crafty miscellanies that go in by one ear and out at the other. The more radiogenic, the quicker forgotten. As the common listener is thus whisked from programme to programme, he is sometimes beguiled into believing that he has grasped the intention of the music by swallowing some honeyed, "poetical" epithet or succulent metaphor, or at least by imbibing date and occasion of composition. Most of Bach's fugues defy such aids to dull ears. There is nothing for it but to listen and listen, as Bach passes from one pursuit of theme for its own sake to another. There is rarely a prophetic meaning or religious doctrine or mass-consciousness round the corner; not even a time-spirit, for fugue has never been fashionable, or historically necessary at a particular time. Yet the faithfulness of the music to the chosen text is more than stimulating. It is one of the assurances of the power of the human mind, both to overcome the most humdrum or recalcitrant material, and to make the revealing categorically imperative. Such music claims close hearing, not the quaffing of an idle moment.

Chapter II

THE NATURE AND STRUCTURE
OF FUGUE

FUGUE originated as a method of beginning or continuing a piece, namely, by releasing a phrase in varying points of the harmony—top, bottom or middle—usually by a process of weaving two or three strands cumulatively round the first, which has given rise to the fallacy that fugue is merely a texture. By the time of Bach, fugue had extended to a complete composition, and its structure, although entirely elastic in size and shape, admits of broad definition. The simplest way to form a concrete but reasonably comprehensive conception of Bach's fugue, on the slender scale, is to listen to the first two fugues of the "Forty-eight." Certain common features are noticeable at once: the initial tightening of a weave of sound around a short but characteristic phrase which appears to be taken up by different "voices," close or more separate recurrences of that phrase, now palpably the main theme, with fresh features of accompaniment, and the disposition of these entries in stages of statement, development and a less explicit return.

In most respects the two fugues follow different courses. In the C minor, which happens to be the more normal of the two, the two-bar theme, conventionally termed "subject," is a rhythmic entity, and its impact is felt clearly each time. It is usually attended by the accompanying figure of the second entry, which becomes a "counter-subject." Between these entries come various short connecting passages or "episodes," here derived from subject or counter-subject. A subtle oscillation of primary and episodic phrases thus makes itself felt, and may be compared with the interplay of set refrain and impromptu incident in a concerto-movement, on a miniature scale.

In the C major fugue, the subject is altogether less integral, and its persistence in the texture becomes a stylistic feature rather than a rhythmic impact. Development is effected by the delivery of the subject in close canon (*stretto* or tightened entry) at incredibly variable intervals of rhythm and pitch, with free movement elsewhere in the texture. A succession of resourcefully and contrapuntally contrived interlacing sentences, punctuated by a change of key midway (bars 12–13), unfolds with steady relevance from start to finish. There are no interludes, and incidentally no counter-subject, the subject being perpetually both Point (i.e. a series of pricks on the paper) and Counterpoint.

In the C minor fugue, then, counter-subject and episode seem essential attachments of fugue, in the C major close canon, each exclusively. The former is the commoner type in Bach, from the earliest organ fugues to "The Art of Fugue." The *stretto* or close-entry type recurs in the keyboard works, but very exceptionally without any episode. However, both fugues are characteristic of Bach and have several parallels, and it is obvious that each represents a different tradition. This divergence may briefly be traced back to its source.

Imitation of phrase was constantly pursued by Bach's predecessors, Pachelbel especially, in treating the successive lines of a hymn-tune. Sometimes only one line was taken. Variety had then to be sought in the fresh harmony of rhythmically close imitation at convenient and varied melodic intervals. In certain fugues, some the greatest, Bach kept almost entirely to his subject by this traditional method. Among choral fugues "Gratias agimus" (B minor Mass) springs to mind. In the "Forty-eight," the first fugue led to the D and E major fugues of the second Book. In general, however, fugue on the keyboard could not readily harp on one theme, without the vocal declamation to give it meaning. The movement of the performer's wandering fingers, spacing out subject-entries with free interludes, had structural common sense behind it. In Bach's organ fugues such episodes tend at first to be perfunctory and insouciant. The establishment of a firmer relation between these and the subject-entries marks his first progress in fugue. The piquant relevancy of the C minor fugue is thus the product of a mature choice of matter and style, not of fugal routine. Alternatively, episodes set up contrary interests, as in the second F sharp fugue. In either case Bach's approach to fugue was by way of subject and episode, and "research" or subject-centred fugues became a matter of making episodes redundant. The latter form the exceptions that prove the rule, which is a balance of subject and episode.

The typical stages of a Bach keyboard fugue may thus be codified roughly as follows, allowing for the variant turns of other fugues. (References below will be to the first Book of the "Forty-eight," where not otherwise stated.)

1. The subject is delivered in each of the imaginary voices which make up the texture. The second voice answers the first a fifth higher (or a fourth lower), apart from an initial modification of detail which will be explained in Chapter XVI. Usually a bracing stretch of key to the dominant is effected or implied. A slight but characteristic *codetta* or extension may follow (C minor, bars 5–6). Otherwise the remaining voice or voices will continue the process of statement and possibly rejoinder in a fresh compass, as in a choral opening. The accompaniment of the second entry may establish itself as a counter-subject, as in the C minor, but equally often fresh counterpoint is expedient. To speak of "the counter-subject" as an inevitable concomitant is both pedantic and unscholarly.

After this minimum exposition, an extra entry in the same orbit of key may be convenient (E flat), or a further *set* of entries, more casual in number and order of appearance and enriched with new detail, may form a spontaneous counter-exposition (C major, bars 7–11). The C minor fugue establishes its intentions in a single set of entries, and this type is fairly common.

The provenance of subject and fugue is thus indicated, in brief or on a broader scale, by a highly stylized method which it is Bach's art to conceal by cross-rhythmic interest, variant voicing (as between top, bass and middle), a modicum of interlude, and all the fastidious detail which makes the music living and unpredictable. Subsequent entries need not be multiplied by the number of chosen voices. A single entry in a fresh key is token enough of one diversion, and one final entry is sufficient. There is no need whatever to re-establish the basic weave as at first. In the D major fugue, indeed, there is no proper "final" entry at all.

2. After due exposition, the subject may be expected to develop in fresh contexts of key, accompaniment and voicing, which may range from the two brief allusions of the C minor to the sustained argument of the C sharp minor. The circle may be completed by one deft entry in the main key (B flat fugue), or it may gradually enhance the sense of conclusion (C minor, bars 20 to end; C major, bars 14 to end). The general intention is to vary the settings of the subject, not to involve it, as in a Beethoven sonata-development, in fantastic contrasts of mood, release from which will be the concern of a reprise. Contrapuntal interest (exploiting subject, counter-subject or fresh figures) may press the impact of the subject further, but in Bach it will be invariably anticipated in earlier entries.

3. It is in keeping with this singleness of conception, in which a prodigal cultivation of material and a resourceful exhibition of one motive may equally be means to creative fulfilment, that the intervening episodes are primarily connecting passages. Their purpose is to lead from one entry to the next, and this usually means leading into the next key. If, as in the organ fugues as a whole, the basic phrases are extemporized, this wayward rhetoric will enhance the return of the subject. But episodes may be made more organic, whether they refer to the subject (B flat fugue) or set up their own interest in the first episode and develop that (E flat fugue, bars 8–10). In Bach's maturest fugues this balance of subject and episode is a constant interest. Yet fugal episodes must not be considered on the same plane as the episodes of a rondo, which are essentially an escape from the main subject into a new theme and mood. Here they are, at most, a means of spacing out the entries. In the fugue in C, episodes are not called for, the transforming counterpoint of the subject in canon with itself (elsewhere, of a counter-subject) being variant enough.

An acquaintance with these later developments may prompt passing identifications of a maturer touch, promise of a more refined art, as one listens to Bach's early essays in fugue.

Chapter III

ORGAN WORKS

I. APPRENTICESHIP

WHEN he was fifteen and had to leave school, or at least to earn while he learnt, Bach became a chorister at Lüneburg. At the neighbouring church Böhm exhibited chorale-adornment, and young Bach began composition with some sets of chorale-variations: the antithesis of true fugue, in its set pattern of fixed phrases repeated. Nevertheless, by promoting contrapuntal figures ("Christ, der du bist der helle Tag," verses 2 and 3) and firm harmonic progressions ("O Gott, du frommer Gott," verse 8) these variations stored factors of poise and gravity, without which organ fugue may become volatile, elusive or obscure.

Gratifying as the organ fugues sound on the piano (with a second player), with the graded emphasis of inner parts there available, Bach cannot (or should not) have thought of the texture except as a changing manifold of more and of less subject-centred harmony and interlude. To "bring out the subject," as if the rest were unfit for human ears, mars the intrinsic contrasts of organ voicing, as between top, manual bass, pedal bass (normally in octaves) and barely audible inner voice. Constant changes of pipe-combination similarly disturb the continuity of style, and even the broadest dynamic grading is apt to jolt the ear as the big diapasons come on or off. Pronounced artificial overtones (mixture stops) in the foundation tone of a fugue are also tiresome and in fact baroque in many cases. Whether or not Bach's organs promoted such colouring, any decision on the type of tone and organ needed—I do not propose to express any detailed opinion at the present stage of fresh but scarcely established experiment—must submit to the test of clarity. Most modern organs call either for compromise, if the main strength of the

12

organ is to be used at some point, or—the one stop on which Parratt used sometimes to play the G minor to demonstrate the sufficiency of the music in this extreme simplicity. The bigger fugues call for warmth of tone sooner or later, but this does not mean the addition of a premature or preponderant 16-ft (lower octave) tone or a discordantly open Swell. The best registration for a fugue is that in which one is least conscious of it. I recall such a rendering of the "Dorian" D minor by Walford Davies on the late lamented Temple Church organ, without disrespect for the present age.

Bach's first appointment was as violinist in the orchestra of the younger Duke of Weimar—a fruitful contact—but he then obtained the charge of the new organ of twenty-six stops in the New Church at Arnstadt. Here the choir-boys from the local school were heftily beyond the choirmaster's control, and he soon stopped rehearsing anthems. This left him free to wander over the noisy keys. Preludes and fantasias accrued, and also fugues.

The new organ had a pedal "trombone," but apparently the new organist's technique discouraged a pedal entry till the last moment. So much may be inferred from the crude FUGUE IN C MINOR (beginning with four quarter-beats*). The long, repetitive subject, vigorous in outline, suffers delivery in tonic or dominant eight times before the pedal enters, none distinctive. At the pedal entry Bach drives a coach-and-four through the counterpoint, substituting sallies of jaunty syncopation or blunt emphasis. Finally, a dashing sweep of whisking clusters of sound drops on to one sonorous chord. Yet behind this shallow craftsmanship there are vitality and pattern in the subject, the later counterpoint, and the final bravura. Another early FUGUE IN G (beginning D–E–E–E) maintains its text and four-part texture faithfully to the end of its ninety-six bars, with varied key and episodes, but it goes on too long. It usually rests on the shelf, while the C minor still attracts many aspirants, eager to muddle through. On a wet morning its boyish stoicism and dash are at least heartening. W. T. Best used to captivate his Liverpool audiences by drawing a fresh

* See Note on page 19.

stop for each entry but keeping *piano* up to a quick outburst of
tone before a thundering pedal entry.

After a few years at Arnstadt and one at Mühlhausen (which no
organ fugue records) Bach became organist to the reigning duke at
Weimar. Here he settled down to develop his organ technique,
and in the process wrote most of his extant works for the instrument, and presumably many others. Several works have survived only in copies, and we can but guess the tale of lost autographs. The twenty-odd fugues available show that the fugal
pattern suited Bach's slowly developing creative impulses. In
what order these were written cannot be determined with certainty, but early, late and later trends are manifest, and the
persistent effort at one style after another, each reinforcing the
next, conveys an assured feeling of progress.

The still popular "short" FUGUE IN G MINOR of sixty-eight bars
must be in the early Weimar period, but it leaves the youthful
C minor far behind. The five-bar subject is plain but melodious
at the start, and the recurrent counter-subject makes durable
harmony. The four-part texture is capricious, the manuals
dropping a part when the pedal enters, and recovering it at a most
casual point (bar 45). But this porousness is concealed by the flow
of what counterpoint there is. A timely change of key to the
major (bar 33) lends power to the final entries in subdominant
and tonic. The longest and last of the stray interludes is readily
absorbed by the returning subject, supported by fresh counterpoint. Altogether the subject is competently exhausted and
abandoned by turns. Here is a fugue for the capable young
organist of all ages.

The rhythmic sweep of a contemporary FUGUE IN G in $\frac{12}{8}$,
commonly known as the "jig" fugue, may carry many listeners off
their feet, if only at the last entry, but the forthright rhythm and
pertinacious sequence which attend each entry are apt to pall, and
the extensive episodes are based on slender sequential* material.
Bach seems to have said all that he wished to say here, and more,
in the brief and balanced fugal finale of the fifth French suite for
keyboard. The short and contrasted "little" FUGUE IN E MINOR,

* See Glossary.

which begins with two mordents or flourishes round one note, moves with a heavy gait, not relieved by a change of key, but it has perhaps a refreshing gravity and disdain of mere finger-activity, for which the poignant sequences of the prelude prepare the ear. It is the slow learner's opportunity.

These, then, were the varied trends of fugal experiment. Which would go further? In the first place, the way of exhaustive virtuosity, as exemplified in the fugues in G (starting with D–D–D–B), D and D minor (flowing quarter-beats), with which may be placed the fugue which ends the Toccata, Adagio and Fugue in C. The FUGUE IN G runs to 149 bars, chiefly by sheer repetition, with a key-interest that extends to the mediant minor (bar 83) and slight sequential episodes derived from the arpeggio figures of the second bar. The style is laboured and in fact North-German, but at a good spanking pace the final entries in the tonic can sound positive and not redundant, the last (pedal) being an acceptable rhetorical substitute for the subject. The playful and elusive FUGUE IN D also achieves its 137 bars by ready accumulation of entry, with a very considerable key-interest. After tonic and dominant for seven entries, the normal route to the submediant and mediant minor (bars 53, 64) leads on to the remote key of the leading-note minor and the equally remote and, as it happens, very rare supertonic major (bars 79, 91). After these excursions and an expectant penultimate episode (bars 101–18), the full pedal entry in the tonic, oddly anticipated by two bars of vibrating tonic harmony, seems decisive, and the coda inadequate and redundant. In all editions the fugue is preceded by a prelude, on the strength of a manuscript belonging to Nicolai, accepted by Griepenkerl for the Peters edition. This prelude encloses a very voluble section of sequential treatment with a rhapsodic introduction and close. The final emotional intensity posits a fugue of calm resolution. The Fugue in D is incredibly insouciant in this context. If it is an intentional rejoinder to a somewhat pretentious prelude, this Ustinov touch is not the hand of the Bach we know elsewhere. Apart from the challenge to muscular control (toe and heel), there is not a strong call to revive this fugue, but, when it is played, it is best rendered as a *jeu d'esprit* in itself.

The now almost famous TOCCATA AND FUGUE IN D MINOR
(fugue in quarter-beats) has of late years travelled near and far
from its original provenance, chiefly on account of the Toccata,
whose ungovernable repetitions have a persuasive touch of wild
nature about them; Pirro detected thunder, wind and hail there!
One can readily understand a conductor-arranger thinking, "But
how much more vivid on the live orchestra!" and going to it
with gusto. On the organ, the Toccata sweeps the listener
masterfully enough into the most prodigal of fugues. The entries
of the two-bar rotary formula which poses as subject are so much
spaced out after the answer that it takes twenty-three bars to
cover all four voices, and throughout the 113-bar fugue free
episodes continue to occupy far the greater room. In the final
section, the subject returns no less than three times in the tonic,
the second time exposed floundering on the pedal, solo. The rest
is whirling rhetoric. The tonality altogether misses the firm disposition which might have kept these diversions in shape. The
answer is in the subdominant, and this move to the flat side of the
key, never adjusted by a single entry in the dominant, is confirmed
in later entries, which go as far as the leading-note minor.* Some
listeners will detect a curious anticipation of a weakness of
Schumann. The general listener may not worry at first, but, once
recognized, the unbalance gives an enervating tilt to the music.
There is something about this dashing fugue which is greater than
these idiosyncrasies, as audiences have not been slow to perceive,
but it is the appeal of the flamboyant and unexpected, not of close
weaving or firm design.

The weaknesses of the FUGUE IN C MAJOR ($^6_8$) are more deep-
seated. It starts with plenty in its favour: an imposing toccata in
the virtuoso style and a piquant adagio in A minor, which regains
C major in an impressive aftermath. But the subject could only
maintain a fugue in which it was systematically and artfully
neglected. It must hold an all-comers record for length (nine
bars) and tiresome insistence. Since it modulates from tonic to
dominant, the answer must reverse the process.† This gravitation

---

* Cf. the fugue of the Concerto and Fugue in C minor (Bach Society edition,
Vol. 42), of uncertain authorship but to my ears genuine early Bach.
† For the explanation of this type of answer, see Chapter XVI.

to the tonic soon begins to pall, however, and it is aggravated by a counter-exposition of answer, subject and answer, seventy-one bars in all. The remaining seventy bars relieve the monotony of key but not of subject, and the separation of entries by long episodes prolongs the tedium. Where is the "wonderful pathos" which Schweitzer (in his early enthusiasm) divined here, as in the D major fugue; or the "gay and genial" qualities which Parry found in the same fugue? No nine-bar phrase can suffer sevenfold exposition and retain its geniality, if any.

Somewhere at this point, indeed, Bach, tired of bravura, turned to Italian composers for fresh models. In the FUGUE IN C MINOR (beginning with three Cs) he took a subject by the Venetian composer, Legrenzi, and worked it into a double-fugue, based on Legrenzi's subject, a second subject, and the combination, all on a small scale. The upshot is wearisome. The first fugue wears thin and closes in a state of decline; the artificial second subject does no better; and the combination is equally inconclusive, as the subsequent cadenza of free rhetoric seems to admit. Legrenzi's subject modulates to the dominant and thus the answer slides back to the tonic, as in the fugue last considered. Hence the second subject, in order to combine later, does the same. Each fugue suffers from this brake on the harmonic momentum, except for one genuine answer modulating from the dominant in the third fugue. But this raw encounter, worth tons of theory, struck a creative spark, for Bach returned more than once to double-fugue, with all the impediments removed, and his last work was a quadruple fugue.

In another fugue he tried double-fugue from the start. He expanded to over 100 bars a short FUGUE by Corelli IN B MINOR (from the fourth sonata, Op. 3). The two subjects appear at two bars' distance. In this loose two-strand weave the main subject, a, is melodious; the other subject, b, is incisive and determines the harmonic gait of a. Towards the end b appears a third higher than usual, or doubled a third lower (bars 75, 94); after which, a return to the normal combination falls rather flat. Bach was not drawn, as Handel often was, to this kind of double-fugue, for his only return to it was at the end of the Passacaglia, where an immediate second subject was an inevitable addition to a theme already exploited as ground-bass. He preferred to let each subject set up its own current of rhythm first. In one example he developed two motives together in a different sense. In the fugal PRELUDE ON A "MAGNIFICAT" TONE, Tonus Peregrinus, the Tone (first phrase) is at once accompanied by a counter-subject, which not only combines with the Tone at several intervals (bars 11, 57, 76 showing it relatively a third, a fifth, a sixth lower than originally) and with melodic inversion (bars 10, 55, 75) but supplies the material for most of the abundant episodes. The Tone itself furnishes blunt cross-rhythm by means of close canon (bars 56, 76), and for climax enters on the pedal, here an extra "voice," in

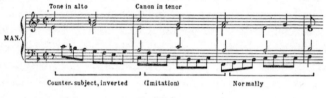

Example 1

the splendid deliberation of half the usual speed, a mannerism duly maintained (else an excrescence) in the second phrase of the Tone. Thus Bach capped the workaday efforts of Cabezón, Scheidt, Pachelbel and others, assembling numberless preludes on "Magnificat" Tones in all the modes,* with a masterful fugue of 136 bars on an "impossible" subject. This is not to class such exuberant craftsmanship as "sublime" (Schweitzer). Its voluble rhetoric is, indeed, remote from the original outburst of *Magnificat mea anima Dominum.* There is a choral fugue on the same Tone, shaped into a neat three-bar subject, in a setting of the German version† by Zachow, Handel's master. It has an instrumental bass throughout to keep up the rhythm, and by ignoring the second phrase makes the key F major.

Another work of Italian origin, the CANZONA IN D MINOR, derives its method from Frescobaldi's "Fiori musicali." Here a

---

* See Chapter XVII. Cf. the early *Magnificat* (Leningrad), No. 9.
† *Denkmäler Deutscher Tonkunst,* Vols. XXI–II.

subject and a rather trite semitonal figure are developed together in a two-beat measure, and then reappear in triple measure, expanded fugally with a fatal similarity of harmonic sequence. Bach never repeated this scheme in the same fugue, but he remembered it, perhaps, in "The Art of Fugue," when, after eleven exhaustive essays in duple metre, he put the main subject into triple rhythm for the first pair of "mirror" fugues.

The Italian contact was less immediately valuable for the double-fugue than for a certain shapeliness of outline with which the contumacious bravura of Buxtehude, for example, was not concerned. The next group of fugues reveals the consummation of this more melodious "Southern" style.

NOTE

(*Page* 13) The lack of an authoritative and coherent edition of the organ works calls for such practical indications of identity where there are several fugues in the same key. The citation of the number of bars may be an additional check in some instances.

Chapter IV

ORGAN WORKS

II. GROWING MASTERY

THE seven fugues which show a more Italian and vocal style may well be the surviving portion of a larger output, for three or four of them cannot have taxed Bach's invention, once begun. All seven have preludes in a developed pattern, or in an almost lyrical mood, not in the extempory cast of the earlier preludes. Some preludes are perceptibly more advanced or pronounced, and therefore presumably later, than their fugues, but our concern is with fugal progress. On that ground the fugues may be placed in the following conjectural order: (*a*) F minor, C minor (starting with two-beat notes), C minor (starting off the beat), C (four ascending notes), and A; (*b*) F major; (*c*) D minor (the "Dorian," ascending from keynote). Certain signs of a surer final grasp are unmistakable, and in the lack of any other evidence the maturing process followed the temporal succession. Even if the composer sometimes took a step sideways or backwards, it is the advance that matters, not when it occurred. The next group, indeed, are almost reactionary in style, and may have overlapped the present one. The Italian conquest remains a coherent achievement from similar polyphonic impulses.

The PRELUDE IN F MINOR develops in two generous stages which call for more, and *faute de mieux* the one extant FUGUE IN F MINOR must fill the gap; whether rightly or not, is hard to say. The new vocalism displays a concise, rather trenchant subject, a good reserve of passing counter-subjects and an assured five-voice polyphony. All the same, this 138-bar fugue overdoes it, if a listener is to be served, not just a congregation waiting for something else to take place. The sixty-odd bars of connective matter are mainly short and thin extensions of entries, especially the trite

sequence of the last episode-link. The subject reaches full
counter-exposition and passes into the relative major (bars 47,
73), but is otherwise confined to tonic and dominant, which
exposes the rather forced counterpoint. Two final entries in the
dominant, leaving the tonic to be regained in the peroration,
make an odd finish, definitive only in the return of the pedal.
This fugue overworks its subject, and acceptable harmony jostles
with many desultory incidents. If nothing but the prelude
prevents it from being dismissed as an overgrown plant super-
seded later, it is better to leave the prelude in its fullness, a majestic
query.

The prelude in C minor (four beats) is, much more, a work of
great power. Its massive and composite refrain, recurring section-
ally in the middle of the piece, rivets sectors of richly coloured and
close-woven double-fugue, which lead strikingly back to strong
pedal entries in the tonic from concentrations of now dominant
and now subdominant tonality (bars 53–84, 85–119) and then are
overwhelmed by the full refrain. After this masterful experience,
the FUGUE IN C MINOR sounds pedestrian and prolonged, and again
the prelude (evidently a later work) is best left apart from a fugue
that it shows up. Yet compared with the F minor, this fugue has a
firmer shape and character. The repeated figure in the second and
third bars adds thrust to the subject, and the counterpoint improves after a lame start. There are three main stages of 58, 81
and 20 bars. The long exposition, for five voices with an extra
entry, is staggered by three gracious episodes after the answer, and
the weave is weakened by the dropping of a thread in the second
episode, casually recovered later (cf. bar 151). From bar 59 onwards a fresh descending figure, anticipated in the last episode
(bar 48, alto), is developed into extensive and ambling episodes
and also serves as counterpoint to subject-entries, whose late
access to the relative major (bar 104) is a relief to the ear. After a
singularly tedious episode, a tonic entry at the base of the fabric
produces an effective finish, with the descending figures still
reverberating and a sustained dominant on the pedal to create
suspense and bring the rambling fugue home at last.

The four-voice FUGUE IN C MINOR is an utter contrast. It is

vivacious and trenchant in turn, and never at a loss, but it is not a fugue in any sense yet encountered. After 56 bars of eloquent exposition and counter-exposition, the latter spaced out by organic episodes, a new development (cf. bar 24, soprano) acquires a plain counterpoint of ascending semitones, so suggestive that it carries all before it for forty-eight bars before letting in the subject. And the sequel proves to be, not the sealing of this development with the stamp of the subject, but its blank dismissal by an incredibly literal repeat of the exposition, beginning with the answer and adding one entry in the tonic. This plain ternary course would be good enough sense if the opening was simply a fugued refrain which recurred more concisely after an extended episode. But that is not the aural impression. The counter-exposition definitely prolongs the polyphonic argument in fugal style. Bars 57–104 thus appear as an extraordinary episode, not a loose "middle section." Then the fugal restatement *crumbles*, as such, from the lack of any distinguishing detail, apart from the primacy of the answer and its pivotal key, the dominant, in each pair of entries. A well-established fugal subject thus loses all its freedom in an utterly regimented recovery. Regarded (alternatively) as fugal but not fugue, the returning refrain of twenty-six bars, after forty-eight of sturdy and concentrated interlude, is meagre and unsatisfactory. A similar problem of structure arises in the late E minor fugue. Here the spontaneous rhythm and flowing outline may keep most listeners contented throughout, yet this baffling 19-bar fixation remains at the crucial point. The fugue has a singularly beautiful and balanced Fantasia in front of it. One sympathizes with Elgar's orchestration of the two movements without considering the transcription at all necessary. Bach's texture abides no question.

The FUGUE IN C MAJOR (prelude in four beats) is altogether a more searching composition, in spite of its plain subject and urbane treatment. For prelude, Bach, with his singular ear for amplified structure, transformed a workaday prelude* into a compelling piece by the addition of three bars of vibrating harmony and a corresponding close, briefly suggestive of a

* Printed in the Peters volume concerned (241).

vaster setting. The fugue develops gradually, entries being spaced out by mainly brief extensions, cumulatively no more than a quarter of the 111-bar fugue and far less than in the three previous examples. Leisurely stages of interlinked exposition and spacious counter-exposition widen to entries in minor keys. The

* The pedal normally plays an octave lower than written, coupled to a manual playing the written notes

Example 2†

recovery of the dominant in the pedal begins a broad section of return, whose triumphant finish, after a thrilling moment of care-less rapture in the top part, is announced by the pedal and com-pleted by a top entry with the most sonorous of closes. The serene theme thus emerges exultantly fundamental and then ecstatically soaring, after severe trials of counterpoint, pungent harmony and not a little key-travel. For more than one wedding assembly that could be named, the fugue has provided a heartening symbol of the common round sublime. For listeners generally, it is a most satisfying work. Eminently one of this "Southern" group, it reaches its objective with a mastery which places it beyond period. It might have been written at almost any stage of high maturity, Weimar or Leipzig. (It is much quoted by Vincent d'Indy as a model of fugal composition.)‡

Some details may be drawn to notice. The exposition unfolds in accomplished counterpoint. The counter-exposition, mainly in the dominant and in full harmony, is maintained by a fresh counter-subject, which is constantly changing its interval from the subject, with interesting harmonic results that add piquancy to successive entries. (The tenor of bar 35 recurs as the top part at bars 62 and 100, is relatively a fifth lower in bar 41 (tenor), and

† See Note on p. 24.
‡ *Cours de composition*, section on Fugue.

finds further variants in bars 42, 89 and 106.) Additional cross-rhythms arise impromptu (bars 45, 52, 73) or derivatively (bar 79, cf. 16). The approach to the dominant from its relative minor (bar 62) prevents any immediate impression of restatement. As the key falls to the subdominant (bar 84), intimations of recovery take firm shape, and a simple but riveting sequence invokes the final tonic entries, quickened by soprano rapture. The whole fugue is seasoned with a stringent and often tart harmonic flavour. Bars 28-9, 41, 52-4 (quoted in Ex. 2) and 78-87 are worth special notice. The precise setting of the familiar theme can never be taken for granted. This lasting freshness guarantees the fugue a long life.

The FUGUE IN A MAJOR is a striking contrast, while preserving the Southern style. Its jaunty eight-bar subject wanders on for 182 bars without any episode worth mentioning, relying mainly on a melodious top part and counterpoint, a close canon, and some eventual key-interest. The style remains imperturbably perfunctory to the end, grudging of anything like contrapuntal device.

Bach's fugal writing thus reached maturity from by no means faultless attempts at a new style. The sequel must be reserved for another chapter.

NOTE

(*Page* 23) The phrasing of music examples in this book is mine, with the piano in mind for the keyboard works. At the risk of being "fussy," I have sought to emphasize the characteristic quality of each line in the polyphony, and to stimulate, by agreement or disagreement, a vivid and positive conception of a relationship too often regarded as one of pitch and time only. I have not "edited" the recurrent *alla breve* time-signature (half-circle *with a stroke* down, implying *two* main beats), but there are so many examples in which four beats (i.e. a slower bar) sound right and two sound hectic that it is at once musicianly and scholarly not to regard any *alla breve* mark as binding.

Chapter V

ORGAN WORKS

III. MASTER-WORKS

THE Toccata in F is the greatest example of the genre by any composer alive or dead. A vigorous organ bravura (hands and feet) and simple contrapuntal imitation are pointed by sweeping harmonic phases in a wide and spacious design. The reverberating "Neapolitan" close and grinding cadence make an overwhelming finish to a piece of over 450 bars. Such trenchant music cannot be heard as a mere prelude, and it is commonly assumed that the Toccata was written separately and after the FUGUE IN F. There is much to be said for the common practice of playing Toccata and Fugue quite independently. The fugue is almost equally self-contained, demanding a prelude only on the convention that some sort of ear-rinser is required before listening to the train of subject-entries. If it is played after the Toccata, it must be heard as an utter contrast, challenging its massive effect by probing thematic research and a contrapuntal harmony of its own piquancy.

It is a double-fugue on an ample scale, except that the combination of theme is effectively brief. The first fugue is just that type of bland exordium which, well sustained as it is, calls for something to cut across it. The second fugue stabilizes this transition, and passes quickly to a vigorous development. The third fugue forms a ready climax, with a broad combination of subject to summarize the first two fugues, but it does not rely too much on the combination, the counterpoint being in many respects fresh, and for most of its seven entries the key is kept on the move, so that there is not the slightest feeling of vain repetition of the main subject. The first seal has been set on a type of fugue to which Bach returned signally later, transcending and yet respecting the singleness of mood inherent in monothematic fugue.

It is not certain that the fugue in F was planned in advance, but it is easy to understand Bach's train of thought. In the first fugue the sustained subject calls for a counter-subject, and it receives a provocative one, the discord of the second bar being treated as a free chord and never properly resolved (cf. bars 27, 34, 57). This seems to prompt other dissonances later in the way of bluntly accented non-harmonic notes (bars 62, 83, 105, bass; 138, tenor; 153 and 158–63, inner parts). In this far from emollient atmosphere, exposition is succeeded by a broad, complete and fully harmonized counter-exposition in the four voices. The subject, with its perpetual subdominant turn (bars 3–4), has nearly rung its own knell. The development of an independent episode would

Example 3

now be a strained effort. But a fresh *subject* is possible, if it can sally quickly off the mark. This would at first amount to a formal fugal diversion, with its own subsidiary episodes. If, however, the new subject can attend the first subject at its inevitable return, its own fugue becomes rather the nervous preparation for a more integral sequel. Hence the need of this second fugue is to wander

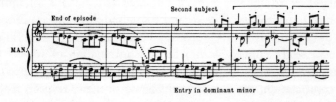

Example 4

swiftly and competently. Entries soon move into a chain of minor keys, dropping to the rare dominant minor, with an abundance of fresh counterpoint and with episodes resourcefully derived from a figure in the codetta (bar 79) or semitonal impromptus. The springy new subject has run to nearly sixty bars of *divertissement*, but the absence of the pedal has kept the fugue steadily detached and on probation.

The obscure reappearance in the tonic of the first subject and its counter-subject, below the surface of this pedal-less texture (bar 128), is therefore a negation of all the apparent constructive purpose, to present without confusion the impact of main and subsidiary subjects and their combination. If Bach *was* awake at this point, his intention must have been, on the contrary, to start the third stage thus unobtrusively (but presumably with more organ). The upshot is that it is in the *answer* to this mealy-mouthed entry, now frankly in the soprano, that the addition of the second subject on the pedal provides the expected and neces-sary fresh impetus for the return of the solemn first subject. There is no resting on oars. Blunt and surprising variations of key (minor keys and the subdominant) and of scale-degree (bar 147) keep the ear in alert suspense. The second subject meanwhile has lost its once essential first bar, which confines the harmony to tonic or submediant chords; this leaves the first subject free to

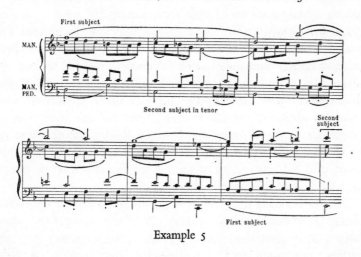

Example 5

enter in a rich train of sonorities and sweeping figures. In one entry, indeed, the continuation of a previous feature leaves no room for the second subject. The main subject thus reappears uncompromisingly on the outside of the harmony (top or bottom) six times without strain. This is where the formalist is found wanting and the composer steps in. The combination of theme is for strong harmony; it is not essential, and if it proves a hindrance to further harmonic periods, it must be pruned. I quote the penultimate stroke and the beginning of the last and inevitably pedal entry. This finale is a document in the musicianly use of available contrapuntal resources. The whole fugue is a revelation of that central impulse which alone can give meaning to intellectually conceived structural devices and decide upon the essential turn of thought at the critical point. With the Toccata it makes one of the indispensable things in that desert island which the imaginative mind furnishes with the bare essentials of cultural life.

In one other fugue, the D MINOR, Bach raised the vocal style to splendid and unparalleled heights. Here the vivacious and unpretentious Toccata seems redundant, for an attentive audience. The fugue begins basically and expands exhaustively in its own time. It is conveniently always mis-called the "Dorian," but it has no contact with the Dorian mode except D.*

On first hearing, this fugue of 222 bars, the longest of the master-works for organ or keyboard, may appear as an endless series of rather obstinately spaced out entries: eight in the eighty-seven bars of exposition, but four in the seventy-nine of the development and three in the fifty-six of recapitulation, not counting additional canonic entries. After the significant control of episode in the C major and F major fugues, the devotion of more than half the present fugue to the severest episodic development calls for some justification. Even the last entry is swept inexorably into further episode, now coda.

The reasons lie in the growth of the subject, a shapely seven-bar theme (a) with fits of syncopation. A counter-subject (b) passes from a stray rhythmic figure (b1) to a trim sequence (b2). A further counter-subject (bar 18) persists later (bars 30, 71, 81).

* The MS. *looks* Dorian, B flat appearing as an accidental and not in the key-signature, but the sound is utterly D minor.

Counter-exposition, repeating the order of announcement (A.S., T.B.) with reversed answer and subject, admits free counterpoint to loosen the *a–b* nexus. Of the next four entries, the first two on

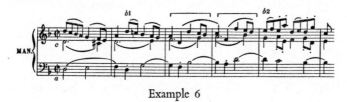

Example 6

the sharp side of the main key and the next two on the flat, the first and third introduce, as counterpoint, the entire subject, in canon at the octave at a bar's distance, with *b2* in attendance on the canon. The other two entries rely on fresh soprano lines for distinction. In the last three entries of all, the canon alternates with a vibrating inner counterpoint. Of the fifteen complete entries,

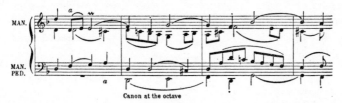

Example 7

only the seventh repeats another (the third) closely, and that in answering key and higher soprano octave.

Such are the exceptional possibilities which invention and contrapuntal skill provide for the subject. It would not be practical to devise independent and characteristic material for episodes on a similar scale. Apart, then, from one passing incident (bars 195–202), Bach uses the variant potentialities of the canonic sequence that follows the answer (bars 15–17) as the nucleus of richer phrases which begin, conclude or contain an episode. The basic harmony of four typical episodes, the last here transposed to the tonic for comparison, occurs and recurs as follows, apart from key. Doubling of parts a sixth below or above is shown by an asterisk. "Inverted" refers to an exchange of top and bass.

Example 8

Exposition

Bar 15   E1
,,   26   E1 inverted*
,,   36   E2

Development

Bar 88   E4
,,   110   E2*
,,   125   E1 inverted* (canon in tenor)
,,   138   E4
,,   156   E1 inverted
,,   163   E3, tenor and bass, in soprano and bass (canons in alto and tenor)

Counter-exposition

Bar 50   E3
,,   67   E3, soprano and tenor (bass canon)
,,   78   E2 inverted

Recapitulation

Bar 178   top and bass of bars 67–70
,,   184   E3, soprano and bass
,,   211   E4, with tenor in alto, soprano in tenor*

Thus the entries maintain counterpoint for the seven-bar subject, while the episodes specialize in cross-rhythm. Sometimes the last appearance of a subject supplies its own firm cadence to a fugue. Here, however, the subject has been extended from the first by the canonic episode, and it only remains to tighten up the version chosen with doubled strands and to let the sequence obtained go grinding on until it rests on the penultimate chord,† after which sonorous organ rhetoric can take charge of the finish. (A simple accountable cadence would fall flat after the relentless sequence. There is no limit to fugal musicianship!)

† See Ex. 44, p. 189.

Hence even the full pedal for the nineteenth and last entry (counting canons) leads into the episode by way of coda. The trenchancy of the D minor, on top of the F major fugue, is a measure of Bach's mastery of the Southern style.

In the FUGUE IN A MINOR $\binom{6}{8}$ he returned to his earlier bravura manner, not disdaining the bustling sequences around repeated notes associated with the name of the Venetian harpsichord composer Alberti, yet subjecting these to a live embellishment. An abundance of episode ranges from short extemporary incidents to the more organic developments of bars 31–43, 83–96, 101–12 and 120–30. The coda leaves the balance on the extemporary side. Meanwhile the twelve subject-entries (fewer than usual) are maintained by fresh counterpoint "on tap," florid versions of the subject (bars 51, 61, 71, 116), false anticipations (bars 95, 113), fresh accent (73), and key-interest up to the leading-note major (71). The confinement of the subject inside the harmony in the recapitulation gives freer play to contrapuntal invention. The subject seems to have flowered from the same stem as the long keyboard fugue in the same key (see p. 110). Once that was determined, the fugue must have been a relaxation for Bach to write. A seemingly extemporary but actually much re-written prelude prepares the ear for exuberant fancy in the fugue, unlike the relentless art of the D minor.

The prelude in G (beginning with R.H. arpeggio) is a graceful and well-filled pattern of sound, fugitive and yet characteristic. It was originally and distractingly followed by the fugal finale of the E minor sonata, as an interlude. The subject of the FUGUE IN G (anticipated in Cantata 21) is less melodious than that of the A minor, and the composer does not let it run on too long. Exposition stops at one extra entry, but middle entries range as far as the very rare tonic minor, equipped with a Neapolitan-sixth half-cadence which proves literally and effectively arresting. Two entries in the major, with varied close canon, establish a complete sense of poise, which bears sometimes a striking extrinsic value after the hearing of hysterical or trifling music. Episodes amount to nearly half the fugue, but only one (bars 39–52) is substantial. This sound, compact work, vigorous rather than tuneful, flows

easily from its prelude, from which (e.g. bars 16–17) it partly
derives its material.

The fantasia in G minor stands altogether by itself. It is passionate, mysterious and probing by turns. The normal emergence of
characteristic figures is interspersed with high rhapsody and
semitonal modulation that hints at tragedy. The final cadence
leaves an intense impression without precedent. What follows?
Nothing for certain. The original editor of the Peters edition,
Griepenkerl (d. 1849), states that in no scripts were the fantasia and
fugue in G minor found together. However, on the back of an
"old" copy of the fantasia the theme of the fugue has been
written, with an indication that it should follow. On that
evidence, Griepenkerl boldly printed fantasia and fugue together
for the first time. There is also a copy of the fugue transposed to
F minor, with the pedal raised where necessary. To go with the
prelude in F minor? We can only conjecture.

What is more, the provenance of the FUGUE IN G MINOR is a
baffling mystery to the alert listener. It begins unusually, off the
beat. It is awkward to make this start from nothing. But if the
fugue follows the fantasia, the latter casts its sublime reverberations over a fugue of swinging step and exuberant cliché, influenced, as Spitta noted, by Reinken's fifth sonata (*Hortus
musicus*). The whole texture of the fugue is facile where the fantasia spelt strain and adventure. The works may therefore well be
left apart; the fantasia in its brooding grandeur, the fugue in its
careless buoyancy. For reasons stated, there is no strong compulsion to make sense of the pair.

The fugue appears to have been bound up with a visit Bach
made to Hamburg in 1720, in connexion with a church appointment. According to later accounts,* Bach sought out the veteran
organist, Reinken, one of the adjudicators, and played to him at
the Catherinenkirche, whose four-manual organ, with its five
rows of cumbrous and inaccessible stops on each side, Terry
found unchanged two centuries later. That the G minor fugue
was played at that time is strongly suggested by the subsequent
quotation of an academic version of the subject as having been

* The obituary notice of 1754 and Forkel's *Life* (1802).

given to an organ candidate at Hamburg, with the comment that
it was familiar and the player who first used it well known.* The
fugue thus certainly *became* a Hamburg fugue, and seems to have
been written thus incidentally for Hamburg. It displays the
organist-composer's mastery of voluble organ polyphony (with
thirty-six revolutions of one chord in bars 61–3) and at the same
time an audible release of theme, for the subject is kept on the
outside of the harmony in all but three of the eighteen entries.
The unmistakable derivation of the subject from a Dutch folk-
song† is further evidence of a more popular approach than usual.
The differences between the folk-song, too melodious and unsym-
metrical at first for consistent entry, Bach's more harmonic
version—the fruit of four centuries of evolution, as we shall
observe later—and the Organ Board's "adaptation," invite
comparison.

Example 9

As a whole the four-voice fugue maintains its racy beginning.
The vigorous descending curves and gracious symmetry of the
subject extend to seven expository entries, assisted by the counter-
subjects, *b* and *c* (Ex. 10); *c* acquires a new downward twist later
(bars 56, 73). The weave is rather oddly loosened where least expected, in the last two entries. After this, the subject passes through
three major keys and three others. The harmonic replenishment
of the major entries is a relief to the ear, and false entries add their
diversion. At the end of this extensive tour, unceasing entries in
the tonic (S.T.A.B.) make a fool-proof re-statement, attended by

* Johann Mattheson, *Grosse Generalbass-Schule* (1731).
† *Zeitschrift für Musik*, September, 1924. Quoted by Terry in his life of Bach.

garrulous counterpoint. Episodes are first derived from a figure in the fourth bar (bar 32, cf. 107) or the first bar (*passim*), but later based on a simple ascending formula in imitative style, which readily returns (bars 57, 68, 82). The flatward conclusion of these incidents in reflective style prompts a swift resort to the

Example 10

tonic. This tediously quadruplicate statement is spread out by nugatory episodes (bars 106–9 are specially redundant) but finishes with a blunt vigour. Every suspicion of hurried workmanship in these last twenty-two bars strengthens the case for keeping the Fantasia separate.

The supposed Hamburg connexion of the G minor is a reminder of Bach's growing dissatisfaction with his ducal patron at Weimar. He ended by accepting the post of Capellmeister to Prince Leopold of Cöthen. He ceased to be an organist, and for the chamber orchestra under his direction he rarely wrote movements in continuous fugue. He realized, it seems, that polyphony for strings (and *a fortiori* for the "broken music" of strings and wind) is either a reflection of vocal blend and *sostenuto* without the pertinence of voices, or, if truly orchestral, an elusive quantity, with its rapid excursions into widely separated compasses and textures. (Only in his fiercest, most crushing mood did Vaughan Williams begin a fugue on the tuba.) The finale of the fourth of the six concertos written for the Markgrave of Brandenburg's collection is something of an exception, but it is not a proper fugue. The recurrences of a loosely-fugued refrain are separated by displays of solo-violin and flute virtuosity which break away from the main thought, and in the last forty bars the "subject" becomes a mere *point d'appui* for a wider assertion.

The FINALE OF THE CONCERTO IN C MAJOR for two keyboards and strings is an unusual and vigorous fugue. The subject combines an incisive rhythm, a calm, strenuous climb to the submediant and back, and well-defined harmonic implications to enrich any realized harmony. It moves easily through a spacious exposition for the three strands of each keyboard part and three string parts, with two extra keyboard entries after a *soli*-episode in casual extension of a conclusive all-bass entry. Further entries keep the subject below the surface, to avoid exposure of its harmonic trend. Entries in minor keys (two in each) are again pointed by the massing of the basses. On this understanding, one more entry in the united basses provides a firm conclusion to further and increasingly pertinent keyboard skirmishes. Thus a manifold exposition of eighty-five bars is succeeded by a *shorter* key-development and return (twenty-six and twenty-nine bars), but these are reinforced by the rapidly gathering impact of the orchestra, and all gaps are readily filled in a two-keyboard style at once methodical and improvisatory. The various textures have determined both the subject and its deployment convincingly. (Cf. the confusing *solo-tutti* repartee of Holst's Fugal Concerto.)

Bach also stretched the imagination of performers and listeners alike by including FUGUES in his SONATAS FOR UNACCOMPANIED SOLO VIOLIN (Nos. 1, 3, 5).* The bold economy is in keeping with the tremendous concentration of the subject-matter. Schumann's piano accompaniments discreetly realize the harmonic background for weaker listeners, but they miss all the hazards of the mountain track. For progress on a wider scale Bach now turned to keyboard solo. He developed a fresh, compressed fugue, with an independent bass in part, in the THREE-PART INVENTIONS IN D AND A, and elsewhere. From these he came to "The Well-tempered Clavier." The limitation to two hands was no hindrance, and there was no obvious artistic call to return to the organ. Nor, when Bach moved from the Cöthen court to take charge of the music at St. Thomas's, Leipzig, did he have any organ duties. However, at Leipzig he revised three organ preludes and fugues not yet mentioned and he wrote one fresh and

* See Note, p. 36.

monumental example. These will be considered in the next chapter, as isolated efforts in slender contact with their predecessors.

NOTE

In *Das Violonspiel im Deutschland vor* 1700 G. Beckmann shows evidence that multiple stopping (i.e. a chord) was sometimes performed in the arpeggio style suited to the Italian (since universal) mechanically stretched bow, relying on the listener to infer the polyphony. This undermines the commonly accepted assertion of Arnold Schering that actual polyphony was made possible, and therefore may be posited here, in the relaxation of thumb-pressure on the old arched bow (see *Bachjahrbuch*, 1904, p. 675, for evidence of the German and Italian styles of applying and avoiding thumb-pressure). Telmanyi's insistence on a special bow (*Musical Times*, January, cf. February, May, 1955) does not alter the historical position, and Bach's organ transcription (in D minor) of the fugue from Sonata I constantly exhibits a polyphony avoided in the original. The Schroeder bow (1933) was, similarly, utterly out of touch with the simple French bow-technique posited by Schering, and, so far from being a fulfilment of Schering's theories, was, rather, a walking refutation of them (see D. D. Boyden's decisive article in *The Musical Quarterly*, 1950, pp. 18–19).

Chapter VI

ORGAN WORKS

IV. LEIPZIG

CANDOUR compels us to remark that the last four organ fugues greatly vary in quality as well as in content. The E minor, the widening intervals of whose subject have given it the quaint but convenient title of the "Wedge" (beginning with the thin end), is the longest of Bach's fugues, loose-limbed and, indeed, not a proper fugue. The C major (prelude in $\frac{9}{8}$) makes seventy-two bars of its one-bar subject, and suffers somewhat from much binding in this thread. The B minor, a fugue of eighty-eight bars on a very plain two-bar subject, reaches a powerful conclusion after a long-drawn development of thinner content. The E flat, a combination of three fugues, is masterly. It suggests a dissatisfaction with the ordinary monothematic fugue. It happens to be an epilogue to the "Catechism" preludes (1739), but it is sheer fugue.

The E minor is in many respects the most elaborate of the organ preludes. The opening refrain, rigidly repeated at the outset, blends later with contrasted phrases (bars 51, 55) so freely that its concluding bars are sufficient to round off the pattern. They leave the listener with his ears full and alert. The FUGUE IN E MINOR has a certain initial breadth and consistency, but it proves to be, not a fugue, but a fugal piece in a blunt ternary structure. It begins with normal phases of exposition and counter-exposition, an arpeggio figure of the first episode (9–13) supplying the impulse for most of the connecting incidents. A break into persistent and rather commonplace bravura discards polyphony, but this is interrupted (or integrated) by spasmodic returns of the subject in various keys, and also of the arpeggio figure mentioned. After over a hundred bars of this desultory movement, the main subject returns exactly as in the exposition. The literal reproduction of polyphonic detail for fifty-three bars becomes increasingly tedious, especially the final sustained dominant which replaces a pedal entry. The general impression is of hasty work, structurally confused and inimical to fugal texture, and not redeemed by its solid counterpoint and grave theme, good only in its place. Here, again, the prelude may well be regarded as sufficient in itself for most occasions, and blunted by the wayward development and bland *da capo* of its fugue.

The FUGUE IN C is well placed. The prelude is a serene work in a tuneful pastoral style, amplified by accomplished polyphony and punctuated by a semitonal cadence which reverberates in the fugue. The concentration of the fugue is in keeping with this confident note. It is soon evident that it is of the same order of obsessional imitation as the first of the "Forty-eight," whose nature was considered in the second chapter. Yet it is a more extreme instance. The subject is the barest modulating formula, and becomes merely a constituent factor of style in a development otherwise controlled. To speak of excessive repetition of subject would be almost as absurd as to call the opening of the Fifth Symphony monotonous. The subject-entries themselves supply most of the diversions, or rather the sense of cumulative diversion which calls for some drastic recovery. Besides an early oscillation of key and fresh counterpoint, melodic inversions of the subject and answer, with free treatment of semitones, establish piquant reversals of the semi-vocal ascent (bar 27, etc.), with trenchant harmony to compensate for the easier descent. The key slips flatward and creeps into the tonic *minor*, which it holds evocatively in faltering suspense. Something must restore a sense of creative activity to the main symbol. The pedal, so far unheard, enters with the subject at half speed, and later with the inversion of this, with all sorts of odd canons and counter-canons in the manuals heaped round the recurring two-bar span. Searching harmony shakes the polyphony out of its rut, before a plain sustained tonic pedal establishes a final and acceptable sense of gravity. Such portentous augmentation of theme is a little grotesque. The fugue remains a remarkable *tour de force* in perpetual imitation, almost impressionist in its repetition of the same melodic blob—*sempre tremolando* with a difference. After the blunt repetitions of the early fugues, the subtle art at work here is the more apparent.

The FUGUE IN B MINOR (prelude in $\frac{6}{8}$) owes much to its prelude. The richly wrought opening refrain is increasingly forceful in repetition, like that of the prelude in C minor (see p. 21), and its divisible and portmanteau character enables it not only to admit lighter diversions of interest (bars 17, 56) but ultimately (bars 69, 73) to comprehend them as steps towards its own fulfilment. No other single piece makes such an intense summons of personality. The subject of the fugue avoids any comparison by being extremely quiet and plain, while engraving the minor chord firmly on the ear (B, D, F sharp, D–B). Shapely counterpoint, including a counter-subject which has come to stay, carries the music through an ample exposition and adventurous counter-exposition. In the latter the re-engagement of all four voices for each entry is varied by the wayward leaps of the subject up and down the polyphony (T.S.B.A.B.) and by the unusual range of key (subdominant and two major keys), but the final entry in the dominant and the steady maintenance of the pedal separate this entire exordium from the procession of manual entries that follows. In the long development, two groups of ascending entries (T.A.S.) each move from the dominant to major keys, stimulated by scales and other rhetoric, including the arpeggio feature of bar 29*b*, heard trenchantly later. There is a wilful and escapist touch here: something has gone out of control. The recovery of the original subject in the tonic, with its former counter-subject and

Example 11

a fresh one, meets this emergency none too soon, presumably supported by more organ. The answer indicates that the new counterpoint is integral, not a passing efflorescence. Parry sees here an intensification of the feeling of human powerlessness which he associates with the subject. This interpretation makes the wayward middle entries more intelligible, and the new note is certainly inexorable. Intense and distinct entries (supertonic and subdominant), flanked by relevant episodes (cf. bar 32), converge in a relentless, cumulative delivery on the pedal; a single soprano entry, the suspension of whose initial note avoids bathos after the bass *continuum*, invokes further suspense for the close. The relaxed tone of the middle section enhances the passion of the finale. Thus the cumulative thought of the fugue points the more scattered refrain-pattern of the prelude. Together they alter the pitch of living. Centuries of distressed, slavish existence and crying need seem to find habitation in the austere but enduring phrases in whose cultivation the Germans have read their own spiritual epic. The imagery is more than meets the ear. Bach's craftsmanship has given the underlying aspirations permanence.

Some such approach, from a serener world, is germane, too, to the FUGUE IN E FLAT.* As almost every listener to Bach must know, this is a composite work, in three distinct but connected fugal movements, the subject reappearing in the other two. A possible anticipation, both in subject and structure, is the final chorus of a cantata (*c.* 1693), "Gelobet sei der Herr," by the Zittau composer, Johann Krieger. This works out a kind of triple fugue on three separate subjects that combine later. The first is quoted. What is more, Bach's contemporary at the

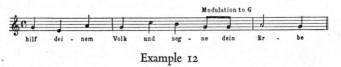

Example 12

Weimar court, J. G. Walther, an admirer and collector of Krieger's works (as were Handel and Mattheson), wrote an organ fugue in A on the same subject. The derivation of Bach's main subject from this is most probable, and the triple fugue suggestive, though more remote.† Frescobaldi's is the structural precedent.

* See Note 1 on p. 46.   † See Note 2 on p. 47.

The E flat remained Bach's sole triple fugue, in the unusual
sense of three distinct fugues in one orbit. Not that the appeal of
the fugue is primarily to the intellect. The broad tripartite scheme
(comprised in 36–45–36 bars) is unmistakable, owing to the
changes in metre. Equally clear are the recurrences of the main
theme, expository in the first fugue, adaptable in the second,
where it forms a free additional subject, and increasingly all-
absorbing in the third fugue. The triple *fugue* is nevertheless
subtly contrived. In the opening movement a broad, vocal half-
familiar theme acquires an ample exposition of rare dignity and
clarity. Contrapuntal figures in sturdy half-beats (bars 4, 7, cf.
Ex. 13 below) and informal close canon in the second stage (bars
21–36) keep the subject fresh. Its return on the pedal with the
initial note restored in pitch (after a lapse in the previous soprano
entry) is both conclusive and characteristic—

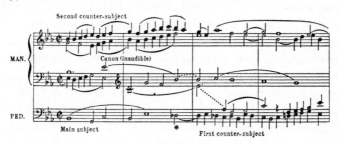

Example 13

From this well-knit but essentially expository movement
emerges a second fughetta of another character, for manuals only
as in the fugue in F, and in a fresh, more animated metre. (It is
misleadingly barred throughout, the metrical accent falling on the
second half of each bar. The harmonic sense points this almost
the whole way.) The new subject is vibrant, elusive and almost
impressionist, while presenting a perceptible thrust of ascending
thirds in rising sequence. For counter-exposition melodic inversion maintains an informal course, with piquant semitonal
alterations (and hence ambivalent tonality) to strengthen the now
descending, effortless sequence, but it pulls up unequivocally in
the dominant. In this expectant mood the subject finds a piquant

role as the accompaniment of the returning subject of the first fugue, now forced into a brusquely syncopated pattern but fast becoming the established principal motive in a rich variation of contrapuntal detail. After an erratic course, the key drops easily into the relative minor (bar 70, cf. 50) for three patent entries. In

Example 14

this key, then, a fugal movement in a more stately tempo begins, admirably pompous for the moment. (Again the true bar-lines should mainly be placed half way through the existing bars.) The new one-bar "subject" is a sequential formula of falling fifths, with a perpetual tendency to form a cadence. By means of skilful harmonization it gains a full "exposition" on its own, with restatement later (bars 111–13), but it remains a perfunctory figure. The main subject, syncopated and re-accented—to avoid tedious echoes of the first fugue—thus re-enters easily between the fourth and fifth entries, in answer form. Soon the one-bar subject recedes to the level of counterpoint at a variety of intervals, along with a good deal of scale rhetoric. A pointed key-scheme disposes entries of the combined subjects, or (bar 108) of the main subject in canon with itself, ending buoyantly in the dominant. In the final and resounding entry of the *idée fixe* on the pedal, the initial fall of a primal semitone (cf. bar 26) instead of the formal third, is one of many compelling features. Once more an informal fughetta has served to reveal the quality of the main subject.

The fugue in E flat, then, is not triple in the sense of developing three subjects of equal importance. Rather, it brings the exposition of one main theme into relation with two other fugal developments, which are characteristic enough to justify a fresh movement but, like episodes in a normal fugue, arise for the sake of the chief motive. It is a mark of Bach's intense grasp of "that precious intangible, the initiative" that he could thus extend fugue into a feast of fugues without a sacrifice of integrity, as Beethoven did later (op. 133). The total impression is of prodigal and yet purposive affirmation. Of what nature is this affirmation? Schweitzer's rash and unsupported conjecture (fifty years ago) that the three-fold fugue is a mirror of the divine Trinity collapses before the perfunctory nature of the subjects of the second and third fugues. Nor can any passing allusion to a chorale (e.g. "Was mein Gott will") be counted significant, after a set of preludes on specific chorales; and the English custom of referring to the "St. Anne's" Fugue is absurdly parochial. Yet, as the wide historical associations of the primal curve and the didactic context lead one to expect, this fugue seems to confirm or revive a sense of immortal longings and unshakable beliefs, for listeners in every contingent relation to this difficult life, confident as Bach was and remained, or losing hope. Whether a final burst of underlying dogma or pure constructiveness, such a vitalizing experience is part of that civilizing inheritance by which successive generations are heartened against artistic cynicism, philistinism and every shade of insouciance. They crown the study of Bach fugue up to this point, in the observation of consummate musicianship and creative assertion.

Bach occasionally drew upon fugue for developing religious concepts in the symbolic but self-contained music of the chorale-preludes. The "Catechism" preludes* contain several instances. The MANUAL PRELUDE ON "ALLEIN GOTT" ("To God alone") in A is a miniature double-fugue on the first two lines of the chorale, the two fughettas being linked by a common counter-subject; all in twenty bars of startling compactness. The three prolonged preludes with pedal on the three-fold "Kyrie" have a fugal basis. The first, "KYRIE GOTT VATER" ("O Lord, God the Father"), shows the structural method. A running fugal commentary, with the subject based on the first line of the chorale, links the spacious delivery of the chorale in separate phrases, which take the place of episodes. It may perplex listeners that there is no clear

* See Note 3 on p. 47.

disposition of key. The harmonic texture is founded, not on any major or minor scale, but on the church modes,* and key-centre is a matter of pitch-gravitation, not of explicit starting-point. The final basis is the Phrygian mode (E to E, white notes), transposed up to G, but at the beginning the general basis is the Mixolydian mode (G to G), transposed up to B flat. The usual comforts of key-centre and related keys are missing, and the strange modal harmony jostles with many "modern" touches. Hence the music may seem to meander from one centre to another, and to oscillate in style. And it does. Nevertheless, this is a refreshing adventure after the glib tonality of some fugues, while incidentally exposing the real convenience of working to a clear key-system, by conflating the modes in two prevalent patterns, major and minor.

"CHRISTE, ALLER WELT TROST" ("Christ, the whole world's comforter") moves on similar lines, with the chorale put into the tenor (God in the midst of them). The subject here has a more pronounced curve, the harmony is more modern and less angular, and the counterpoint more flowing. The key-centre and mode again fluctuate: the tune and opening are Phrygian in G, but the close is in C. "KYRIE GOTT HEILIGER GEIST" ("O Lord God, the holy Spirit") similarly begins in B flat and ends in Phrygian G, but the harmony is so much more definite here that the termini may be set down as B flat major and a very chromatic G major. The broad grandeur of pedal chorale and cumulative polyphony is impressive. A syncopated sequential figure develops (bar 4, cf. 14, 41) along with vivacious counterpoint, and the closing harmonization is striking and definitely modern. One cannot but admire Bach for facing the modal implications of these "Office" hymns. Consider the modal output of G. F. Handel! Yet Bach did not go further with this neo-modal style. It was too awkward for any extended movement.

The MANUAL PRELUDE in F minor on the Communion hymn, "JESUS CHRISTUS, UNSER HEILAND" ("Jesus Christ, our Saviour") is an austere but accomplished excursion on the first line of the chorale, the subject being kept mainly below the surface and soon

* See Glossary.

appearing in reversed accentuation. The companion prelude (in D minor) is an amazing contrast. A free, vivacious two-part fugue for the manuals is punctuated by the successive phrases of the chorale on the pedal, spaced out in halting, processional steps. The fugal subject moves in a set sequence from bar to bar, but in varying detail within the bar. By all precedent of associated word and tone the typical stretches, from tenth to sixth, are the exultant leaps of bold conviction (*credo quia impossibile*, as Schweitzer suggested); and perhaps this alone explains Bach's absorption. While the pure musician will appreciate the fusion of unceasing, ingenious contrapuntal activity and intermittent, majestic instancy, for Bach it was an ecstatic pioneering experience, guided by the traditional and unanimous call (as of a company on a long march) to the sanctuary. The gleam of the impossible still beckons.

The recurrence of a simpler and more extended figure of audacity links the last prelude in idea with the well-known PRELUDE in D minor on "WIR GLAUBEN ALL' AN EINEN GOTT, SCHÖPFER" ("We all believe in one God, Creator"), sometimes idiotically described as the "giant" fugue owing to the ponderous ascent of Audacity on the pedal. This eloquent and freely recurring bass reinforces the independent fugal development of a lively, modern version of the first line of the chorale named. The manual fugue expands easily on its own, but the bass proves increasingly integral, and crowns one episode without any fugal ado (bar 40). The assertion of sound-relationship is highly impressive in itself, but so is the symbolic challenge to the doubts that beset man, as he moves about a cruel and reactionary world. A traditional safeguard of belief (reduced to a phrase and modernized) blends with the composer's personal tokens of firm and vital decision. The age of rationalism had its relentless logic, but also its noble hypotheses. Bach reflects both.

The Eighteen Chorale-preludes which Bach revised at the end of his life contain one eminently fugal example: the THIRD PRELUDE ON "NUN KOMM', DER HEIDEN HEILAND" ("Come now, Saviour of the Gentiles"). The general pattern resembles that of "Jesus Christus" (with pedal). The chorale, spread out in the bass, disposes the course of a manual fugue on a busy, almost contentious subject, which may by a stretch be referred to the opening line of the chorale. The thematic development is resourceful, but the inversion of the subject sounds rather forced. The outcome is reasonable, orderly music, rousing to a Lutheran who takes the significance of the chorale for granted, to others a neat feat of structural economy.

The second of the six sonatas "for two keyboards and pedal" (i.e. pedal harpsichord *en route* for organ) ends with a breezy movement whose distinction from fugue as so far understood is worth noticing. A firmly enclosed fugal refrain (a double exposition of 29–29 bars) returns succinctly later, and at the end with slight curtailment (14–29 bars). Between these three entries comes a piquant and independent episode of twenty-seven bars, repeated a fifth lower after the middle entry. This blunt alternation has nothing of the subtle unity of fugue, but fits the Italian style. Nor is the finale of No. 3 in D minor a fugue; the "exposition" of thirty-six bars simply returns in part or whole after three symmetrical episodes. In the remarkable finale of No. 5 in C, again, the opening statement of seventy-three bars not only reverberates amply in the last fifty-three bars, but also contains two complementary stages of thematic release in the manner of a classical sonata-movement. The initial fugal subject becomes little more than a recurrent phrase in a wider rhythm. This harnessing of fugue to sonata-form is prophetic (cf. the finale of Mozart's quartet in G, K. 387). Fugacious but not fugue. No. 4 in E minor ends in a tuneful fugue (see p. 31).

On the organ, then, Bach formed his first fugal style, chiefly while at Weimar, and continued it sporadically at Leipzig, sometimes in a specific religious context. We may now turn back to the intermediate and remarkable spurt of fugue-writing for keyboard which possessed him at Cöthen, between the Weimar years and the Leipzig appointment which he held for the last twenty-seven years of his career.

NOTES

1 (*Page* 40) The long-winded and rather awkwardly constructed prelude in E flat is a mere prologue to the "Catechism" preludes, and I do

not understand the "inward connexion" between prelude and fugue
discerned by Spitta and by Griepenkerl, who printed the two together
in defiance of Bach's order and in simple reliance on a "tradition"
handed on by Forkel from Bach's sons, untrustworthy authority.
Organists seem to have a passion for unwanted preludes, and this fugue
is exceptionally self-contained, as its position clearly suggests.

2 (*Page* 40) See D.T.B. VI. 1 and compare D.D.T. XXVI–VII
(Walther, fugues); also the Scottish Psalter, 1637, any Lutheran hymn-
book, any hymn-book in English, Buxtehude's fugues, and the
"Chandos" anthems. Bach's echo of the Krieger-Walther subject *may*
be a coincidence of mental habit, confirmed respectively by the openings of Henry Lawes's tune to Ps. 9, the chorale "Was mein Gott will"
(starting E–G), "St. Anne's" ("O God, our help"), Buxtehude's fugue
in E, Handel's "O praise the Lord," and doubtless other works. Yet
one can readily imagine Bach taking the subject from Walther, re-
pointing it—without the twist to the dominant—and then deciding
that it was sacred-folky enough to be suitable for a postscript to his
"Catechism" pieces, and strong enough for triple fugue, and that not
merely the transparent accumulation of theme that had satisfied the
worthy Krieger.

3 (*Page* 43) These and the Eighteen Preludes are published separately in the Novello and Peters (supplementary) editions. Elsewhere
they are all bundled together with miscellaneous preludes. The
"Catechism" preludes contain two preludes on each chorale (three for
"Allein Gott"), one without and one with pedal.

Chapter VII

THE "FORTY-EIGHT"

I. EXQUISITE MINIATURES

IN 1722 there appeared "The well-tempered Clavier," known as the first volume of the same ever since its publication in 1800 with a later set of preludes and fugues, which originally had no titular reference to the first.* The extraordinary finish and astounding emotional variety of this first collection must not be taken for granted, nor its all-key scheme. At the time the tuning of the keyboard was an issue. It was becoming clear that, instead of having a few keys usable and an outer circle discordant, it was essential to the future expansion of musical thought that the comma of error should be distributed evenly amongst the twelve keys, thus making available a complete set of common relationships both in every key and between keys. What was wanted, it seems, was for composers to show the musical gain of being able to go into any and every key *in* a given work, rather than of using every key in turn as the home key. However, Bach was carried away by the plan of composing steadily up the scale, major and minor. Possibly he was encouraged by precedent, even if it was more nominal than creative. He may have seen an identical collection (but not that of the Thuringian organist, B. C. Weber).† He must have seen J. C. F. Fischer's *Ariadne Musica* (1702), a collection of miniature preludes and fugues in all but five keys, for the subjects of the "fugues" in F and E there evidently suggested Bach's for Nos. 11 and 33. But the salient factors in the production are Bach's initial or growing confidence in his capacity to produce so many fugues at his own standard; preludes could be based on a stylish improvisation, where a more concrete conception was lacking, but not a fugue. Only a major creative impulse could have dictated so large a framework for this new venture, and found it no greater measure than could be filled in one way or another. Technical effort could furnish any number of fugues on different subjects in similar patterns. Buxtehude had done as much. But Bach's twenty-four are anything but mass-products. On the contrary, there are scarcely two which might be confused, either in text or treatment. This said, there will be less need to stress the equivalent or possibly greater effort of compiling twenty-four more such keyboard fugues later.

For creative purposes, then, the newly emancipated twenty-four keys, brought into service by an acceptable extension of the existing "Mean Tone" compromise with the natural or scientific scale, made *conveniently distinct* points to which to peg down an unprecedented cluster of new fancies in a prelude and fugue apiece, some quite separately, others perhaps in an intentional succession. It is impossible to establish any evidence of key-quality by comparing the collection either with the organ works or with the second volume. To take two examples, the D minor fugues vary from period to period, apart from a vague austerity, and the fugues in F sharp minor and C sharp minor do not resemble each other, respectively, either in subject, development or texture. The works must be taken as they come, without any predispositions of mood owing to a common or rare key.

On the other hand, there is a certain amount of evidence of a planned contrast in each pair of preludes-with-fugues, and between pairs. This contrast most affects the nature of the fugues. It is at least noticeable that, while the fugue in C major is precise, economical and ingenious, the C minor is off-hand and episodic; that the C sharp major flows easily from entry to episode, while the C sharp minor avoids episode by a *tour de force* in counter-subject development. Again, after the D major, magnificent but scarcely a fugue, the D minor demonstrates inversion and close canon; and after the E flat major, volatile and artless, comes the absorbed "research" fugue in E flat minor. Similar contrasts may be observed in the remaining pairs. They are unofficial but unmistakable, and, in so far as the book may be taken to give an order of succession, help to explain how Bach came to think of, or to place, a fugue or a pair of fugues after its predecessors, whether freshly or on the basis of an earlier draft in another collection (e.g. the keyboard manual Bach wrote for his son Friedemann). It may thus be established that Bach avoids having two fugues of a concentrated professional tone consecutively. There is every evidence, on the contrary, that he wished fugue to express a spirit of release and free movement of idea. He was still more chary of the "research" style in the second volume. Only in the frankly encyclopaedic "Art of Fugue" did he group together technically similar patterns of close canon or double-fugue.

Tabulation also suggests a certain balance and rejoinder between the two halves of the book. The first half contains seven fugues in three parts—the obvious texture for two hands, if there is to be any passage-work worth considering—one in two parts, three in four, one in five. Seven fugues are well under fifty bars and thus exceptionally succinct—confirming Gerber's tale of rapid, "armchair" composition—and of the other five only the C sharp minor and E flat minor are extended. Four fugues concentrate on their subject, the rest rely on episode to maintain interest. In the second half of the book there are now four fugues in three parts, seven in four and one in five; Bach drew more on polyphony here. But again seven show miniature proportions, and only the G major, A minor and B minor are extensive. Two fugues, the G minor and more particularly the A minor, specialize in their subject. One can thus observe Bach's experience favouring first three parts and then the richness of four or five, and preferring a balance of subject-entry and episode but occasionally treating the subject more searchingly, in the vocal tradition. In every fourth fugue (at least) a certain gravity or intensity of mood recurs, from the C sharp minor to the B minor, and tries to prevail against all the ready calmness and vivacity of the remainder. So far the book reflects, romantically, the struggle of the human spirit in a recalcitrant world.

The steady variety and opportunism of the pieces in their actual order having been stressed, it will be convenient here to group the fugues aurally according to their structural nature. This will show most clearly which fugues exhibit a common method, however divergent their melodic content, and will thus save a good deal of verbal repetition. Provisionally, then, we may distribute the fugues of this book as follows—

1. Fugues with episodes in equivalent measure to the subject-entries (15)—

    (a) Mainly organic or extemporary episodes—
        (i) Short: C minor, E flat, E minor, A flat, G sharp minor, B flat.
        (ii) Long: F, A.
    (b) Mainly independent episodes—
        (i) Short: D, F sharp, F sharp minor.
        (ii) Long: C sharp, F minor, G, B minor.

2. Concentration on the subject (9)—

    (a) No thematic devices—Short: E.
    (b) Canon or inversion with slight episode—
        (i) Short: D minor, G minor, B.
        (ii) Long: E flat minor, A minor, B flat minor.
    (c) No episode—
        (i) Short: C.
        (ii) Long: C sharp minor.

Preludes of various kinds, short in every case but one, go with the fugues. Ten are in the extemporary style of a veritable prelude of wayward harmonic sequences or elementary rhythmic development. Others are more balanced pieces, patterned in two or three sections. The E flat minor is an unusual experiment in the *arioso* style, and the E flat major, the one extended prelude, is a sort of prelude and fugue in itself. The preludes thus summon the listener by dashing impromptu, steady interplay of theme, or the tremendous insistence of the B flat minor. The preparation for the fugue is frequently slender and enigmatic. How does the intimate prelude in E make its bustling fugue more credible? Something very near doggedness drove Bach to write a prelude for every fugue, even if there is evidence that he later planned to make a collection of preludes alone.* Yet it is not difficult to

* See Spitta, *J. S. Bach* (English Edition), II, 666.

conceive him fingering prelude after prelude at the keyboard, as extemporization and invention converged in a more urgent, creative mood. Also, the sometimes quite inexplicable or "surrealist" sequence of prelude and fugue is part of the fascination of the book. Assuming, then, a not-too-committal trend in the preludes as such, we may turn to the fugues, on the plan given, without often doing violence to the integrity of prelude and fugue.

In Chapter II the FUGUE IN C MINOR was given as a concise example of fugue in which the distinction of the episodes from full subject-entries is a subtle one. To appreciate the craftsmanship of this fugue calls, indeed, for a fastidious concern for detail. The listener needs ultimately the performer's exactness of ear. In this and other three-part fugues, then, we shall call the "voices" S., A. and B., to suggest a rough but never literal analogy with the interplay of vocal registers.

The subject (A.) is short, but pernickety enough to need the wear and tear of varied entry, counter-subject and episodic fragment to bring out its vitality. Its accompaniment in the second entry soon proves a useful counter-subject, contrasted in rhythm and melodic curve and pulling the harmony firmly towards the new key-note from the falling-point of its scale (I = IV I basically). A further, almost plodding counter-phrase makes a general support and a serviceable bass (bars 15, 20). The disposition of the five remaining entries with only one substantive modulation exposes the economy of phrase. The four combinations of top and bass which make good sense* are eked out by the variants of minor and major, of subject and answer (the former in one key, the latter moving transitionally to its key), of upper and lower octave, and a final drone-bass in lieu of counterpoint. The fourth entry thus avoids repeating the second by the looser effect of its major key and more distant top and bass. The seventh entry just dodges the third by an exchange of upper parts midway.

All the "episodes" but one embody the rapid scales of the counter-subject, propelled by fragments of the subject. The

* a/b, b/a, b/c, a/c, where a is subject, b counter-subject and c the subsidiary phrase, too unmelodic and fragmentary for soprano.

sequence after the sixth entry skilfully diverges from the sequence after the third, and its automatic extension (letting the scales and fragments run on) adroitly prolongs the expectation of the next entry (B.). A unanimous break at the end of this entry prompts a hasty cadence, but, when the bass has reached its final point, the subject can still go on pirouetting on top with a little inner support. The episode after the fifth entry is less volatile, brief as it is. It is an ingenious expansion of the *codetta* or extension after the second entry, with the former S.A. parts inverted to B.A. and then A.B. The otherwise now trite harmony is converted into a more piquant succession of pleasantly resolved discords by pitching the ascending scale (A.) not an octave but a twelfth above its previous position and then changing key and voicing. The soprano adds muscular cohesion to this double ascending sequence, bracing the music before it relaxes to direct entry. The scholastic device of inversion at the twelfth may betray the hand of Esau, but the kid gloves are Jacob's. Thus a natural finger-movement proceeding from the counter-subject gives the subject a perpetual jog, but with a highly polished wit, not blunt insistence. The masterly insouciance of this fugue is irresistible alike to performers and listeners; every examination will enhance the sense of deft consistency. Here one learns afresh what fugal *style* really is. A fiery prelude in the Czerny manner is a suggestive, intentionally "fussy" preliminary to the *jeu d'esprit*, braced by bars 28–34.

The three-voice FUGUE IN E FLAT moves on a broadly similar pattern. The counter-subject (second entry, S.) attends throughout, the episodes are nearly all derived from a figure in the subject, and with one modulation the essential top-and-bass harmony is again liable to pall. But the texture here is quite different. The subject is more harmonic than melodic in outline. It frames a modulation to the key of the dominant, to which the answer replies with tonic harmony.* The counter-subject here is more assimilative than the subversive scales of the C minor fugue. In this more impressionist style entries multiply unobtrusively, with one in each voice to round off the polyphonic revolution. One

---

* The dominantward subjects in this collection are considered in Chapter XVI under *Answer* ((*d*) *Modulation*).

free part throughout keeps the subject fresh. The episodes are equally harmonic. Extensions of the concluding arpeggio figure of the subject gracefully modulate to and fro, in descending sequences. Even the more positive and melodic episode after the second entry in the minor is caught up in extemporary sequences of whirling harmony, which recur an episode later. The restatement (virtually of entries 2–4) proceeds under the same influence, each episode a palpable reverberation. The rhythmic anticipation of the first note of the subject now produces a soluble discord on the main beat, accenting the harmonic trend. (The second entry is adjusted to conform.) The renovation of the last entry is therefore both harmonic and rhythmic. A semitonal twist tightens the impact of the pivotal chord-sequence, followed (as in the C minor) by a unanimous break. Here a further twist in the bass evokes a decorative close.

The fugue thus exhibits a velvety harmonic disposition, whose setting in the repartee of entry and episode is characteristic of Bach's finesse. A too contrapuntal touch (*answer where no answer need be*) would have made the subject too prickly. The dependence of fugal structure on texture is a matter on which text-books say little or nothing. It is reassuring to discover that this apparently artless, fugitive music can at almost every turn be observed to be not only refreshing but *right* in the context. The appeal of the fugue is not at all limited by its slender size, and is quite as much a document in musicianship as the more professional-sounding fugues. It may sound a light postscript to its sturdy and extended prelude, but this is no trifling music.

The two-voice FUGUE IN E MINOR also has a primarily harmonic texture, emphasized by the fluid character of the subject. Again, as it happens, the subject frames a modulation to the dominant, but here the answer provides no variant turn. The counter-subject (S.) shows a clear melodic swoop to its second bar, and it is the making of the first episode, but in the entries it soon becomes part of a set turn of harmony, moving dominantwards of whatever key is in power on the fifth beat. The two typical episodes (bars 5–10, 15–19) also tend to be smooth harmonic sequences, flustered by scales. A steady variation of key freshens the plain combinations of phrase. By means of an effective unison bar (suggesting a return to one strand but preserving the texture) Bach divides the fugue into two closely corresponding halves, thus bringing out the differences of modulation to major and minor keys respectively. After this, one tonic entry is sufficient. A proper entry would move into the dominant. But in the second bar the entrance of the bass in canon creates a diversion. The right hand resumes the subject, a fifth lower, thus aiming straight at the home key. While the commentator is wondering what has happened, a neat goal has been gained. This is more invention than fugue, yet its impatient sweep from key to key in consistent counterpoint earns it a place in the collection. Like life, fugue is not all gas and gaiters, or beauty beyond compare.

The FUGUE IN A FLAT has a subject of one bar, which spells out two or three chords without any frills and with the barest rhythm, and that against the metre. But its treatment is the richest so far considered in the volume. Free counterpoint in two to four parts produces five entries without effort; pungent harmony reinforces the next entry, the first of a procession of variants, in which the original curve is frequently altered in detail, to allow a more elaborate harmony; finally with quiet authority the subject recovers the balance of key after the diversion of a cadence. These plastic entries are held apart and in place by sequences of various kinds. The exposition is dismissed by a sequence firm enough to return twice in fresh voicing (bars 11–12, cf. 14–15, 19–20), renewed the first time by inversion at the twelfth (cf. the C minor). Later come elegant impromptu extensions (bars 25, 31). The general harmonic flow never stops, but detail is fanciful enough to prevent undue anticipation. With provocative humour, in the prelude Bach draws upon a rather threadbare harmonic phrase for a formal binary piece, before proceeding to an even plainer fugal text. But the discourse is another matter.

In the FUGUE IN G SHARP MINOR (in which the bar-lines would have been better placed halfway through each bar as written) Bach returned to a characteristic subject, here with a jaunty side-step to the key of the dominant. The answer lapses a degree at once, and so moves sharpward from the *sub*dominant to the tonic.

With these in mutual rejoinder, supported by a symmetrical counter-subject and broad subsidiary phrase (bass of second and third entries), the exposition readily doubles its first four entries now (T.B.T.A.), except that the fifth entry echoes the fourth with odd exactness. The other half of the fugue passes through two fresh keys, distinctively enough to call for a return to the original subject and answer. A short, organized and relevant sequence (bar 20) introduces these excursions and the recovery later. Other spaces are filled by simple sequential extensions of the "conversational" tag that ends the subject, first ascending but later descending. The same figure appears with piquant harmony in the last entry, and provokes a marked rejoinder in the bass, to restore poise for the cadence. The prelude is serious and almost yearning, with its diminished seventh in the first bar and an intenser version in the penultimate chord. But the doubly dominant figure of this engaging fugue should be played lightly, or pungently to a fault, otherwise the twenty-fold recurrence of this cadential tag would be insufferably didactic.

The FUGUE IN B FLAT pursues an unfaltering course with a forthright subject of the manually active kind, an apt counter-subject and an adaptable third part to cement the joinery. The subject, melodic at first, settles down to a "chime" round dominant and tonic harmony, emphasizing the key. This prompts not only a rising sequence of escape (bars 17–18) but systematic changes of key, none settled until an entry in the subdominant prompts a recovery of the main key, with the chime readily reverberating towards a conclusion, artfully delayed by the bass. Contrapuntal blends of the chime-figure and the first bar in sliding secondary sevenths furnish mobile interludes (bars 19–21, 30–34). So sprightly a piece, not too shy of the predictable or even commonplace bar, is a definite addition to fugal experience. (Here, again, the accent falls on the *second* beat of the bar more often than not.) There is a whirling, grandly pointed prelude, ending in the air. The prosaic descent to *terra firma* (many editions) is the invention of some Biedermeier.

The vivacious and volatile three-voice fugues in F and A are more extensive examples of the same type of organic episode.

The FUGUE IN A conveys a feeling of spaciousness, with its counter-exposition (B.S.) and minor entry in fifteen bars, and a fresh start with a liquescent counter-subject, after a clutter of false (i.e. partial) entries. Episodes arise mainly from the diffusion of the ascending fourths of the subject, borne along later by the new counter-subject in fresh contexts. Irregular moves to minor keys converge in one answer-entry, continued in free style; there is no point in reviving the original chase of theme. An ungainly curve of ascending fourths springs to life in varied counterpoint, uniform or capricious. Setebos contemplates the sprawling Caliban. How much more sprawling he might have been may be observed in a Pachbelel fugue-subject later (Ex. 54A). A methodically polyphonic prelude exercises the ear in detecting a singularly recurrent blend of phrase in variant voicing and key, with flowing episode.

In the FUGUE in F the triple metre—it should be a clear three beats after the four of the prelude's $^{12}_{8}$—is inimical to the half-bar sequences and close imitation of four beats. Bach accordingly makes the most of the entire subject, and develops imitation and sequence in broad stretches of a whole bar or two. The subject is derived apparently from Fischer's "fugue" in F (see p. 48), where the rhythm is uniformly ♩. ♪ ♩. Bach's less stilted subject preserves the steady underlying sequence of thirds falling from D–C–B flat–A, bar by bar. A counter-subject fills in the cadence for the third and fourth bars. Counter-exposition (S.A.B.) diminishes the harmonic echoes (the fifth and sixth entries closely reflect the third) by textural variants (octave), and is extended by a further entry (A.) in canon with the bass, shaking its harmony out of its rut. The conjunct movement of the subject invites such a canon at the octave in the third bar. The cue passes to minor keys in longer chains of entries. The counter-subject survives only in its rhythm. The subject avoids monotony by ornamental touches (bars 49, etc.). The ornament at once forms material for imitation and sequence, propelled by plain ascending scales (B., S. and A.). The last soprano entry similarly extends to a graceful ascent before its cadence. Such is the compelling quality of fastidious detail in an otherwise directly melodious fugue. The canon, dismissed in a foreign key and unrelieved by canon at the fourth, places this out of range of the "research" fugues of the next chapter. Subject and counter-subject are displayed resourcefully both in entry and episode. The ripeness is all.

We turn to fugues whose episodes are less derivative or purely connective matter. The four-voice FUGUE IN D of twenty-seven bars is a striking example, for those who have the patience to follow a movement of thought which is concentrated into a minute and a half. (Here, again, the metre would be clearer if the bar-line were half way through each bar.) The subject is a flourish (an after-thought), a leap and a punctilious descent. It soon covers five entries and the usual foreign keys in blunt harmony (but adroitly avoiding a pivotal *subdominant*-dominant bass every time). After that, nothing but the flourish, the leap and the punctilious rhythm remains. An episodic figure which emerged after the first minor-key entry (cf. bar 3*d*) thus takes command, attended by the flourish and the stretch upward—the main curve has served its turn—and terminated by a grandly punctilious cadence, or rather chain of cadences. Bach never wrote such a fugue again. (What academic withers he would have wrung, if he had made a practice of it!) But how justly the fugue becomes music; the grandiloquent subject being ridiculous in formal restatement, the episode develops a sense of finish, exploiting the four-strand weave in movement in chords as well as in polyphony. As Wilde once remarked, there is nothing so innocent as indiscretion; and, though drafted earlier, this indiscretion is admirably placed after the monumental C sharp minor fugue. It seems to have attracted players of all ages, as much as if it were forbidden fruit. Such rousing polyphony-harmony calls, indeed, to be brought into daily life, by any name. The prelude seems a niggardly preparation, too canny by half, and suspiciously like a *violin* Study, reduced to "*cembalo*" (cymbal) level.

The three-voice FUGUE IN F SHARP (which again would be better barred at the half-bar) holds subject and episode in delicate balance. The shapely subject gains five expository entries, reaches the relative minor, and returns home via the subdominant, like the B flat fugue (similar subject, rising to tonic). An apt counter-subject in the exposition returns at the very end. But the flowing figure which marks the separation of exposition and counter-exposition maintains a steady interlude-element, penetrates (in inverse curve) the counter-exposition and subsequent entries at the expense of the counter-subject, and forms sundry sequences. The firm curve of the subject emerges from these interludes without a sense of strain, but the "episode" has the last word. The latter develops an obstinate drone in its later form (cf. passing chord of bar 21*d*). This finished masterpiece needs its six sharps, free from the trite associations of F and C, which the standardization of keyboard pitch brings to unconscious or conscious memory ("absolute pitch"), whatever variations prevailed on keyboard instruments in Bach's day. An equally distinctive prelude shows a subtle melodic line, and a penultimate touch of the tonic minor, a passing shadow before the fugal image of untroubled life.

The interludes of the four-voice FUGUE IN F SHARP MINOR are comparatively slender, but their organized sequences produce a consistent counter-interest. They derive from the imitative figure in the spare bar after the second entry, and from the counter-subject. The subject shows a firm, conjunct vocal line, and the

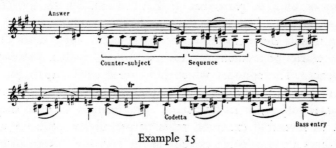

Example 15

counter-subject forms an independent sequence and counter-stress. The unusual entry of the fourth voice (after an episode) with the subject instead of the answer has a stabilizing effect. Seldom does a melodious subject make a good bass, as here, and the plastic counter-subject follows suit. All this would lose its character in a conventional chain of keys. Instead, a complete and more continuous counter-exposition is effected (A.S.T.B.), with fresh features in abundance. The subject is twice inverted (A.B.), with new incidental twists of key, and the counter-subject develops steadily throughout. After this virtual expansion, the return of the normal subject at soprano level, attended by expectant bass (dominant), is final enough. This fugue is so far one prolonged exposition, without any positive modulation beyond the dominant. (Further stirrings in "Look here, sir!" department). Yet it does not sound incomplete or monotonous, but rather a rich discourse in a confined orbit, prepared by a short concentrated prelude. When pain and anguish wring the brow, play or remember the F sharp minor. (This is not purely fanciful. The paired-notes figure of the counter-subject is paralleled both in the "Lament" of the early and light-hearted Capriccio, "On the departure of a beloved brother," and in many references to the Passion in the church music.)

Alternatively, there is the longer-drawn emotional stress of the F and B minor, which are also for four voices. The FUGUE IN F MINOR presents a tortuous semitonal subject in a vocal style, and a trenchant counter-subject, whose harmony with the subject colours the whole fugue and whose rhythm determines the episodes. Further counter-phrases are obscurely involved, with constant crossing of parts (bar 7, T.A., cf. 13, 19, 28, 47; 13d, tenor, cf. 28). Exposition thus reaches six studious entries. In two middle entries in the major the counterpoint is fresh. The two entries of restatement thus pass muster, with a drawn-out cadence. The episodes which hold these entries apart are all derived, rather officiously, from the ascending formula of the counter-subject (or its inversion). The formula varies in shape, but its sevenfold extension relies perpetually on sequence and becomes a too palpable exercise in the provision of ornamental counterpoint. These voluble episodes make the fugue tiresome. No one else could have written it, but it is certainly too long.

The FUGUE IN B MINOR has a more elaborate and pungently semitonal subject, with a twist to the dominant at the end, which is answered by an equally tortuous and symmetrical passage to the tonic. Its accompaniment contains two elements which at once separate, a busy climbing figure, marked by the rise or fall of a third, and a descent in whole beats, which has an antiseptic effect on the otherwise too "spotty" semitonal growth; the second of these stays seriously with the subject. Entries thus move freely, and a normal four spreads out to three more (A.T.B.), in three-part texture. (No four-part writing counts until the penultimate entry.) Middle entries arise with equal freedom. They move across from the usual major keys to the dominant and then establish an unusual centre, the subdominant *major* (bar 57). This last makes a firm *point d'appui* for a formal recovery, with fresh counterpoint as well as the earlier material. But these strained entries occupy rather more than half the 76-bar fugue. Episodes spring partly from a stray and wiry figure that follows the second entry, developed in sequence and imitation with some trenchancy. An interminable sequence which follows this after the exposition (bar 17) is extended at the first opportunity and recalled later (bars 26, 65); and the thirds of the original counter-subject develop into a consistent figure, at first as the cohesive factor of a couple of close but false entries (bar 34, cf. 69). Most episodes sound laboured or, as in the false entries, frivolously academic. For all its forcible style, the fugue in B minor is too uneven to make a climax of the second part of the book. And the prelude, a patient pilgrimage over hard places, suggests that Bach was in a searching mood at the outset.

The continuity of the three-voice FUGUE IN C SHARP MAJOR is possibly an easier achievement, but it remains. In outline the subject falls in steps from dominant to tonic, after a preliminary flourish, and that natural compulsion persists. An exuberant counter-subject, soon inseparable, provokes a discord that makes that descent necessary, followed by a whirling sequence of cadential harmony; and a recurrent plain descent adds grit. An extra soprano entry answers the third entry, after an interlude with a more direct cadence. Two entries in the minor are closely followed by dominant and tonic entries. These might be final, but for the absence of any confirmatory signs. But the next full entry, artfully delayed, leads into a full recapitulation, with a change in the interlude to bring the fourth entry in the tonic and a diversion of the natural cadence of this (basically V VI–II–V–I) to promote a summary and organic finish. (As in the original subject, the soprano finally *descends* to the tonic, as in the air, "My heart, ever faithful," in Cantata 68.) This precise restatement avoids vain repetition by the alteration of textural detail and final key. In these three stages, entries are urged forward by sequential episodes, mainly a broad development of the counter-subject, with a prevailing outline of a descent in thirds and one other interval (bar 7, cf. 16, 31, 49; ascent in 12, 28b). The rest grows out of the subject, with increasing resource in the episode before the restatement. Here the all-too infallible descent of the subject is attached to fresh degrees and held in suspense by a vibrating chordal figure around one note in Alberti style (see p. 31), below or above. Thus an assured return must balance this frustration. It took Bach to continue after the middle tonic entry (bar 27) without using more than a harmonic formula. The fugue is a document in episodic craftsmanship, and a worthy plea for C sharp major, after a brilliant prelude of recurring phrase, spontaneous scintillation, luxurious suspense and a thumping resolution of impetuous beats after harmony in bars.

The three-voice FUGUE IN G shows at first a pronounced cultivation of its subject, but in the second half the full subject does not appear, and the flow of impromptu sequence and persistent episode exceeds, if anything, the more official agenda. It would be absurd to call this a "research" fugue. The counter-subject rises symmetrically with the subject and fills in its capricious sevenths as they kick against the metre. Counter-exposition (A.S.B.) is framed, without any loosening of the weave, round the subject inverted at the fifth, with the inverted counter-subject in Jeeves-like attendance, brushing up detail in the second entry to make the *outré* sevenths more wearable. For the rest, minor-key entries are balanced by a leisurely and informal recovery. The first of these is the last heard of the full subject. The second inverts the subject at the *third*, with the counter-subject back in telling conformity. An absent-minded entry, "omitting" the second bar, now makes close canon workable. Repeated later, this plausible concentration begins a concluding display of irregularity: inversion, half an inversion, and vague entry a third higher than usual, with rhetorical compensations. These opportunist sallies are readily held apart, then, by episodes based on the characteristic sequence which divides exposition and counter-exposition. Jaunty cross-rhythm combines with revolving chords on Alberti lines (bar 15, cf. 31, 48, 65); or the centrifugal drive of an Alberti bass whirls a roll of scale at random like a Catherine-wheel (bars 34, 74). The increasing exhilaration takes the thematic evasions in its stride, and the consequences of an early inversion are buoyantly faced. Never was there such an unfaltering call to use the rotary muscles! Was it, perhaps, through this ascension of the Alberti figure to the ether of Olympic laughter that Tobias Matthay gained a new conception of manual control on the keyboard?

Our survey of fifteen examples of the collection has revealed a fresh type of fugue, depending on a delicate adjustment of entry and episode, not merely on contrapuntal animation and breezy aside; the product, not of scholastic research, but of a much rarer quality, a pinpoint musicianship unknown to our sophists. Conscious absorption of such technique as there has been space to tabulate is uncommonly stimulating towards the general under-standing of problems of musical style. The more one probes the pattern, the more vividly does the mind at its centre declare itself. In the other nine fugues, the composer focuses more obvious attention on his subject, and these demand a fresh start. Their haphazard appearance, from C to B major, is evidence of the spontaneity of the more concentrated method, but it will be convenient to take the nine together, in the order already detailed.

NOTES

1 (*Page* 48) I have adopted the common English title for the total output, as avoiding the title Bach reserved for the first set, and never-theless lumping together two volumes which it is now impossible to dissociate, any more than one dissociates Beethoven's early and late piano sonatas. Whatever possessed Bach to cover the twenty-four keys again, he must have been aware of some sense of continuing a previous 24-prong creative movement.

In his edition of the "Forty-eight" for the Bach Society's complete edition (Vol. 14), the editor mentions Schwencke's copy of the second set (*c.* 1781) as the earliest to use the title of "Well-tempered Clavier."

Presumably it is from this copy that this title (with "Second Part") is quoted in *The Bach Reader* (H. T. David and A. Mendel), p. 173, amongst contemporary documents of Bach's life. Repeated inquiries have failed to gain any information on the source of this quotation, which ends "Anno 1744" but is not therefore to be taken as contemporary.

2 (*Page* 48) The manuscript, in the library of the Brussels Conservatoire, bears the impossible date 1689. The set has been credibly dated *c.* 1750 by Bukofzer (*Music in the Baroque Era*, p. 298, *n.*).

C. Guillet, of Bruges (d. 1654), wrote twice twelve Fantasias on the twelve modes—doubtless an infectious scheme.

F. Suppig, Dresden organist, wrote a *Labyrinthus musicus* "in all the keys," dated 1722 (Paris Conservatoire). More maze than music, perhaps, but still a straw to show a gathering wind.

Chapter VIII

THE "FORTY-EIGHT"

II. CONCENTRATION ON A SUBJECT

THE three-voice FUGUE IN E contrives to convey a striking sense of orderly travel in under thirty bars. The subject's rhythmic jerk catches the ear each time, and the plain dominant-tonic harmony of the first two half-bars (except in bars 4–10, the fugue is misleadingly barred) makes a strong rhythmic unit. The jerk forward is usually supported by a steady "screwing-in" figure, which at first belongs to the previous entry but later detaches itself as an impressionist feature. A counter-exposition (S.A.B.), two entries in the relative minor, and a recapitulation so succinct (closer third entry) as to leave room for more, space out the fugue in balanced stages. Entries are adroitly separated by sequential developments of the screwing-in figure, as background or for its own sake. Hence the classification of this as a "subject" fugue. Yet the outcome is (or should be) a lively spasm of flying polyphony, in which one symbol acquires many nuances. The thoughtful prelude is a surprising *point d'appui*. But the absence of a calculated and perpetual roundness of impression keeps the "Forty-eight" on our desks quite as much as its more integral qualities.

In the FUGUE IN D MINOR (three voices) a parsimonious economy of material soon declares itself. The very subject seems to rise grudgingly to the mediant before making the crucial leap to the submediant on the off-beat, and the counter-subject encumbers that ascent by the contrariness of suspended and other non-harmonic notes. An extra entry (S.), freely re-shaping the melodic curve, sets the type for repetitions of phrase in which the leap of a sixth (or fifth) is treated as the main issue after an adaptable first bar, and may be repeated in descending sequence. The next entry (S. answer) is countered by inversion in close canon

(A.), with a pungent semitonal sequence, which prompts an equally two-minded bass, with alto in direct canon, to form a graceful cadence in the dominant. In what proves the other half of the fugue the process continues in singularly fresh detail, with subject and inversion on equal terms. The graceful cadence is steered into the tonic, reinforced by a sonorous concentration of the opening bar to summarize the argument. The order of events is chiefly of canonic opportunism, controlled by a nice balance of tonic and subdominant trends, not determined till the last bar of all. But pathetic sequences based on the second bar, and odd false entries, form slight interludes, and a poignant blend of counter-subject and inverted subject enhances the arrival of the last canon. The austere *Affekt* is flecked with lyrical touches, and the resource never sounds strained. Rather, the merits of the awkward, sentimental relative, a "dry old stick," are preserved for all time in terms of an elegant pathos. A frail prelude, plaintively semitonal towards the end, sets the tone for prelude and fugue more precisely than usual.

The four-voice FUGUE IN G MINOR, also insistent and pathetic, shows a more melodious vein, but the texture is conventional. A typical stooping subject—spanning a piquant seventh—with an efficient counter-subject, gains a plain exposition, middle entries in the major and an increasingly tense subdominant, and a clear recovery, with a modicum of close canon and relevant episode. The basically conjunct ascent of the subject on each beat lends itself to close canon at two beats' interval; either canon at the fifth, forming thirds above the prior entry, or canon at the octave, forming thirds below, with a further canon to that (bars 17, 28). After these close pursuits of theme, the subject can still return twice (A.T.) as the pertinent background of a vital soprano line that rises and falls with the mechanical ease of the keyboard but still has its climax and quittal, as something attempted and remembered. The plain anticipation of the soprano descent in the bass is a relief from the plaster of the counter-subject. The bland persistence of subject seems almost a sketch of self-righteous gloom. The opening phrase was used (fugally) in the early funeral cantata, "God's time is the best" (106), to convey false pessimism in face of death (with C the third note, twisting to F sharp). This coincidence permits a reference to a professional mourner of almost "Bunbury" standards of hypocrisy. The association is highly fanciful; but this smug fugue is more tolerable if it is partly ironical. As a wholly serious pursuit of a Point, it strikes a note of forbidding, obsessional strain.

The four-voice FUGUE IN B (in which, again, the main metrical accent comes on the third beat) recalls the F sharp fugue in texture, but keeps much more to its initial text. The subject, with its dominant-tonic harmonic basis, recalls that of the fugue in E in outline. The answer here, however, avoids a literal repetition. The composer's choice is acceptable to the ear, and logical enough by the conventions (see p. 166), and it leaves an exact answer in useful reserve. The counter-subject is constantly felt, defining the harmony. Exposition is followed by an elaborate counter-exposition (T.A.S.A.B.), keeping up a polyphony of four or three voices. Fresh soprano and bass interest is a constant feature, but meanwhile the subject undergoes change. At the third entry it is inverted at the fifth, and precisely and elegantly harmonized to suit the accentuation of the subdominant. The answer to this seems to be establishing the inversion, but musical sense has been strained for this purpose, and a normal tonicward entry intervenes. The next entry moves from a subdominant start to its relative, the supertonic minor, the only foreign key of entry, but enough to justify the recovery of subject and answer in a facile setting of spaced-out hands, a restored counter-subject and pertinent scales. As in the fugue in F sharp minor, inversion forms a special variant in a somewhat precious fugue. A decorative sequential episode separates exposition from counter-exposition and recurs later. An intimate melodic development is thus carried along by a flow of extemporary figures.

We come to two contrasted fugues where bookish methods are more conspicuous, the E flat and A minor. The three-voice FUGUE IN E FLAT MINOR has a shapely vocal subject, rising and falling with a strong suggestion of tonic harmony. It is announced in free counterpoint. Counter-exposition (B.A.S., S.A., S.A.) is manifold but compressed. The plain canon in the soprano maintains the opening harmony in a tight two-strand weave, elastic in rhythmic detail. After a canon so elastic as to be negligible as such, apart from cross-rhythm, a more normal canon modulates to the major. Melodic inversion now determines the connecting thought of a fresh chain of recognizable but not too literal entries (S.A.B.), ending in the tonic. Inversion in canon follows, regularly (B.S.) and elastically (A.S.) in turn (bars 44–9, cf. 19–26). From a "masterly" accumulation of partial entries, first of the subject, then of the inversion, the subject emerges on top of fresh polyphony, its descending line prolonged by alto syncopation.

Subject and inversion being now exhausted as basic symbols, doubling the stretch of rhythm (as in numberless settings of Tones and Chorales) is the only way to freshen the essential counterpoint, supported by the original subject-rhythm in an increasingly accessory role. A complete restatement (B.A.S.) thus takes shape in a broad disposition of key (subdominant, mediant major, tonic), qualified in detail. The soprano lapse during descent prompts further sequences and a final semitonal ascent to make things even. With all its daring construction on a consistent motive, the fugue suffers from its elegant tenuous theme, so much happier as its lyrical self than facing the gymnastics of inversion and canon. It is noticeable that when, over twenty-five years later, Bach contemplated a fugal demonstration, he took a subject that began as in the present fugue, but without any frills (D–A–F–D); and that gymnastics fit the more elementary subject better. Surely Bach remembered the exhaustive but exhausting canonic experience of the E flat minor when he hit upon a subject for "The Art of Fugue." Here, indeed, the arresting prelude brings the listener to the fugue in a state of intense anticipation; and the consistency of the fugue is striking in its austerity. But it is so overdone as to thwart its expressive ends.

The stalwart subject of the early four-voice FUGUE IN A MINOR, the longest in the collection, is built for wear. Apart from a recurring descent of four notes, the counterpoint of the exposition develops freely around the subject, absorbing it in the prevailing weave. It remains an overpoweringly breast-forward theme, and counter-exposition (S.T.B.A.) takes to inversion. The falling seventh and third (bar 2) reverse awkwardly (G F^{l}–A^{l}). By making it F sharp, Bach secures instead a pivotal chord for a new key, G, in which the entry closes. With this door open, the subsequent entries begin in one key and move to another (relative major to subdominant, vice versa, neutral to tonic). Once more, an awkward transition has become a structural development. By closing the door at the end, however, this development ranges itself with the exposition. Yet the next change is neither of key nor of basic text. It is a systematic re-entry of the normal subject or answer, with a close and complete canon at the octave (S.T., A.B., T.A.). The canon is soon submerged in the counter-point. Indeed, except for the recurring span of three bars, countered two beats later, one might scarcely be aware how organic the counterpoint is. A further canon in the major inten-sifies the canonry in the third bar (bar 46). Undaunted, Bach treats the inverted subject with a similar canon, with an avoidance of the previous voicing of the organic phrases and making them more transparent (A.T., B.S., S.A.). Key-variation spices the disposition of entries but returns to the tonic.

So far, competent calculation of the possibilities of consonance in the close duplication of the successive scale-degrees of 12–34–56–71–23 (or their reversal, 54–32–17–65–4) has guided the out-line or inner content of an otherwise improvised keyboard polyphony. A short episode (bars 61–4) seems to draw breath and ask experience, "But will the slide-rule go any further?" It can move further. Canon may be pitched a *fifth* apart from the leading voice (56–78, etc., or 87–65, etc.), making thirds above or below it (bars 65, 68), with accidentals freshly adjusted to the key of the *canon*; the old canon on the inversion can begin in a remote key and be twisted elsewhere (bar 75); and entries may conven-iently be pitched so as to converge and accumulate on one pivotal chord (43–2, 56–78–2, 23–4). But here the traditional technique hangs fire. Canonry has reached a state of rest or movement along one line (D minor), and an arresting cadence is essential. In answer to a "Neapolitan" move to an utter halt on the dominant chord (see Ex. 43A), further canons at the fifth are useful to keep up the sway of key until the pendulum rests on the tonic. A final temptation to multiply token groups of 54-3, 32-1, 56-(5) and 34-5 above the tonic bass (pedal) proves irresistible, leaving a major finish.

Here, then, the theme is subject to perpetual stress by total inversion and canon—the "model" is evidently a fugue in A minor by Buxtehude—and this is so pronounced that each transformation must be any intelligent listener's concern. Yet what has here been observed so far affects only two parts of a rich manifold. The quips and quirks of canonry are amply clothed in voluble and shapely phrases. The prelude strikes a somewhat monotonous note, but the fugue will only stale in hands which treat matter beyond the subject as of no consequence. There is a genuine quality about this crusty old theme, which no wear and tear can expunge. If dated 1707-8 (Spitta), the fugue is a *tour de force*.

At the same time the five-voice FUGUE IN B FLAT MINOR will be something of a relief to the ear, among fugues of the research class. A brief but suggestive vocal phrase reaches a dignified exposition with a margin of extension by dovetailing sequences. Further entries in the relative major and subdominant are spaced out by a plastic polyphony of 3-5 voices, which is strengthened by an inner harmonic rhythm, and by the repeat of an earlier sequence (bar 42, cf. 6). Restatement begins, but is diverted by an aurally rather obscure set of close and partly coincident entries in the subdominant, balanced by a double entry and extension in thirds. A lengthening soprano descent by step, tensely harmonized, closes in a further accumulation of coincident canons, pressed home by diminished sevenths and minor ninths, with a suggestion of the subject in canon to make the very cadence organic. The freedom with which this vocal and yet ultimately clanging polyphony spreads into a complete fugue, drawing scarcely at all on keyboard rhetoric, apart from varied chording, is a perpetual wonder. The urgent, massive prelude, the most penetrating in the volume, makes a fine opening summons.

The two fugues left, otherwise so different in scale and method, have one feature in common: the elimination of episode. The inner logic is uninterrupted in each case. In the four-voice

FUGUE IN C, the rise and fall of the subject is rhythmically notched (third and sixth beats) to secure its impact in any situation. Exposition in homogeneous counterpoint merges insensibly into a counter-exposition whose canons at one beat's interval (S.T., B.A.) provide new harmony and lead to an entry in the relative minor, whose pungent cadence makes a halfway point, as the dominant does in the D minor fugue. The music proceeds pithily to its destination with suggestions of many keys and many fresh and typical canons, sufficiently punctuated to avoid confusion and ensure coherent point for each appearance of the chosen symbol. One cannot but admire the swiftness with which the "subject" develops its own atmosphere and multiplies new allusions. This close fugue has a rare spontaneity. Once accomplished, Bach in his wisdom did not try to repeat the type, and in general fell back upon the new kind of entry-and-episode exhibited in the C minor. The famous prelude in C major, whose melody is implicit and, so far from lacking in nutriment, makes the adventitious air of Gounod's "Ave Maria" a grotesque tribute, quietly flows into the listener's ear in readiness for the concentrated pursuit of theme; cleansing it, indeed, of any Gounod.

In default of any other evidence, in "The well-tempered Clavier" Bach moved from key to key from C major, when the project was fresh. No fugue can be declared early and immature, and the miniatures are in no way inferior to the longer examples. Yet the FUGUE IN C SHARP MINOR may well have been, what it sounds, a late development, deliberately placed in a key to which Bach did not turn spontaneously at first. It stands by itself, as the emanation of one subject and the revelation of latent power.

Like the B flat minor fugue, this five-voice fugue builds a striking opening out of its spare and vocal subject, with shrewd deployment of the voices around subject and answer. The maintenance of the full five-strand texture is reserved for the *answer* of the sixth entry, which promotes a counter-exposition, moving from tonic to relative major on the same conjunct lines. Now comes the rub. The B flat minor can space out entries by relevant connective matter. No pliable figure has emerged from this exposition; and the development of an independent episode would soon become a too conscious contrast with the set style of the opening matter. Hence the subject (*a*) must be equipped with figures in the form of counter-subjects, whose promotion will be distracting enough to take the music beyond its original argument. An oscillating but symmetrical figure (*b*), descending in sequence, appears at once, and a rhythmic tag (*c*) attaches itself later (bar 49). These form the pervasive ingredients in a fresh series of entries, spaced out by incidental extensions of *b* in rising or falling sequence. The key drops to the subdominant in the fourth entry, and thence to its relative major, the submediant. The tonic recovered, there is a corresponding stretch of key northward, to the supertonic (S. in canon with T.). Otherwise the prevailing subject-harmony, in the varied voicing of *a*, *b* and *c* and free elements, keeps to the tonic, except for one further subdominant entry. The main interest lies thus in the varieties of top and bass, and the position of the subject in the polyphony. (Bar 82 oddly repeats bar 74.) The delivery of *b* and *c* at varying intervals is scarcely possible; *b* would not fit *a* at another degree, and *c*, invertible at the twelfth, would make a faulty progression in octaves with *b*. Instead, *c* enters at odd extra places between entries. (Bach's counter-subjects have a perpetual way of not entering where they should, and slipping in where they are never expected.)

The triple counterpoint of *a*, *b* and *c* thus austerely maintains the subject for sixty-five bars beyond the exposition without calling on other matter. It remains to exhibit this section as in some sense episodic. The tireless half-beat rhythm of *b* is exhausted, but it must be replaced. Instead of symmetrical entries of three bars or more, the subject is applied in a series of close canons, with *c* underlining the cross-accents and entering elsewhere. Modulation to the mediant minor (further south than in any other minor fugue) implements further entries. A final subdominant entry, with *c* moving lingeringly to the chord of the tonic (already established in the bass) seems to anticipate the prolonged close of Beethoven's C sharp minor quartet.

A long art, little to be acquired from precedents, carried the composer here from an absorbed and apparently unpromising exposition to a procession of vivacious variants of the subject, and on to a texture less energetic but more emotionally charged and no less insistent in another way. It took Bach to exhibit all the main combinations of theme, not as a climax but as a steady *ballon d'essai*, and then to reveal the subject in a fresh and more intense light. No category had been given for this fugue! It remained *sui generis* in the volume and was never repeated.

Such are some of the structural qualities of the first twenty-four of the "Forty-eight." They need, perhaps, a special devotion to be played or studied in bulk and in close succession, as here. Bach administered to the high gaiety of an industrious community, but he also developed his already accomplished technique over an exceptional range of precise intimations. The cumulative experience, however deliberately covered by the listener, remains; and Bach himself sometimes liked to play each book straight through.* The variety of approach and the concern for consistent detail are constant and striking features. Scarcely a single work can be dismissed as ineffective or incoherent or even as dull. These are not two dozen examples of a given mould: they are two dozen phases of expression in a major creative effort dedicated to a broadly fugal texture and structure. No true account of one fugue applies to another. It was the strange *individuality* of the fugues, indeed, which still most impressed the musical world of 1750. They spoke too characteristically to sound like fugues.

Shortly after this, Bach became choirmaster at St. Thomas's, Leipzig. Here for twenty years he was mainly engaged, apart from rehearsing choir and orchestra for the Sunday anthem, in the composition of church music. We shall consider the fugal choruses concerned in a later chapter. We turn, then, to the "Twenty-four preludes and fugues" of 1740–44, which formed the second volume of "The well-tempered Clavier" as published in 1800.† Serially they exhibit an obvious identity of plain title from C major to B minor, and suggest a similar structural enterprise. They also issue some sort of challenge to the earlier set, by more emphasis of some fugal types and less of others, by usually wider proportions, and by various signs of an organized advance from the succinct style without loss of consistency. They cannot be heard, as a whole, in general isolation from the historical volume which preceded them by twenty-two or more years. Whatever fresh impulse carried Bach the whole way from C to B a second time, he must have been deeply conscious of the fugal track of 1722.

NOTES

1 (*Page* 73) In Vol. 1 of his Lexicon (1790–92), E. L. Gerber states that, when his father was at Leipzig University in 1725, Bach taught him fugue-playing, from the Inventions to "The well-tempered Clavier," which he played through altogether three times. "Bach thus turned hours into minutes." A happy testimony to the integrity of the basic intimations of the collection.

2 (*Page* 73) Forkel (1802) gives no date. C. L. Hilgenfeldt gives 1740 in his *J. S. Bachs Leben, Wirken und Werke* (1850), apparently from an autograph he had from C. P. E. Bach. C. F. G. Schwencke's copy (Berlin National Library) gives 1744, and this more solid evidence has been generally accepted. The B. M. autograph has no title-page. In relation to the contemporary publication of the "Catechism" Preludes, 1739, and "Goldberg" Variations, 1742, the later date seems the more likely. The point is scarcely important, except that 1740 widens the gap from "The Art of Fugue"—making it a still more sudden revelation of fugue in itself—but the now forgotten conflicting evidence, assembled by Spitta, may be re-stated as the true basis of the arbitrary later date now lightly accepted for fact. On the question of title, see page 63n.

Chapter IX

THE "FORTY-EIGHT"

III. SUBJECT AND EPISODE AGAIN

B Y 1740 the question of tuning was long settled. Earlier suites in B flat minor (Havingha, 1725) presuppose the modern equal-temperament system. We may take it that Bach began by writing preludes and fugues in various keys and then warmed to the plan of completing the key-register again.

As fugues accumulated once more, the thorough-going episodic type was favoured less, and the "subject" type more, the proportions being four to eight in each half of the book, a direct reversal of previous trends. There is, however, as Spitta noted, less technical display. The "subject" fugues range from the canonic type set up by the first fugue of the "Forty-eight" to the unobtrusive development of counter-subjects and auxiliary subjects. In this exploitation of counter-theme, Bach adopted the fugal line which led him to some of his finest discoveries later. The majority of the fugues are on a wider scale here, but the same consistency of style continues to impress the ear. There is very little note-spinning for the sake of keyboard practice. Rather, the implications of a subject are pursued more freely here. The fugal types are distributed as follows, if we take fifty bars as a working borderline between short and long fugues. It will be found that Nos. 2–9 are "subject" fugues, Nos. 10–13 episodic. There is no patent balance of types in each pair or quartet of fugues. Each piece is separate. Some fugues fill a gap in key by the transposition of an earlier existing fugue or draft. Comparisons of texture show a decided preference for three-part fugues, modifying the previous balance. The Chromatic Fugue and No. 8 of "The Art of Fugue" similarly forgo polyphonic density for the sake of a more dashing style.

1. Episodic—
   (a) Organic episodes—
       Long: C, E minor, F sharp, G, B flat, B minor.   (6)
   (b) Independent episodes—
       Long: F, F minor.   (2)

2. "Subject"—
   (a) With episodes—
       (i) Short: D sharp minor, A, A minor.
       (ii) Long: A flat.   (4)
   (b) Canonic—
       (i) Short: C minor, C sharp, D, D minor, E flat, E.
       (ii) Long: B flat minor.   (7)
   (c) Development of counter-subject—
       Long: C sharp minor, G minor, B.   (3)
   (d) Second or third subject—
       Long: F sharp minor, G sharp minor.   ·   (2)

The preludes exhibit no less a more persistent kind of invention. Four preserve the old ruminant, non-committal style. Four others contrive to be brief. The rest are developed pieces, many in measured dance-suite form, preludes only in coming first. They are duly balanced by extensive fugues or, as in the fugue in D, by a concentrated example.* Nevertheless, an almost froward habit furnished a prelude again for every fugue. A laboured manner is often perceptible. In many cases the prelude seems anything but a preparation, in the educational sense. Here, again, Bach later contemplated assembling the preludes separately. It may be said that this is just disagreeable comment in defence of the modern composer, who is too proud to condition his audience. But why did Bach abandon the prelude idea in his "exhibition" set, "The Art of Fugue"? It is idle to deny that for the sake of a full and symmetrical volume Bach was prepared to put in preludes of inferior interest in comparison with their fugues; sometimes, one suspects, because a prelude in the right or near key was

* See Appendix.

already available. The modern listener does not need these preludes. Some liberty, then, should be given to the performer who is bold enough to withhold a prelude from a fugue which needs no introduction for an attentive audience, and who can thus adroitly link a greater number of fugues, freed of their discursive preludes.

We may now turn to individual fugues, beginning with the discursive type. Of six with organic episodes, two or more "provide no new material for the critic." The FUGUE IN C resembles the first C sharp major in subject, texture and shape. The subject is chiefly a syncopated ornamentation of wayward descents from the dominant. The garrulous sequential figure of the second part (F E | D : G F | E) forms the counter-subject (as | E : E D | C : C B | A), and develops episodically in ascending sequence (as | E : E D | F : F E | D). A free and brusque exposition expands in entries in minor keys, flanked by connecting episodes based on the two features of the subject. A sonorous counter-exposition, reversing subject and answer (B.A.S.), might thus be the beginning of the end. The last entry lets in the first episode, which now moves to the tonic with the leisure of a fluent speaker, and in the earlier fughetta, of which this fugue is an extension, the music thus draws to a close after bar 67 (simplified). But on second thoughts Bach wished to continue. The counter-exposition is too recent to make a normal recovery possible. Instead, a token restatement (*Fudgit*) is contrived in all voices by a new, sequential development of the first figure, now descending. The unquenchable counter-subject gives this sequence colour, and rollicking "Alberti" figures and scales press the last entry to a close. The fugue so extends another fifteen bars without strain of matter or rhetorical device. In this North German fugue Bach shows his sympathy with the rhythmic and imitative potentialities of his vigorous subject, but also his power to make traditional thematic processes a means to a fresh and no less relevant conclusion. There is a florid prelude, extending the original (bars 15–33).

Bach returned, less happily, to this balance of entry and episode in the FUGUE IN E MINOR. A long but characteristic and shapely theme acquires sonority in union with a symmetrical counter-subject and supporting part. After being heard in major keys, it crosses back to the primary keys (from dominant to subdominant) for spread-out entries (B.A.S.) in trenchant poly-phony (cf. bars 43, 51, 53), but after a pronounced stop the tonic is recovered in a dashing style which extends to an extemporary coda. Episodes are derived, rather glibly, from the triplet whirl of the fifth bar, as the basis of ascending sequences, and from impromptu sequential figures (bars 38, 55). Prout quotes the fugue in full, as an example of organic development. Yet Bach noticeably abandons the whirling sequences midway (bar 50). The contrast between the opening two bars and the remainder of the subject becomes a problem. Bach was bound to develop bar 5; but this almost ruled out any other expansion. The five middle entries and episodes all depend too much on corroborative detail. There is an austere binary prelude with a nice six-bar coda, spoilt by the sectional repeat.

The FUGUE IN F SHARP flouts tradition by beginning affectedly on the leading-note, and that with a trill,* and the subject also contains a slightly precious modulation to the subdominant and back, which the plain and recurrent semitonal accompaniment enhances. Counter-exposition (S.B.A.) maintains good sense on this score by modulating episodes to promote the tonicward entries and by a fresh soprano line. An immediate entry in the relative minor key, again, avoids its subdominant turn by a fresh twist in the bass, and the same stimulant revives the next entry. Symmetrical diversions make a restatement (B.A.S.) possible, the first entry a frank echo (of the third) but the others carried along by a new bass, with a ready cadence. The first episode, between exposition and counter-exposition, is independent except for a reference to the flowing ascent of the subject. It returns between the middle entries. The remaining episodes arise from an exten-sion of the stooping figure at the end of the subject, organized in three or four sequential stages over an ascending bass. These extensions are a strain on its basic phrase, but the ambling serenity

---

* The same trill exploded later, from a tenth below, in the subject of the fugal finale of Beethoven's sonata op. 106 in B flat, discussed later.

of the shapely, imitable subject and its varied harmony is a match for its eleven entries in any unhustling age and perhaps also in the present one.

The subject of the three-voice FUGUE IN G is a delicate piece of liquescent sonority, surrounding a simple hovering and falling of basic pitch (D; E–D–C–B). A descent of syncopated or suspended notes (from the dominant or, later, mediant) forms a constant counterpoint and firm harmonic rhythm, and a parallel descent on the main beat (third entry, A.) stiffens the texture of the prevailing sequence. The details represent the ornamentation of an earlier fughetta. Entries in the minor succeed the minimum exposition required for such predictable harmony, and a single entry in the tonic reaches finality in an elegant cadence. Organic episodes arise easily in such a "preludial" atmosphere. They are derived from the *opening* arpeggio, thus spacing out the recurrent entry-sequences by a chain of two-bar sonorities, imitations and impromptus. The last episode, extended to twenty bars by the addition of bars 53–64 to the original fughetta, escapes from the full subject in a happy blend of unquenchable imitation, dominant's persistence and bravura, which enhances the formal cut of the following entry. A consistently harmonic subject has boldly claimed contrapuntal chase. This delightful trifle makes a definite score in favour of fugue and J. S. Bach. The prelude is formal but vivacious in detail. Two alternative preludes survive for the fughetta (vol. 36 of the Bach Society Edition), one a miniature sonata form, too elaborate here, and the other short but elementary-crude.

The long three-voice FUGUE IN B FLAT, starting most casually on the supertonic, arises almost as smoothly from its subject, with a free counterpoint of remarkable variety. There is eventually a full B.A.S. counter-exposition (bars 21–43), but the bass entry extends in an imitative passage with an unusually formal cadence (bar 31). Minor keys follow. A final entry extends with the same formal cadence as before. There is thus a suggestion of an unbalanced "dance" pattern of thirty-one and sixty-two bars, in binary style, crossing the normal fugal design. There are two fresh starts, at bars 21 ("real" dominant entry) and 32 (after cadence). The cadence is not a passing conceit, since it recurs later. Does the "real" entry at bar 21, then, belong to the exposition proper? A performer may so decide, but the intention of bars 32–43 is not clear. The episodes and coda are maintained by sequential treatment of the initial arpeggio phrase and of the paired-notes figure of the subject, and of an almost Sibelian fusion of the two (bars 69–70). It took Bach, indeed, to resume counter-exposition at bar 32, confident of spacing out further entries without fresh basic material. An extensive prelude, rounded off after considerable random development, prepares well enough for a spacious and wayward fugue.

The three-voice FUGUE IN B MINOR quickly banishes any expectations of structural *tour de force* or even textural finish. A jaunty subject, resembling that of the G major fugue in its eventual descent from the submediant, acquires definition and symmetry for that descent, first from one busy, trilling counter-subject (second entry, A.) and then from another and more per-manent figure (fourth entry, B.), vibrantly harmonic in character; the opening of each entry remains free. Entries in the major follow. A set of entries in the primary keys, spread out by episode and extended by coda, occupy the remaining half of the fugue. Episodes arise sequentially in turn from the trilling counter-subject, an impromptu figure with resolving ninths (bars 32, 42, 87), a piquant semitonal phrase (bars 50, 92), and further impro-visation (bar 59). In the coda the third episode forms a half-cadence to the second, before a token reference to the subject, already an established hoax, provides a finish. The collection thus concludes with a careless fugal sweep, relying a good deal on stray invention and an indefatigable bass, with some episodes organic and some independent. It is the kind of fugue Bach might have extemporized and then polished in detail, as No. 48 of an exhausting fugal achievement. The prelude is a long and laboured two-part Invention.

No such doubts can be held about the three-voice fugues in F and F minor. The subject of the FUGUE IN F ascends the octave in three playful leaps ($a1$) and then descends swiftly in continuous motion ($a2$). It runs to four entries in free counterpoint, designed to conceal the somewhat square-toed harmonic tread of subject and answer, and spreading out by means of an imitative phrase (*b*) after the answer, and *a*2 (cf. Ex. 39A). But the subject will not go into the minor: the changing detail to and from the upper tonic would be too corrective. The remaining entries (A. B. S. B.) are thus in primary keys—tonic or subdominant. Hence the main sense of development must arise in episodes, from which the subject emerges as a recovery of text and key. The long episode after the exposition, variably based on *a*2 and *b*, readily conveys this feeling of foreign travel. The next two episodes each use a sustained bass (dominant of coming key) to arouse expectation. The last full tonic entry (S.) begins in this context in the minor, in majestic five-part chords, regaining the major later. A normal entry would now be impossibly scholastic. Instead, the bass expands *a*1 and *a*2 in turn. The right hand supplies flowing bravura and prim polyphony on this basis (cf. Beethoven, op. 110, finale). The fugue thus ends precisely where it should. The casual subject can be conclusive when necessary. A shapely and richly polyphonic prelude makes a solemn and overpowering reflection, which may test the listener's patience before the fugue makes its escape.

The shorter but more varied prelude in F minor is also *maestoso* and indeed uniformly strained in feeling, as the semitonal harmony of the cadences confirms. The FUGUE IN F MINOR thus begins under the shadow of an emergency. However, it carries its burden lightly and imperturbably. The four-bar subject combines a plain pattern of rhythmic figures and whirling sound with a pronounced harmonic tread (1–23–4) of tonic-dominant-tonic. Varied counterpoint qualifies its polka stamp, and the first and typical episode is harmonic and in fact cadential in trend, besides reflecting the reiteration and falling seventh of the opening bars. The episode leads to and from two entries in the major, and later admits and quits the final entries (bars 66, 78). Two tonic entries, the second with soprano skirmishes over reiterated dominant bass, might be making for the end, but the fugue resists the cadence in firm renewal of episode, based on the opening "stamp" of the subject, flying impromptus, and the soothing sequences of the first episode, which return in fresh detail to complete the last entry. The first episode thus supplies a point of perpetual diversion and cadence, rather like the slick sequel that Aristophanes attaches to all Euripides's lines in *The Frogs*. The balance of contrapuntally vivacious entry and demure episode, each springing from a common source, again vindicates the intimate type of episodic fugue and carries the vigorous polyphony to its unexpected length without faltering. The "choice" of prelude seems the more hasty and incomprehensible.

Chapter X

THE "FORTY-EIGHT"

IV. VARIED CONCENTRATION ON A SUBJECT

OF the fugues that centre on the appeal of the subject, four contain a modicum of episodic interest. The subject of the three-voice FUGUE IN A, rising contentiously to the dominant, is excellent counterpoint, both as cross-rhythm and as containing a sequence of thirds which may be made harmonic in one context and non-harmonic and dissonant in another. It achieves four entries of increasing harmonic sparkle and polyphonic ornament, and two entries in minor keys. The florid figure of the second bar extends in descending sequence, or by melodic inversion, which avoids its officious dominantward trend (bars 6, 13). In this argumentative mood, intent on the harmonic bearing of each phrase, a set of entries in the primary keys (B.S.A.S.) follows. An effective tightening or loosening of pitch in the subject itself (bars 17, 23) warrants pernickety semitonal detail in the fresh sequences which arise from the florid figure and its inversion, and the piquant avoidances of the conventional harmony (bars 17, 21, 24) are stimulating to the alert ear. In this masterful manner the final soprano entry closes, without any palaver, an admirably compact fugue, whose corroborative detail is steadily engaging. The gentle pastoral prelude seems as blandly irrelevant to the sturdy fugal argument as the first prelude in E.

This may be one of the untoward moments of a collection committed in advance to a prelude and fugue for each key. The almost atonal prelude in A minor is much more committal. All analogies from the chorale-preludes suggest a thought of guilty humanity in the perpetually dissolving progressions, cadential at the last possible moment of each section. The FUGUE IN A MINOR fulfils this sense of disturbed consciousness, but its assertions of phrase and key are quite positive. The subject is immediately penetrating, with its blunt falling seventh and cadential half-beat figure, and it is firmly harmonized by a fine travelling counter-subject of descending fifths in a pronounced rhythm, with an imitative third part. After three-voice exposition and an immediate entry in the relative major, a further answer seems to resume exposition. A coherent set of primary entries (A.S.B.) balances the foregoing. These trenchant sallies in varied registers, with final soprano flourishes to fill in gaps in the subject-rhythm, readily dispose the impact of the fugue. They are briefly driven apart by sequential or imitational developments of the half-beat figure and of the trill phrase in the counter-subject, cemented by soprano bravura and deft organization. The final slip of the vagrant subject into the subdominant is countered by a fusion of falling seventh and half-beat rhythm in the alto. A masterly compression of tense feeling into twenty-nine bars matches the buoyancy of the A major fugue.

The FUGUE IN D SHARP MINOR gropes deeper. It presents a halting subject, drawn along by a symmetrical counter-subject (b) that is steadily on the beat. The latter extends in a figure of rising fourths (c) which develops later (bars 12, 36). After a close exposition, freely continued with c in the background, an abnormally continuous series of middle entries maintains the prevailing strain in an unusual blend of primary and foreign keys, some repeated, with free counterpoint in three or four parts. The last of these entries, moving distractedly to the tonic (bar 32), extends in rising sequence over c and subsides with some ceremony, thus intensifying the appearance of the subject (B.) in a declamatory style, flecked with blobs of harmony. Finally the subject and its inversion are combined in unisonal rhythm (S.T.) and so lead to the close.

It took Bach to contrive that these last two entries should follow the rest without a loss of emotional power. This seemingly prolonged (because concentrated) fugue of forty-six bars is almost a tragic piece. Presumably Mendelssohn had it in mind when he came to write his E minor fugue. Bach wrote it first in D minor, and then "passed" it for the rarer key.

The four-voice FUGUE IN A FLAT is the expansion of an earlier fughetta in F, here represented by the first twenty-three bars. The subject introduces rising fourths in descending sequence, recalling the bald subject of a Pachelbel fugue in F (see p. 211) at the start. It is supported by a plain semitonal descent, which remains more or less throughout. The flowing counterpoint of the next two entries continues in the counter-exposition, whose loose order of voices (B.S.A.S.) and progressive tightening of texture after one entry reflect the final entries of the fughetta. At the bass entry the semitonal line is a fifth higher than before, making fresh thirds but also piquant sevenths with the subject. The last entry, the first to realize four parts, has (as one might expect) a conclusive ring. Development must therefore go further afield. The key jumps to the relative major, moves via the dominant *minor* to the more normal supertonic minor, and thence to a set of primary entries (B.T.B.T.) of which the first and third turn into the sub-dominant minor, the latter recovering poise by means of a spectacular "Neapolitan" progression to the tonic (see Ex. 43B, and cf. Ex. 43A). A further diversion is the cross-accent of an entry one beat early (bar 38), with the counter-subject moving "on time" and thus making sevenths and thirds in fresh places (the reverse of bar 14). Finally, the plain harmony of the original counterpoint is amplified in thirds in an extra part. The episodic links are interesting. After the exposition, a figure in the extension of the original answer forms a steady bass, and as the record-holder in sequences—seven limbs—reflects early craftsmanship; but the upper parts vary. (In bars 10 and 12 D flat and G flat appear, temperamentally, half a beat earlier than in the fughetta.) The next episode treats the same figure more discreetly, in a close interplay of exchanging strands (bar 27). The extension of the subject by the development of the concluding formula in sequence or imitation fills odd corners (bars 15, 20, 26, 34, 39, 44). The relevance of all this connective matter adds power to the semitonal tread of the last twenty bars, which has been forecast from the answer onwards. The finely tempered subject of a flowing fughetta is carried into startling contexts of key, counterpoint and texture, motivated by rhythmic keyboard polyphony. The total impact is bracing, not chastening. A grand and spacious prelude announces the baroque style.

Seven fugues present the subject in close canon, with a minimum of episode or none. Significantly six are on the short side; only one offers the sustained thematic virtuosity of the first A minor fugue. The first two fugues in this group, the C minor and C sharp major, carry compression of subject to extreme limits. The ultimately four-voice FUGUE IN C MINOR has a formal one-bar subject, which secures ample three-voice exposition and counter-exposition, chiefly through sequence and imitation, a scintillating syncopated rhythm (bar 8, A.) and extra entries. But now it needs fresh impetus. It obtains this by widening to *two* bars, as in the Leipzig organ fugue in C. On that broader basis (A.) the normal subject and inversion can mingle freely, with closer entry and semitonal variants, without being fidgety. In this intimate style of augmentation there is no need for "pedal" pomp or for entry in all voices. Bach effects one more entry at half-speed in the real bass now added for the first time, as in the organ fugue. With this amplification, the scintillating figure and tense counterpoint become acceptable. Close canon and a poignant semitonal inversion (B.) maintain a polyphony which happily dissolves in a liquescent but pungent cadential chord, the subject being exhausted. Thus a bustling North German fugue is succeeded by the succinct and singularly complete revelation of a vocal phrase which would appear incapable of more than a fugal incident. A good augury for further creative evolution.

The FUGUE IN C SHARP is the expansion of an earlier trifle, a fughetta in C,* from nineteen bars to thirty-five, with much fresh and characteristic detail. The subject is now two bars, but its impact is qualified by immediate entries at the half-bar, and by many odd half-entries. A new ascending figure in bar 8, notched at the end and soon inverted, leads to one more group of entries. After that the subject disappears as an entity, remaining in the texture as a salient curve of four notes, sometimes in diminished or augmented rhythm. The ascending figure is almost as prominent. The sustained dominant bass of bars 28-9, terminating

* See Note I on p. 93.

and yet not terminating, punctuates this free coda of nineteen bars. The total impact is more diversionary than in any other fugue, even the first D major. The prelude, originally (and in a copy made by J. C. F. Bach, b. 1732) a self-contained prelude in C, begins in conventional preludial style but continues in a compact fughetta. The fugue is a baffling sequel, not particularly likely to establish a once untouchable key by its subject or treatment.

The FUGUE IN D at least remains faithful to its subject. Entries in minor keys follow the exposition closely. After that it becomes apparent to observant ears that the composer has set out to vary, by contrapuntal methods, the harmony of the essential D[1] G B A of the subject by diversions from the obvious subdominant-dominant progression. The method is partly of close canon at various intervals with semitonal variants, which serves to replace subdominant harmony by tonic, supertonic and special effects, and to suggest ambiguity of key; partly, also, of using the second bar of the subject with like trenchancy as counter-subject (bars 3, etc.; 6 (T.), etc.; 40). A canon at the fourth appears in various senses (bars 14, 22, 33 and 45); at the octave, producing a ninth on the "wrong" beat (bar 28); and in addition at the sixth and second (bars 33, 45). In the final S.A.T.B. canonry the key, already slipping (bar 43), falters subdominantwards, and this oscillation is continued in a coda equally canonic under the surface of a firm soprano descent. Episodes based on imitational treatment of the second bar space out a few entries (bars 16, 36). A steady and resourceful variation of detail (not less significant for being exactly observed) attends a singularly uniform expression, whose serene monotony of style will be the concern of the modern performer, aided by the tightening cross-rhythm. (This fugue, again, needs the bar-line at the half-bar.) An energetic prelude, bustling and pompous in a developed ternary structure, provides another surprising *point d'appui* (cf. Ex. 37A).

In contrast, the FUGUE IN D MINOR is a fine, brief excursus on a passionate theme of rising fourths and semitonal descent. The latter is pointed by a counter-subject (see Ex. 42B) in quarter-beats, which overflows into episode (bar 8, cf. 22). The initial sextuplet figure, or its inversion, is also a useful accessory for half-entries and odd cross-rhythm (bar 10). The symmetrical fourths of the subject-outline enable a fresh start to be made with a canon at the fifth at one beat, with the counter-subject at heel; melodic inversion with similar canon below implements falling fourths and inexorable climbing semitones. But after further skirmishes on previous lines the counter-subject justifies itself as the binding issue of the sextuplets. Meanwhile the semitonal texture makes the absence of foreign keys unnoticeable. The rising, falling fourths are all-absorbing. A vigorous prelude, an expansion of a Preambulum (B.S. vol. 36) completed in the London copy,* gradually steadies the ear round D minor before three voices crowd it with wild and whirling entries and half-entries.

The prelude in E establishes in two balanced stages an atmosphere of rare serenity, strangely set down by Spitta as "cheerful activity." The FUGUE IN E which follows is one of the clearest in intention ever written. The salient vocal phrase moves without any conscious elaboration to its various compelling cadences and master-conclusion. The fugue remains one of the most striking images of an immutable purpose in the universe. (I played it to some companions on a camp piano around 11th November, 1918, and on a Sunday in May, 1945, it still seemed the best safeguard, in abstract sound, of the belief that whatever may happen to the contrary there will always be a sane world to make and keep, and incidentally—observe the cadence—a free England.) The sheer musical appeal comes home to very many who have little perception of *stretto* and diminution. The haunting quality of the fugue possesses the mind when the concrete steps of Bach's high argument remain imperfectly grasped.

However, there is no harm in finding precisely what is to be heard so compactly, or in understanding the problem of maintaining four-voice fugue on such a brief and colourless subject, which Bach must have taken, key and all, from Fischer's *Musica Ariadne* (see below). In contrast with Fischer, Bach at once measures the smooth span of the subject (*a*) by a rising figure in half-beats, with a rhythmic notch at the end (*b*). The resultant harmonic progression, tied only to a tonic chord for the fourth

* See Note 2 on p. 93.

note, rises easily to upper voices, with a fresh bass each time. Close canon after two and four beats reduces counter-exposition to three compact bars of tense harmony, but it leads to a further series of four-beat canonic entries in pairs (A.S., B.T.), re-pointed by fresh semitonal counterpoint, and by beginning and ending in a minor key, with a lingering cadence. The problem is now how to enlarge the contrapuntal or harmonic scope of a theme already expanded in either direction. Canon at the fifth at one beat is a possible but bald sequence. Bach makes it fruitful in minor keys by decorative treatment of the subject (S.A., B.T.). Halving the measure of the subject, set across the metre with canons at two beats, the second doubled in thirds, conveys a sense of swift and sonorous incident, and animates the normal subject (A.) with fresh figures in an ascending sequence (B.), forcing a close to development, in the mediant minor. Recovery is now replenished by close canon *with* counter-subject, recalling exposition and counter-exposition in four packed bars. The soprano part extends its more isolated entry in lingering falls, supported by *b* and prompted by the bass in a final gravitation of pitch and key. A sudden thinning of texture adroitly dissolves the halting harmony in an exposed descant in declamatory style (almost inescapably "never, never" for English ears) before the initial fall finds its decisive cadence.

Example 16

By such means the plain theme of Fischer's fughetta acquires a 27-fold affirmation without repeating a single bar. Episodes are replaced by a series of diversions (bars 16–34) which only a musician could compose. It is the total impression of right, relevant and physically concrete decisions which conveys to the imaginative listener some glimpse of perfection, fleeting but complete. He may pass on to more adventurous, more gymnastic fugues, but he will return to the E major as the true epilogue of the "Forty-eight," Bach's serene fugal self.

Numerically seventy bars long, the FUGUE IN E FLAT is still one of the shorter fugues of the book. Its eight broad repetitions leave a simple impression. A considerable but symmetrical subject, vocal but also percussive in style, ascends the polyphony confidently in free harmony, with a recurrent counter-phrase to force dominant harmony in the fifth bar. Counter-exposition follows up a third answer crisply, avoiding the tedium of fourfold restatement by close canon in each pair of entries (T.B., A.S.). The harmony is freshened, but the key keeps to the tonic. Hence rapid modulation attends the next sequence (cf. bars 2–3), and an answer slips down to a subdominant entry (T.). Another pair of entries (S.B.), recovers the canon in primary harmony, prolonged by a falling soprano descant, with some poignant flats inserted to keep the texture bracing to the end. A small circle of entries is spontaneously rounded without fuss or confusion. The buoyancy of this fugue is for all times and seasons. It scarcely needs its gentle, swaying prelude. C. E. Horn mangled it in his *Rich and Poor* overture, absorbing bars 1–29 in his own fatuities.

The prelude in B flat minor is a spacious and consistent creation. It employs a repeated-note figure similar to the salient phrase of the first prelude in the same key. That prelude leads to a rapidly developing fugue on the briefest of subjects in an elastic 3–5 voice texture, with impromptu cadential passages and a spasmodic flow of close entries, more rhetorical than insistent, to punctuate the expression. The present four-voice FUGUE IN B FLAT MINOR is a deliberate, prolonged and cumulative pursuit of theme, like the first A minor fugue in method but not in manner. Its considerable subject gains sixteen substantive entries and eight in canon (to the 17–12 of the A minor). While the general nature of the development—close canon, melodic inversion and key-variation—becomes clear in repeated hearings, various phases must be distinguished. They must be defined in terms of thematic processes, but they are not less musical for that.

The subject (*a*), rising from the tonic in two stages, rhythmic and decorative, gains an ascending semitonal counter-subject (*b*) in liquescent style. The tail of the subject being useful for varied sequential treatment in episodes (bars 15, 21, 37, 77, 84), entries must concentrate on the main thrust of the subject, which invites dispute. In an extra entry (T.) close canon at the seventh (A.) defines the prevailing counter-thrust. A little later, melodic inversion reverses the original thrust to a fall from the dominant. For purposes of canon the subject, steadily conjunct, can be doubled in thirds or sixths at several points, not only at one beat's interval. The following are the comparative degrees of the minor scale in the outline of subject and possible canons at one and two beats' interval, represented as bluntly and uniformly on the beat—

Subject | 1 : 2 : 3 | 4 : 1 : 2 | 3 : 4 : 5 | 6,5 :

Canons (i) at seventh   : ♮7 : 1 | 2 : 3 : ♮7 | 1 : 2 : 3 | 4   : 5,4 :

(ii) at octave | :   : 1 | 2 : 3 : 4 | 1 : 2 : 3 | 4   : 5   :

Bach plumps for a uniform counter-thrust (canon no. 1). He disposes entries in a compulsive order of key, with moderate interludes before each main stage. Returns to the tonic mark the initiation of canon, inversion, and the inversion in canon, and close a final bout of canon by inversion (bars 27, 42, 67, 89). Intermediately the single inversions move on the flat side of the main key, the remainder on the sharp side, if any.

In this balanced context the thematic components of entries change as follows (bars 27, 42, 67, 80)—

(i) *a* in direct canon in minor and major (T.A. and, more audibly, S.B.), with the leader-entry fixing the key.

(ii) Inversion of *a* (T.S.S.B.) and *b* (A.T.A.S.) at the fifth; the key meanwhile slips flatward via the subdominant and submediant (major) to the rare leading-note *minor*, calling for an episode of redress.

(iii) In the inversion in canon (T.S., A.B.) the canon is on the surface and the more audible. The relative outlines harmonize as follows (*b* drops out, except for its semitonal tints, bar 82, A.)—

```
Dux      | 5 : 4 : 3 | 2 :  5 : 4 | 3 : 2 : 1 | ♮7,1
Comes    |   : 6 : 5 | 4 : ♮3 : 6 | 5 : 4 : 3 |  2      (See Ex. 17).
```

(iv) Canon by inversion (a simpler blend to hear than two thrusts in similar motion) begins unobtrusively in the major (S.T.), with the subject almost in canonic "smog"—

```
Dux      | 5 : 4 : 3 | 2 : 5 : 4 | 3 : 2 : 1 | 7,1
Comes    |   : 7 : 1 | 2 : 3 : 7 | 1 : 2 : 3 | 4   : 5,4
```

The reverse order of theme regains the tonic in a context of suspense, induced by an episode, and again obscurely (B.A.), with distracting soprano—

```
Comes    |   : 6 : 5 | 4 : ♮3 : 6 | 5 : 4 :   | 3 : 2
Dux      | 1 : 2 : 3 | 4 :  1 : 2 | 3 : 4 :   | 5 : 6,5
```

For conclusion, some reinforcement of rhythm is expedient. But with such a decisive start, a doubled entry cannot counter a single entry with one free part, or vice versa. *Dux* and *comes* must both be doubled, reducing the polyphony to a contrapuntal duel. This is possible with the subject doubled below in sixths and then by an imperceptible change in thirds, as in many duets; meanwhile the inversion, in canon, is doubled below in thirds throughout. (Trial-and-error dismisses doubling the subject in sixths throughout. See Ex. 38F, p. 181.) This blunt but grand counterpoint leaves the music to move resoundingly to the conclusion which the subject has so far rejected (bars 15, 93). An unusual but just outcome has been found for a steady elaboration of theme, whose integrity is able to stand the cross-rhythm and cross-melody of canon and inversion, free polyphony and a certain amount of brilliantly diversionary episode. Vocal in range, the fugue nevertheless needs the keyboard to do justice to its increasingly percussive quality. The fugal tactics have unmistakably been planned ahead in their several stages, and the subject *may* have been framed with a view to canonry, but the absorbing impression is that the subject deserves what it receives. There is no less of Bach in the placing of the sustained tonic bass in the first canon to the inversion than in the more tangible

Canon at the second

Inverted subject in tenor
Ornamental tonic pedal in bass

Example 17

manipulations of theme. It is the beginning of that release of spiritual force in reserve which, alike in recapitulation and coda, distinguishes every Bach master-work. The fugue is the manifest peak point of the collection, as a riveting structural accomplishment, and it remains the greatest of all the longer fugues centred on one subject, as the E major comprehends the shorter examples.

NOTES

1 (*Page* 86) Bach Society edition, Vol. 36. Bars 3–6, 9–10, 14–17, 25–31 and 34–5 of the fugue are entirely or substantially new. The figuration of bars 2, etc., 8, etc., 19, etc., 32, is new. The original piece has fugue for seven bars and coda for twelve. Bull's spare Ricercar in F (see p. 208) uses the same motive, with others (cf. p. 217).

2 (*Page* 88) After bar 9, two bars resembling bars 10 (exchanging hands) and 18 are crossed out, and bars 10–18 written at the foot of the page. This is the only considerable correction in the whole manuscript. Obviously by composer, not copyist. (See Appendix.)

Chapter XI

THE "FORTY-EIGHT"

V. COUNTER-SUBJECT AND SECOND SUBJECT

THE five remaining fugues in the "Forty-eight" expand their subject with a difference. The subject persists, but the contrapuntal drive comes from contrasted matter, whether counter-subject or a more independent subject, announced separately. In the C sharp minor fugue such a counter-subject subtly alternates with more casual development. In the B major fugue it emerges more clearly, and in the G minor it is pivotal throughout. The F sharp minor presents three subjects, the G sharp minor two, which combine later. The order of appearance in the collection being quite unrevealing, it will be convenient to take the fugues in the order stated.

The three-voice FUGUE IN C SHARP MINOR (originally in a workaday C minor) is so rich in incident that for many listeners it may pass as a characteristic episodic fugue. Nor is the pivotal counter-subject patent at first. For half the fugue the flowing subject seems all-sufficient, with its firm, syncopated harmonic rhythm (tonic . dominant: . tonic) and its tail-phrase, apt for extension in descending sequences. Exposition in firm expanding harmony extends easily to episode and free counter-exposition (S.A.B.), and then to a further series (S.A.B.) for the subject inverted at the fifth in fresh keys, with one normal entry to round it off. After a long episode, a phase of recapitulation spreads out by similar extensions and variants, balancing the entire exposition. A syncopated figure in the first episode (bar 13) shares the passage-work with the tail-phrase mentioned.

Closer observation will pick on the semitonal phrase (b) which emerges in the long episode (S.A.B., bars 35–8). It has already appeared casually as counterpoint to the subject (bars 20 S. and 30 B.). In bar 20 its D *natural* queers the tonic harmony (E major) on the fourth beat, pointing the recovery in the next bar. At bar 30 *b* has been put down a twelfth, making the sevenths on the even beats into more plastic sixths. These two reconstructions of the subject, with one more melodic inversion in a major key (A.), inform the six entries of the final section. Here *b* appears once in the original position (bar 55), mainly in the second (bars 48, 61, 66), and finally over the tail-phrase, holding off the final cadence. An agile but limited subject thus runs a lively course by free counterpoint and melodic inversion, and then acquires fresh colour by means of the semitonal slant of a placid but subversive counter-subject, as the focal line of voluble interludes. The suggestion of a second subject (bar 35) recedes into counterpoint, but the rigid subject-harmony is broken up. A spacious, dreamy prelude beguiles the ear before this versatile movement.

The four-voice FUGUE IN B expands a good deal more transparently, and its contrapuntal excursions may equally be traced to an initial monotony. The subject is at once plain and insistent, with a trite harmonic rhythm of tonic-subdominant-dominant-tonic. Counter-subjects and diversions are essential. Yet, as in the first C sharp minor fugue, a too marked subsidiary theme would be subversive; it must be, rather, sporadic and ephemeral, needing the subject to give its broken lights permanence and integrity. The first counter-subject (*b*), of falling phrases ascending symmetrically in syncopated rhythm, steadily blurs the primary harmony by suspensions. (The third and fourth entries are oddly alike in texture.) An extra bass entry brings the subject to the bottom of the pyramid, at the same time showing cause for counter-exposition.

Two expected features may now be observed. There is a fresh and graceful counter-subject (*c1*), and it is at once put down a twelfth, making different harmony and turning the dominant-tonic punctuation into a modulation (*c2*). The second and third entries thus quickly drift into related minor keys, the otiose fourth bar disappearing in the process. Further entries continue to defeat expectation by oscillating trends. A "pukka" relative minor entry (B.) returns to primary harmony (*c1*); the subdominant (T.) slides into its relative minor (*c2*); and what should

be another relative minor (submediant) entry begins in the
subdominant, owing to the counter-subject being half a bar
early. All these variants, pertinent as they are, are concealed in a
wider polyphony, which contrives to replace episodic development by a subtle blend of the primary and the decorative. A

Example 18

rousing rhetorical sequence (bars 63–74), intensifying the demand
for recovery, promotes fresh versatility. (See Ex. 42A.)

The first entry here relies on key-nuance and renewed polyphony; the second returns to the simpler harmony (*c1*) but is
compelled by the previous episode to *begin* in the relative minor
of its proper key—the reverse of the counter-exposition; the last
entry strikes a subdominant note in the second bar, and *c2* (tenor)
restores the tonic (no more) but leaves cadence to the coda. Once
again, adroit counterpoint and harmonic forethought have
enabled a plain monotonous subject to hold its own, unexhausted,
through fourteen full entries, the stronger for being based on an
uncompromising three-bar measure. These occupy about half
the fugue. Numerous slight extensions fill in gaps, *c* being good
company for other strands of polyphony and a useful promoter
of fresh figures in the same voice. A subject it is not: it spreads
too much. It is a texture, not a motive, like many of Wagner's
so-called *Leit-motive*. There is something very human about the
way in which the real subject persists to the end, as if to proclaim—

Grow old along with me!
The best is yet to be,
The last of life, for which the first was made.

It soon loses its element (fourth bar) of plastic circumstance, but the earlier (harmonic) grooves no longer pause and press. The substance remains, "heaven's consummate cup"—on the right occasion.

Some common purpose animated Bach's craftsmanship in these two fugues, whose utter contrast of *Affekt* is striking. The wiry subject of the C sharp minor will invert, but it is too independent to bend to more than a fresh twist of harmony. The subject of the B major is so limited as to call for variant counterpoint, and may even have been conceived with this very object. If the key-order of the book holds, between these two came an athletic feat of trebly invertible counterpoint, the four-voice FUGUE IN G MINOR. Not that this is all-apparent at the first hearing. The pronounced rhythm and falling thirds of the subject distinguish it in the densest polyphony. A counter-subject symmetrically fills in the missing third beat, underlines the descending sequence of bars 2 and 3, shows good cause for the repeated notes that follow, and altogether forms an apt counter-phrase throughout. Fresh additional counterpoint brings exposition up to six entries. Middle entries follow, chiefly in major keys, with some doubling of the subject in thirds. A richer doubling of top and bass in tenths inwards recovers the tonic with sonorous directness, but a further entry forms the bass of a more subtle, brittle counterpoint, which breaks up in an affecting cadence. Episodes are derived sequentially from the counter-subject—the rising figure (*passim*) or the final bustle (bar 63). Hence the same element determines the timbre of thirteen entries and six episodes, and one may ask whether such insistence comes from a didactic mood, laboured humour or breezy self-confidence.

There is no obvious answer. But on closer observation the characteristic weave of entries exhibits the counter-subject at least at varying interval, besides doubling strands. Once more, a harmonic fixation seems to have provided the stimulus. Let us return to the sixth entry (bar 28). So far the polyphony has been spontaneous enough, but the basic sequence of the first three bars (V–I IV–VII III–VI) is becoming trite, the mediant harmony of the third bar is rather old-fashioned and awkward, and the

dominant harmony of the fourth is wearing thin. Bach must drop
or re-set the counter-subject. In bar 28 it is put up a twelfth
(S.), thus making the consonances on the first beats of the second

Example 19

and third bars into questioning sevenths, resolving ornamentally
on the third beats. The mediant mannerism has been avoided,
and the last bar begins at least with a fresh seventh to resolve. At
the next entry the counter-subject (A.) is below the subject but a
third higher than originally. The fresh consonances have become
primary dissonances in the context of a fresh bass, again resolved
ornamentally, and the mediant feeling is held off.

It remains to exploit these useful variants in entries in thirds
above or below. These double a strand without destroying the
polyphony and pile readily on to most triads. The various recurrent elements may be distinguished as follows, in the order of

Example 20

their appearance: *a*1, *b*1, subject and counter-subject as in the
exposition, with the usual modifications for the answer-form;
*b*2 and *b*3, the latter put up a twelfth and tenth (at whatever

octave); *a2* and *a3*, the subject doubled a third higher and lower
(or sixth higher); *b4*, *b5*, variants. These converge in two concentrations of theme, the first quoted here in the *tonic* major for
purposes of easier comparison, with alternate semitones indicated
for the minor. This blunt counterpoint follows the absorption of
the basic themes in a freer polyphony. The doubling of both
themes moves in easy sequence. The first combination adds
sonority to the piquancy of *b2* over *a1*, with its gracefully resolving sevenths, and is actually couched in the casual key of the
submediant major; the second amplifies the original harmony
without the naked fervour of the comparable passage at the end
of the B flat minor fugue. Here, then, from top to bottom—
with the most audible harmonic or textural features in italics—is
the accumulation of varied and doubled entry, free polyphony
and changing key-groups, after the exposition proper, *x* and *y*
being free and variable parts—

Bars 20, 28   *x*, *y*, *a1*, *b1* and *b2*, *a1*, *x* in primary keys;
      32, 36, 45   *a1*, *b3*, *x*; *b3*, *x*, *y*, *a1*; *x*, *a2*, *a1*, *b1* in major keys to-
                 wards the sharp side;
      51, 59   *a3*, *a1*, *b1*, *x* and *b2*, *b3*, *a2*, *a1* in keys on the flat side;
      67, 69, 79   *b2*, *a1*; *a1*, *b3*, *a3*, *b1*; *x*, *b4*, *b5*, *a1* in the recovered tonic.

By such swift repartee, capricious and yet economic, the ten
entries avoid all literal repetition and yet succeed in clear order,
spaced out by more casual but relevant developments and pointed
in cadences. The froward sequence has been held in control by
contrapuntal wit. The fugue is at once one of the most pursuant
of its basic harmony and a document in variable counter-subject,
as the B flat minor demonstrates a variable subject as its own
counterpoint. A short but stocky prelude establishes preliminary
poise.

The remaining two fugues take the development of a counter-
theme further, by delivering it at first separately. Bach here began
on the keyboard what he took to a more decisive point in "The
Art of Fugue." The organ fugues in F and E flat demonstrate
the suitability of the manuals for a lighter but sonorous second
fugue in three or four parts, and of the pedals for the final deliberate delivery of a sustained principal subject in a further stage

of converging counterpoint. A three-voice fugue for keyboard obviously aims at a different kind of expression, and no grandeur of returning theme need be expected. Yet with the greater clarity of keyboard polyphony a sense of travel may quickly be suggested in a slighter pattern, given infectious material.

If the FUGUE IN F SHARP MINOR is a triple fugue, this need not imply three subjects of equal importance. The first subject, whose outline falls in springing syncopation from the dominant (*a*), turns after four entries into the relative major. In that gentler context a fresh phrase (*b*), taken up in rapid and wayward imitation, suggests at first an independent episode. But after eight bars it is harnessed to *a* in two balanced entries (A.B.) in primary keys. At the end of these a third figure (*c*) begins to be noticeable (A.). Its flow of sound round a plain descent from a given dominant to its mediant can at once be felt polyphonically (A.S.B.) as it moves flatward from the key of the dominant, then (bar 41) sharpward. The doubly obscure return of *a*, with the rhythmic drive but not the melodic detail of *c*, anticipates a recovery, as in the organ fugue in F. The next entries combine *a* with *c*, at the same time introducing *b* in the second bar as previously (bar 30). The *c* rhythm, which easily maintains scale figures between entries, is exhausted only in the last cadence. The three fughettas converge in triple counterpoint, but the second "subject" is barely noticeable there. It is pertinent to compare the first C sharp minor fugue, whose first counter-subject *c* here strongly recalls, especially in bars 41–3; the off-shoot in bar 51 here also echoes bar 47 there. In the earlier fugue the flowing rhythm, monotonous in pitch, stops before the end, leaving the trenchant curve of the subject substantially in command. Here the more versatile cross-tension of *c* never stops, once begun, and *a* has always to be on the outside to be heard. The conclusion is breezy and casual; piquant rather than powerful. It is none the less Bach for that.

Closer observation of the basic counterpoint will show its strength. The exposition finds *a* falling in syncopated steps from the submediant, with a modulation to the major on the second step, which is at once reversed. In combination *b* colours this with an entry in each bar, underlining the circular modulation (bars 30–31); the second entry keeps to its tonic. Now *c*, falling by step to a mediant, calls for a swift variety of key (bars 36–46). But in combination with *a* it will not go as at first. Instead, it begins a fifth lower, and by bearing on the flat leading-note supports a modulation to the major (bars 55, 61). This leaves *b*, redundant in the first bar, to pull the key back in the second. In the last entry a free bass changes the first modulation (subdomin-antward) and a restorative *b* follows in fresh redress. The triple counterpoint is thus conclusive because it fulfils the under-lying integrity of the first subject, as defined in exposition and second fughetta. These final entries at once harmonize the material impulses of the three fughettas and supply a compulsive series of cadences. The combination sounds careless but the pivotal details are trenchant and persuasive. These spare seventy bars (20–16–14–20) cover at each turn a surprising amount of ground without any of the audible and tiresome formalities of triple fugue, and all within three-part harmony. The work seems now to have been a breezy preparation for the great Eighth Fugue of "The Art of Fugue." There is a florid but orderly prelude.

The three-voice FUGUE IN G SHARP MINOR applies similar methods to a texture so uniform as to verge on the impressionist. Quite apart from the steady six beats, the subject is a symmetrical one of 2–2 bars, but it gains full exposition and counter-exposition by means of free counterpoint and pertinent changes of bass, which avoid the glibness of the obvious chordal rhythm of tonic-dominant-tonic, dominant-submediant-dominant, as maintained in the bass entries. In this basic sense a dominant is replaced by the flat leading-note in bars 7, 16 and 47, and a tonic by dom-inant and submediant in bars 20 and 46, so that variant and normal sequences alternate in steady repartee, spaced out by episodes. The soprano answer (bar 45) is noticeably "other" in this respect, invoking a seventh entry in deepest bass. These sixty bars halt in a highly coloured half-cadence (the as-yet-rare augmented-sixth chord commanding the dominant chord). A fresh line of falling and rising semitones, vaguely anticipated in the first fughetta, gradually pervades the texture (S.A.B.) in a series of primary keys (dominant to subdominant again), with symmetrical counterpoint. An equally semitonal episode, marked by steady imitation in a chain of falling and rising fifths, prepares for the next stage. The alert listener will discern that this fresh series of entries not only combines both subjects in a common iambic rhythm, but has also been devised to break the monotony of the harmonic rhythm of the first subject further, while preserving the balance of phrase. The tonic chord is displaced entirely or at first in the second bar, and in the next bar the dominant is again replaced by leading-note harmony (bars 99, 127, 137). One major entry (A.) divides up the primary entries and breaks the monotony of mode, as in the C sharp minor fugue. Episodes are derived from the syncopated accompaniment of the second subject or impromptu sequences. The outcome is a noticeably extended and voluble fugue and something of a *tour de force* in subject-maintenance, in which the second subject is serviceable rather than characteristic, and the double fugue a stimulating fresh turn but no more. With such a conscious effort to construct twelve entries in varying harmony, the subject can only sound persuasive if it is considered a texture or harmonic Ground rather than a theme. There is far less sense of travel than in the F sharp minor fugue. There is a pellucid and delightful prelude in a clear-cut shape. (See Ex. 43B.)

Bach's second creative impulse in keyboard fugue, then, confirmed the episodic type in the examples in B flat major and F minor, the plain subject type in the A major and minor, and the research type in the E major and B flat minor; but also it appreciably developed the symbolism of a fresh and fertile countersubject or further subject. Throughout the book (somewhat in contrast with the first volume) it is very rare that one becomes aware of contrapuntal virtuosity as a predominant feature. Rather, a subject is projected for what it may be worth, and its limitations of rhythm or harmony, if conspicuous, are either recognized in a short fugue of contrapuntal energy or made the *point d'appui* for renewal and sometimes for something like revelation. Episodes here link and space out entries with wayside development or downright impromptu sequences, and less commonly, as in the F fugue, create tension in the postponement of the next entry. Scarcely any of the longer fugues is without its surprises, whether (to take four consecutive works at random) it is the fresh fugues of the F sharp minor, the splendid later eloquence of the G major, the double entries of the G minor, or the operatic and in fact "Neapolitan" tension of the A flat. Any of these might have been historical and household names in the treasury of keyboard fugue, if there had not been so many others as notable. Together they are a document in that for which no category can be predicted except fulfilment.

In emotional range a more reflective and ruminant mood may be discerned generally than in the first book. The freshness of the first F sharp fugue finds no parallel in its graceful but exhaustive counterpart here. The passing canonic wit of the first fugue in F is matched by the more sober virtues of the second E flat; the second D minor is more forceful than the first; and after the pompousities of the first G minor the trenchancy of the second A minor, around a similar descent of a seventh, is striking. There is no anticipation of the range of the C sharp minor, E and B fugues. There is every evidence that fugue was still much more natural to Bach's style of thought than the dance-measures of a more fashionable keyboard craft. Some pieces are quickly apprehended and occasionally exhausted; others need growing with, and are at their best then. The latter possibility is a stumbling-block to many listener-performers of today, intent on the exploration of new worlds without sifting the ground. The combination of styles remains a salient impression.

An additional testimony to the select quality of the "Forty-eight" lies in the many fugues Bach did not include. Most of these show a less fastidious sense of structure and relevance. Observation of their methods in the next chapter will in many cases enhance our perception of the spare measure which marks the two volumes of the "Forty-eight" so frequently and renders them as two self-contained stages of expression. On the other hand, the persistence of the same renewals (not just repetitions) of theme as have already been observed makes a link between the two volumes and the stray fugal pieces or movements.

Chapter XII

MISCELLANEOUS KEYBOARD FUGUES

A BROAD impression of the fugues now to be discussed is volubility. They conjure up occasions of public, professional extemporization, where the degree of afflatus is measured by the length to which a creative performer's invention carries, or seems to carry, his basic notions; where the irrepressible is the good. Some of the more transparent examples leave no doubt that this kind of gallant adventure in the "learned" style had its social place. It is characteristic of Bach that he busied himself considerably with writing fugues to suit this taste—sometimes by writing out precisely what he had already improvised in broad detail—and that he exhibits a certain seriousness, in the revision of certain fugues, from which the emergence of a masterpiece in the virtuoso style becomes a matter of time and rousing circumstances.

The seven Toccatas come into this group. Each contains at least one nominal fugue, as a clarifying moment of a richer whole. Parry has suggested that the approximation to the organ style in the TOCCATA IN D MINOR and elsewhere implies early work. Certainly the diffuse, impersonal movements of this Toccata will not detain many listeners, although this is one of the works which Bach later amplified considerably in figurative detail.* The TOCCATA IN D MAJOR contains three typical movements: a rambling prelude, combining Toccata or hand-mindedness with imitational writing, a wayward rhapsodic Adagio incorporating fugal elements, and a straight fugue. The last makes a *perpetuum mobile* of a progression (D–F sharp C sharp–E) as *naif* as "Chopsticks." The recurring phrase establishes 2–3 part texture and a centre key, spins from key to key, exchanging its "sleeping" thirds for sixths or more mobile intervals and ultimately for sheer

---

* The earlier draft is given in the original Peters edition.

chords in "Chop-sticks" style, and finally disappears in a cloud of dissolving harmony. An Invention is made of a chordal Ground that every accordionist knows. If hand-mindedness can produce an upstanding fugue (151 bars) of such kittle stuff, how much more of the shapely tonic-dominant subjects of the first E major and minor fugues ("Forty-eight"). This Toccata finale is a triumph of its kind, which no predecessor of Bach could have made so persuasive.

The fugal finale of the TOCCATA IN E MINOR, with its vibratory "North German" subject, scrappy accompanying phrase and monotony of key, might have been any one's work, and that not to his credit. It shows that Bach learnt by workaday experience and not at all from books or coaching. Indeed, the only part of the Toccata in which the common listener may recognize Bach's hand is the earlier *Un poco Allegro*, which strangely anticipates the basic combination of the "Confiteor" chorus in the B minor Mass. The final fugue of the TOCCATA IN G, on the other hand, rises from a "period" prelude and minor adagio to a movement whose plastic three-part counterpoint assures its graceful but initially monotonous subject of very nearly enough variety for its procession of entries and extensions. The subject moves dominantwards, and the reactionary and tonicward answer is neatly held off later.

The TOCCATA IN G MINOR plunges after a brief flourish into a miniature sarabande, which is interrupted by an Allegro but resumed later. From this absorbed coloratura emerges a stalwart four-voice fugue of nearly 120 bars, with twelve expository entries and eleven to follow. A parallel semitonal counter-subject (of which, indeed, one hears too much) stresses the symmetry of the subject, as it climbs to its peak (stepping out the pitch-pattern 1–4 2–5 3–6 6) and then falls back to the tonic. Inversion balances this ritual ascent (5–2 4–1 3–7 7) in the counter-exposition, and subject and inversion freely alternate as—after an inexplicable series of subdominant entries—major keys blend with minor, and the primary keys return. A passionate passage in doubled thirds concludes with the initial flourish of the Toccata (omitting one turn); and so a suggestion of the sarabande is turned into the cadence. The fugue is bluntly insistent, although its self-confidence is stirring and vivacious.

The TOCCATA IN F SHARP MINOR leads into an impressive sarabande-like movement, but the two fugues which follow, divided by a tiresome ultra-sequential movement, are too much for their slender texts. The first subject, tuneful but plain and always on the outside of the harmony, is over-exposed, and it is tied to its trilling accompanying phrase throughout. The second fugue soon exhausts its bare semitonal descent and accompanying figure. It is significant that the "subject" later became epic in "Crucifixus," where, as the repeated ground-bass of sustained choral sound, it found the right place, presenting an *undeviating* symbol of the passing, identical moments of the endurance which the world will never forget. As a keyboard motive, it is an un-convincing *cri du cœur*. The TOCCATA IN C MINOR is a more sub-stantial work. A concise, vaguely pertinent prelude and a brief but absorbed Adagio, combining imitation of phrase with im-promptu sallies, introduce in varied suspense a three-voice fugue of nearly 150 bars. The jaunty subject is repetitive and has a rigid 2–2 bar opening, but it is not tied for ever to its opening counter-subject. After an ample exposition (seven entries) a fresh start is made with a new "counter-subject," more harmonic frills than cross-rhythm. The texture is loose, and other more ornamental figures find a place, along with the relief of major keys. Some of the later primary entries are superfluous! An imaginative pianist can make the fugue sound exploratory to the end, treating the subject candidly as the refrain it becomes; Samuel made the Toccata sound more. Yet the subject does not survive its repeti-tions too well. One suspects that it is the novel structure, not the fugal invention, that earns so lightly for this and the F sharp minor Toccata Parry's "splendid." He responded rather easily, indeed, to anything which, by leaving the beaten track, might be dubbed "characteristic."

Several of the isolated fugues* deserve mention, some being evidently early work. The FUGUE IN E MINOR (Peters 212) bolsters up a plain subject and answer through fourteen entries by

* See vol. 36 of the Bach Society edition, and Note 1 on p. 114.

means of two successive counter-subjects and free polyphony. The subject has, however, a curious twist to the subdominant, so that the answer never gains its proper key. The critical listener is left guessing whether Bach was once callow, or was experimenting with an awkward subject. A FUGUE IN A in $\frac{6}{8}$ (ibid.) is a neat excursion on its blithe subject, employing all the devices of close canon and inversion without strain. The final canon is persuasive in its context of oscillating chord. (Find that in the books!) The 84-bar FUGUE IN D MINOR (ibid.) combines a voluble but shapely subject with a vigorous counter-subject in a balanced series of entries, avoiding literal repetition. A long bravura finish points to a fashion for a burst of hand-mindedness, to which there are many parallels, and a trenchant allusion in the Chromatic Fugue. Another longish FUGUE IN A (Peters 216) is resourceful treatment of a jaunty ascent from tonic to dominant, with inversion of various kinds and a fresh counter-subject midway. There are innumerable entries, but their detail is so varied that the subject seems irrepressible.

Two long fugues (ibid.) take their basis from op. 1 of the Venetian composer, Albinoni, for whose works Bach cherished a later liking, as matter to set to ampler music.* The three-voice FUGUE IN A relies on free counterpoint for its renewal of a theme whose echo of its first bar in its second Bach usually tries to conceal (not in bars 13, 19). The eight entries of exposition and four of restatement (sixty-one bars out of ninety-nine) suggest that he was concerned to demonstrate what counterpoint can do. The style is Bach's; the structure is not: we miss the sensation of the fugue turning on itself in the latter half. Compare, in the "Forty-eight," the second fugue in A, relying for variety on pertinent detail but finished in twenty-nine bars, and the broader and as freely contrapuntal A flat fugue, discovering so much more eventful an issue. The expressive limitations of the suave Albinoni fugue become apparent. It is "examination" Bach, reasonably healthy but not pulsatingly alive. The more extended three-voice FUGUE IN B MINOR follows a very similar course, with two middle entries, gracefully major, but seven primary and minor to follow.

* See Note 2 on p. 115.

The semitonal element in the subject, supplied with a recurrent and trite harmonic directive, wears decidedly thin. It is a little surprising to discover that Bach had taken the trouble here to amplify an earlier draft by means of a more decorative texture (cf. the less semitonal bars 34–6) and the addition of an extra entry and episode in the closing section. But it shows his attention to balance.

Of the fugues with preludes, the extended FUGHETTA IN E MINOR (Peters 200), with a short and sprightly prelude, pursues a long but vigorous "harmonic" theme, whose outline is based on a trochaic rhythm and symmetrical pitch-pattern (1–2 3; 2–3 4; 3–4 5–6 4–5 3–21 7). An insistent counter-subject, entirely plastic in detail, takes charge not only of entries but also of episodes in a balanced structure. A far from negligible fugue. There is graceful counterpoint in the short FUGHETTA IN D MINOR, but the three subdominant middle entries are odd. A four-voice FUGUE IN A MINOR with a substantial Fantasia in concerto style (Peters 208) works out briefly in turn fughettas on a bold, leaping, declamatory subject, a niggardly semitonal descent, and their loose combination. It is apparent that Bach designed the second "subject" to break, in combination, the monotony of the first subject, especially the tonic in the third bar. The upshot is a workmanlike double-fugue of transparent rhetoric but not (*pace* Parry) "one of Bach's very finest fugues."

In contrast, a three-voice FUGUE IN A MINOR in $\frac{12}{16}$ (Peters 211) is a wild and whirling piece, in which little sounds at all premeditated. Groups of entries alternate with equivalent episodes in a common masterful instancy, the outline of the subject moving moodily from tonic to lower dominant with its own harmonic support and a recurrent accompaniment. Three broad and equal stages are noticeable: (i) exposition and counter-exposition (bars 1–23, 24–53): (ii) balancing groups of entries, moving in turn sharpwards and flatwards from the tonic (54–77, 78–104); (iii) a sweeping "episode," converging hastily in entry and cadence (105–53). The somewhat set harmony of the subject is absorbed in an almost impressionist texture, so that the last section is virtually coda. This engaging excursion has a dignified but also dashing prelude in concerto style. The work, copied by Bach's admirer, J. P. Kellner, in 1725, has a mature ring, and it is entirely satisfactory in itself. It is greatly neglected. But Bach was evidently struck with the compressed concerto style of the prelude, and he decided later to convert it (for an unknown

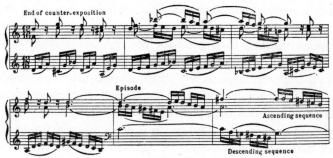

Example 21

occasion) into an opening movement for keyboard, violin, cross-flute and strings, by adding orchestral refrains here and there and by expanding the original keyboard part horizontally and vertically so as to produce matter distributable for the orchestra. These twenty odd additions (fascinating to observe technically) brought the original 98 bars to 149. For the slow movement Bach amplified in C the F major Adagio of the third organ sonata.* For the finale, the ubiquitous fugue-subject did not invite an orchestral arrangement. But Bach drew from it a simple melodic outline which would go with it (and with many other things), and so constructed a vigorous 24-bar refrain for orchestra, which comes back twice in almost humorous interjection and twice in full. For the rest Bach was content (!) to enrich the thin, elusive keyboard texture by grafting on to the existing music the polyphonic refrain-phrase, antiphonal chords and stray imitation, and by improving the final keyboard part in detail (bars 189–206), adding a tiny cadenza before it surrenders delivery back to the orchestra. Thus queerly, by the revisionary process which was so often less trouble to Bach than fresh composition, the 153 bars of fugue grew to 245, and a prelude and fugue to concerto movements

* See Note 3 on p. 115.

half as long again. But this magnification is no reflection on the
original; the fugue, in particular, reduces unwillingly to the
generalities of orchestral vernacular.

Another and longer three-voice FUGUE IN A MINOR, in $\frac{3}{4}$, must
be mentioned, not unlike the preceding fugue in texture. Here a
voluble subject, combining a firm melodic outline (A–E^{l}–D^{l}
C^{l}–A–E^{l} F^{l} E^{l} D^{l}) with harmonic apparatus, acquires a more set
harmony through its counter-subject, and lets it penetrate in a
much spread-out double exposition. Middle entries follow at
leisure, and even more so two entries of recovery, with a coda of
fifty-six bars, nearly a third of the fugue. The ten entries thus
occupy pivotal points in a ceaseless and mainly relevant flow of
keyboard activity. Episodes spring from the chordal figure of the
sixth bar, re-pointed (bar 12, cf. 39, 81, 130; 59, cf. 143), from
bustling sequences, and from a free expansion of the first bar.
The coda thus (bars 143–76) harmonizes established and opposite
transitions flatward (bars 59–72), sharpward (109–13) and cadential
(114–21), before the music makes its final flight of impromptus on
the subject. There is a careless but not prodigal generosity about
the conduct of this fugue which earns it a place in Bach's development no less noteworthy than the more palpably studied works.
A conventional sequence of ten bars, figured at the performer's
discretion, raises the curtain on this animated scene.

The Chromatic Fantasia is no curtain-raiser. It leads the ear,
through dissolving clusters of sound, marked by semitonal
inflections, to the insistent probing of conventional cadences, but
also of release from extremes of flatward and sharpward range
(bars 51, 58), before the music settles down to a graceful decline
over the fixed tonic bass which is the mark of the prelude *par
excellence*. The subject of the FUGUE IN D MINOR comes to a listener
slightly overwhelmed but also supremely expectant. It is at first
semitonal to the point of being atonal, but rhythmically it is
shapely (4–3 bars), and its ruthless stalk is a tremendous advance
on the insinuating subject of the other chromatic fugue, in C
minor (Peters 212), of which only an unfinished fair copy—
exposition and episode—has survived (Spitta). The counter-
subject at once shows that the listless semitones may have an

objective, and the second phrase declares the normal key. The
semitones, indeed, are not definitive. Of the next three entries—
two (A., A.) in leisurely counter-exposition—the first and third
begin in an alien key. But all straighten out in the fifth bar.

Example 22

Middle entries (B.S.A.) similarly make licence a virtue. The first,
emerging from two false entries, begins in the tonic (by dint of an
extra starting semitone) but screws up in time to its proper and
startling key, the sharpened submediant; the second loosens from
the last key to the supertonic; the third tightens from subdominant to tonic, and so far presages a final stage.

Of the last entries (A.B.S.), the first slips from ambiguity to the
subdominant, with compensating pulls sharpward. The bass
entry finds cause to regain its tonic at the usual place, and the
soprano entry creates suspense by dropping into the key of the
dominant, as in the fourth, sixth and ninth entries. All these
twists and turns are delivered with unceasing contrapuntal
sallies and hand-activity. When the last entry has reached the
cadential point with the pomp of a bass in octaves, the whole
counterpoint collapses in a rocket-like ascent from the bass, in
sparkling transition to the penultimate chord, releasing for one
moment the fashionable virtuosity which has been mentioned
earlier as a common feature of the close of a Toccata. At this
critical moment a "strong" cadence would be weak, while impressionism, "the reduction of law to the level of convention"

(Hadow), is a saving grace. The fugue is chromatic, then, *per se.*
Every entry contains an element of uncertainty, and makes capital
of it. *O world, thy slippery turns!* Scarcely two entries begin alike.
The invention with which Bach varies the sense reveals a new
fugal mastery.

The long connecting, distracting episodes, which fill over half
this overwhelming fugue, are based on the counter-subject's
anapaestic ascent and descent (cf. Ex. 41), an eddy of sound
marked by non-harmonic notes in pairs (e.g. the phrase B–D–e–g–
F, where F is harmonic; bar 54), and florid impromptu sequences
(bars 36, 49, 85, 118). Some are urged forward by the previous
entry; others add their own momentum to the often circular modulation they effect *en route* for the next entry (bars 83–9, 113–32).
Their forthright but wayward reverberating sequences are the right
link for the swinging but strained entries, where a more calculated
episodic development would have been disturbing. What with
less control (as in parts of the "Musical Offering" fugues) would
be common chromatic slither becomes, in the context of spontaneous episode, a relentless dialectic, surrounded by supporting
"spade-work." The outcome is a trenchant counterpoint, beyond
any relation to the slick chromaticism of the double-fugue in A
minor or the F sharp minor Toccata.

Two other fugues may be grouped with the present miscellany:
the fugues which Bach extemporized at Potsdam while on a visit in
1747 to his son Emanuel, who was in service to Frederick II of
Prussia. The king, an inveterate flautist, something of a composer
and a knowledgeable musician, wasted no time in having J. S.
Bach on parade and giving him a theme (his own or Emanuel's!)
on which to improvise a fugue. Bach appears to have played
fugues in three and in six parts on this personable subject, which
might well have been his own. He is said to have provided his
own subject for the second fugue, but the six-part fugue he sent
later is on the king's subject, and, apart from the absence of any
reference to its composition *after* the visit to Potsdam, its perfunctory character, especially in the later entries, and the general
absence of Bach's characteristic fugal qualities make it an inconceivable product except under the duress of extemporization.

(All this was fifty years back when Forkel wrote his biography, on which such details are based.)

When Bach was back at Leipzig, he evidently decided to capitalize, if possible, the products of his visit by sending the king a memento of what he had or might have played, with some clever canonic excursions on the same subject, accompanied by the usual doubly allusive titles, and, most acceptable of all, a sonata for flute containing allusions to the motto-theme. Bach slyly called this a "Musical Offering," as if partly in sacrifice to an implacable patron. (An offering it remained, in default of any evidence of payment.) The work was engraved by Schübler of Zella, who also published "The Art of Fugue." The canons include a lively "Fuga Canonica" in three parts (presumably flute with violin and keyboard, or just keyboard), a canon in two well-defined stages.

The THREE-PART RICERCAR or research-piece soon sounds like extemporization and belies its title. Bach flattered the king with a coherent recollection of what he had heard; he could not otherwise have reproduced certain passages in literal proportion. After the exposition, capricious entries in primary keys are spread out in two stages (bars 31–140, 141–85) by means of voluble episodes, including facile semitonal extensions of the subject. Surprisingly and perhaps *post eventum* the sequential counterpoint of the second alto entry (bar 61) consolidates the three last entries. In general, the craftsmanship is diverting but directed to one aim, producing the illusion of creative impulse, mainly by ignoring the subject.

The rather shorter SIX-PART RICERCAR unfolds on similar lines, in a more massive style and with a less diffuse and incoherent development. After the exposition, little use is made of differences of texture, all entries but one (S.) being in 5–6 parts. The final entry confirms recovery from a flatward trend of middle entry, after a long episode. Episodes are of random content as before, except for an immediate penchant for the falling semitone. The last stumbles on the subject of the second A flat fugue, as counter-subject of such a semitonal descent, strange company in such a medley. The fugue is impressive *qua* extemporary, and contains some moments of grandeur, but no heart-searchings. It is one more demonstration that, while semitonal degrees of the scale, and harmony based on them, have their uses as romantic symbols of the world's slippery, treacherous turns, in themselves they pall easily unless they are part of a wider movement. The "Elgar" C minor fugue for organ, midway, is a reminder of a more convincing chromatic style. The present fugue also demonstrates how often Bach thought harmonically rather than contrapuntally, and in this connexion how preferable a plain vocal line is to a more mannered subject with a similar curve, e.g. the subject of the first A minor fugue ("Forty-eight"). The royal touch was a valuable suggestion of the common that might attain to the universal.*

For it cannot be doubted that this chance excursion in fugue and canon round one subject at last made it clear to Bach, once and for all, where the future of fugue and fresh musical thought lay, namely in a set of fugues on a subject expressly designed for the purpose. This would reveal how much fugue could do for a theme *per se*, and also provide (any utility appealed to Bach) a set of complete examples of fugal style for students, worth a ton of theory for each ounce of practice, as Emanuel hastened to claim later when he tried to sell the engraving plates.

Thus the "Musical Offering" was in the first instance the public confirmation (not culmination) of the rhapsodic, diffuse style in which Bach wrote fugue at first and intermittently later, incidentally contrasting fugue in three and in six parts for the same subject. But he went on to fugue of an almost opposite kind, exploiting a theme fugally to the eleventh degree and more. In this "Art of Fugue," as the series was eventually entitled, Bach worked out in logical order with one main subject what he had done earlier at random and with different subjects. His fugal art thus took a fresh turn towards the elimination of the unessential and contingent.

NOTES

1 (*Page* 106) The dozen odd fugues in Vol. 42 (Bach Society edition, cf. Peters, 1959) display a mannered, symmetrical subject in voluble S.A. (or A.S.) B. style. In the first of the A minor fugues, key-range and

* See Note 4 on p. 115.

inversion stretch the theme to 107 bars; the other two (II. 8, 9) treat their subject with more reserve. But the three E minor fugues are more Bachian: one neatly double-themed throughout, one episodic, and the last smooth-flowing, with *stretti* to reinforce, and tempting to complete in three brusque (missing) bars.

2 (*Page* 107) The appendix to Spitta's *J. S. Bach* (English translation, Vol. 3) shows, in a violin sonata, the ephemeral character of Albinoni's own invention. Op. 1 comprises three trio-sonatas.

3 (*Page* 109) Mozart used this later in one of his string-trio arrangements of Bach fugues. See page 228.

4 (*Page* 114) The autograph employs two staves, as for keyboard (possibly with pedal), which *we know* to have been the original instrumental setting. The engraving of the fugue in open score was expedient and possibly demonstrative (see next chapter) but manifestly proves nothing. Hence the open scoring of "The Art of Fugue," as engraved, is no invitation whatever to "arrange" the two-stave manuscript as concerted music.

Chapter XIII

"THE ART OF FUGUE"

I. CREATIVE ACHIEVEMENT

TO the common and professional listener alike, the "Forty-eight" and surrounding fugues would appear to have exhausted all that could be expressed through sheer fugue for two hands, and incidentally to have provided a cumulative assembly of the practical methods of treating a subject, short or long, trivial or enduring. For Bach, to have stopped writing fugue would have been to confess creative decline and mental decay. The "Musical Offering" had been made in a better cause than he at first realized, and now the prospect of a longer and methodical series on one "ideal" subject was attractive to him. But once more and for the third time Bach's advance to a fresh series of extended fugues, now almost entirely dependent on treatment once the theme was settled, must not be taken for granted. It is a further sign of a major constructive impulse, which alone could conceive of making *music* under such limitations, and enrich with new types the methods already pursued in signal examples. It is the last demonstration of the historical imperative that Bach found, unpredictably, in fugue. If, in striving to complete a schedule of some twenty fugues—Bach's pen stopped in the middle of the eighteenth—he shows about half-way an absorption in technical processes at the expense of musical values, this only becomes apparent by the standard of the first ten fugues, which remains impeccable in its somewhat argumentative style. So much may be said in advance on a work on which critical opinion has been singularly confused and often misleading.

It must also be re-stated (what good editions take for granted) that Bach planned the series for normal keyboard performance, as the autograph shows. This statement is not modified by the fact that subsequently he wrote out the first instalment of eleven fugues for the engraver in open score, with each part in its own special clef, thus making the polyphony easier to understand (and to print) but not to perform. That proves nothing more than that Bach wished to demonstrate the inner, informative logic of his new fugal series to the eye, rather than to make it immediately playable in general circles. He had done the same for the six-part fugue he sent Frederick II. The suitability of these eleven fugues to the range of two hands, and to the dancing stamp and free movement of the keyboard, remains a salient fact of manual control and instrumental command which any performer can verify today. There is no serious justification for the varied instrumental arrangements initiated by Wolfgang Graeser a quarter of a century ago, except as emollients for the jaded or unimaginative. They miss both the common every-day touch of the keyboard and the personal advocacy of the solo-performer—imagine the first play-over!—and some wear a specious grandeur.

Of the remaining pieces, which may be termed Part 2 for convenience, much less can be said with certainty. They are written as for keyboard, but at least one pair of fugues is so unplayable by two hands that Bach added an arrangement for two keyboards. What is more, this essentially incomplete Part was evidently not reviewed by the composer for publication with the first Part. It was included (in open score) in the engraving of 1751, edited by Emanuel Bach, not on any authority from the composer but to provide "better weight."* Bluntly, then, Part 2 is a series of experiments written by Bach for Bach. He died without having decided what they would add up to; and the question of artistic aim cannot be pressed with so unfinished and unauthorized a series. The first Part remains intact: musically coherent and instrumentally concrete. We must make the most of it before beginning to conjecture about the rest.

The order of these eleven fugues, modestly entitled Contrapuncti, became a matter of concern to Bach. The "skeleton" subject, which so much baffled Parry, was evidently designed for convenient use as its own counterpoint in various rhythmic senses, but not at once. Bach began with three episodic fugues,

* See Note on p. 136.

the second on the inverted subject. Then he formed a group of technically demonstrative fugues, introducing close canon, counterpoint at the twelfth and tenth, and, with significant reluctance, diminution and augmentation, and he added a long and vivacious canon. Thirdly, he developed two wider fugues: one on two fresh themes, later combined with the main subject, the other on inversions of these three strands in a new order, forming an essentially new fugue on melodically familiar ground. Bach added another long canon, of which he made a simpler version for the engraving. On these lines he completed ten keyboard fugues, numbered in the engraving as follows: 1, 3, 2; 5, 9, 10, 6, 7, with the second canon (at the octave); 8 and 11 with the first canon (by augmentation). To these he added No. 4 later, and made various slight additions to other fugues, chiefly by way of final extension, and doubled the notational unit in some cases, implying anxiety for a slower tempo (ergo, not only practical but precise performance). Bach also changed the order to the published one, which presents three fresh groups: 1–2, 3–4; 5–7; 8, 11, divided by 9, 10. No. 3, richer in content than No. 2, now follows it and is compulsively succeeded by another fugue on the inverted subject. Nos. 6–7 obviously follow No. 5 logically and rhetorically. Nos. 9 and 10, ingeniously manifold in theme, divide No. 11 from No. 8, to which it is too laboriously equal and opposite to be played acceptably in immediate succession. (This change has disturbed some modern critics, but any musician will perceive Bach's point.) The encyclopædic plan has been replaced by a more musical order of appeal. A cumulative unity, unfolding round one common symbol, is Bach's transparent aim so far. (Spitta called the whole series "one fugue.") This coherent and numbered group, then, was sent to the engraver.

The remainder of the autograph consists of two pairs of totally invertible fugues, which we may number 12a, 12b, 13a, 13b; and an earlier draft of No. 10, which should never have been but fortunately was engraved. To these and the two canons the engraving adds, from other manuscripts, two more canons (at tenth and twelfth), a two-keyboard arrangement of Nos. 13a and

13*b*, and No. 14, an enormous unfinished "Fugue on three subjects" whose relevance Emanuel may have understood but certainly never explains; his to reason why not, not why! (The first edition even omits the last seven bars, which show the first three-theme combination.) It was left to Nottebohm, famous student of Beethoven's sketches, to discover that the main subject can also be combined with the three subjects. Tovey established the possibility of a relevant fugue, by completing it tersely as such. Tovey also stretched his peculiar fugal insight to "inventing" the missing pair of totally invertible fugues on four subjects, which, according to Mizler's commemorative notice of 1754, was planned but not written. By making a cumulative combination of theme invertible without total loss of harmonic point, he vindicated Mizler's statement as probably true. In this second and more improvisatory Part, then, Bach envisaged seven distinct fugues, of which he reached a late stage of the fifth. To compensate for the break in the latter, Emanuel threw in his father's last revision of a chorale-prelude, speciously described as "dictated on the spur of the moment" by the blind composer. He did not even bother to quote the revised title, "Vor deinem Thron" ("Before thy throne"). With this intimate but irrelevant piece we are not concerned here.

Such were the gradual steps by which Bach came to the present order of the first eleven fugues, continued but by no means concluded in the remaining pieces, a little off the ground and uncertain of musical aim. This understood, we may turn to individual fugues.

The fugues are in four parts except Nos. 8, 13*a* and 13*b*, which are in three. There is a natural leaning towards polyphony at the expense of keyboard freedom. So stark a subject needs extra covering, and, when it comes to twofold canon or counterpoint, a spare part to cement the joinery becomes essential except where, as in Fugue 8, the threefold combination is the conclusion of the whole matter. The subject is in the minor, an almost inevitable choice to a romanticist, concerned to seek in art some token of life's struggle, and equally to a craftsman who is aware of the greater wearing power of the minor scale, from its foundations in the Dorian mode to the sophisticated variants of submediant and leading-note. In melodic shape the theme is formal and elementary. The opening fanfare round the chord of the tonic tends to carry its own single harmony (modified to subdominant-tonic in the answer form) against any intersecting chord. The remaining conjunct movement from the leading note to the mediant argues dominant and tonic harmony in two clear harmonic beats. The inversion of the subject at the fifth moves from a rather less positive tonic fanfare to subdominant-tonic rhythm. Either of these invites the other in mutual rejoinder

Example 23

and cross-entry, but to effect this at once would be technically *naïf*. In FUGUE I, then, Bach relies on the variable harmony of free counterpoint to colour the flow of entries in tonic and dominant, establishing the four voices by an at first unbroken order of entry (A.S., B.T. twice) and adding others (S.B.) under cover of a false start (A., S.). In this style of rugged honesty, the crossing of the sixth entry by a false bass start leads to a full but re-pointed bass entry, which, intended to be in the dominant, drops half-way to the subdominant and enhances the sense of development. The last entry of all, replacing the final chord of what was first a coda with an abrupt cadence, is thus refreshingly and candidly subdominant in centre until the subdominant chord itself becomes cadential and penultimate. This reluctant surrender of the subdominant to the tonic recurs constantly in the series, sometimes tightened by the addition of the sharpened leading-note (cf. Fugues 2–7, 12*a*, 13*a*). The direct and final punctuation of the intervening fugues is the more bracing. In Fugue 1, most entries are kept apart by versatile sequences, growing out of a simple suspensory figure (bars 17, etc., and 66), or the free and literally

Example 24

arresting rhetoric stimulated by bass fixation in the last episode. This accomplished travelling in a restricted area has no fugal parallel. The subject has been established as a rallying point, firm in principle but elastic in detail. The preliminary experience of spaciousness and carelessness is a stimulating prelude to further adventure.

FUGUE 2 at once sets up a punctilious trochaic rhythm and also a halting effect, produced by placing essential harmony on the last quarter of a beat and then suspending a note in it, discordantly, on the next beat. This "crusty" texture carries the fugue past a transparent exposition (B.T.A.S.)—originally occurring after Fugue 3—an undeviating counter-exposition of subject and answer, and middle entries in the major. The last bass entry extends, as in Fugue 1. What was the final entry (T.) slips inaudibly off the normal beat. Bach added a clear and trenchant soprano entry, a bar after the original half-close (before Fugue 5), and this full close leads more easily to the next fugue. Entries are linked by homogeneous incidents, in which froward non-harmonic notes are noticeable and prepare the ear for similar

discords arising from awkward imitations of theme. The
rhythmic style seems to owe something to a variant in Scheidt's
Tabulatura Nova (Book II, No. 3), or some such trochaic obsession.

A few bars of FUGUE 3 make it clear that it was expedient to
hear Fugue 2, with its glib exposition and steadily *Cold Comfort
Farm* manner, first. The normal inversion of the subject (see
Ex. 23) here appears as the *answer* to an ambivalent curve (23G). It
soon becomes the usual version. Bach wanted to begin pro-
vocatively but had no cause to keep it up. Initial ambiguity is
assisted by a semitonal counter-subject (T.). The subject becomes
a prey to these pathetic twinges, and syncopation and decoration
(bar 23) add to its faltering effect, even in the major. The last
three lingering bars replace a single chord in the autograph.
Short episodes introduce a rhythmic tag (bars 19, 39), which
reappears in Fugue 11, besides stream-lined sequences. Free polyphony keeps the recurrent harmony of entries in sixths in changing
contexts, including half-beats (cf. bar 45). Fresh expression promotes a smoother sense of movement than in Fugue 1.

FUGUE 4, the chief complete afterthought of the series, opens
austerely, with entries steadily deepening (S.A.T.B.) and with a
forbidding undulating figure (S.), compressed to the minimum
rise and fall of pitch, in constant attendance. The usual bracing
effect of entries *in* the dominant is absent from the answers, and
also from the free counter-exposition (S.A.T.B. again), which
moves from major keys to an early subdominant (T.) before
pulling up to the tonic. An episode gains the dominant at last in a
compulsive sequence, but the next entry, in the nearest major key,
turns to the subdominant, owing to the subject's extra stretch in
the third bar (cf. Fugue 1, Ex. 24, B.). This stretch has come to
stay, and a firm chain of entries develops, each of which moves
one degree sharpward. The key-centre thus rises in fifths as far as
the supertonic (bar 80). The subject has stirred itself at last, and
in the process derived a counter-subject from the undulating
figure (bar 73, T.). The key-pressure loosens and a long sequential
episode follows. The next two entries are stimulated by close
canon, with *leader* and *follower* pulling the key in two directions
but resolving in each case on the tonic. A later subdominant

entry (T.) takes the extra stretch and thus automatically heads sharpward for the tonic, leaving the music to subside over a normal entry (A.), not without piquant touches, as in Fugue 3.

Example 25

These stiffening moods of the subject confront a powerful penetration of episode. Besides insistent sequences (bars 47, 82, 97, 120) there are resourceful excursions on a falling-third figure (cf. Ex. 40B), some intruding on entries (bars 20, 43, 53, 88, 115). The stern animation of the subject midway makes it possible to relax in subsequent episodes of twenty-six and fourteen bars with a consciousness of power, and thus to restore the principal image of expression without any more ado than fresh counterpoint, including a declamatory soprano and a tenor that introduces B–A–C–H (in German). Thus eloquently did unconscious cerebration on the first fugal effort (Nos. 1–3, 5–11) produce an extra *fugue* to celebrate the completion of the first main group in integral order.

The composer now turns—at first from the monotony of No. 2 but eventually from the rich incident of No. 4—to develop the subject for what it may be worth as its own counterpoint, with the inverted subject on equal terms with the subject and at first the prior motive. (Where distinction is necessary, "the subject" will refer to the initial curve, as it was in Fugue 1, and "the inverted subject" to its melodic opposite, with such adjustments of rhythmic or melodic detail as may be current. In general contexts, however, "the subject" will refer to the initial theme of the fugue concerned, because that is the musical impact. "Direct canon" means canon in the same melodic sense as the *leader* entry, canon "by inversion" means canon in the opposite sense.) It is possible

to take Fugues 5–7 as no more than an ingenious procession of
reversed melodic curves, halved and doubled metrical stretches in
counterpoint, and a general exploitation of subject-based harmony. But the successive technical difficulties of making music
by such slide-rule methods are interesting problems and un-
doubtedly stimulated Bach towards framing not one but three
fugues, and sooner or later it becomes less trouble to bring an
attentive ear to the many differences of canon.

Formal exposition is now *vieux jeu*, but the voices must enter
on some principle of rejoinder. In FUGUE 5 the interval of entry
is reduced so that the subject presents a three-bar rhythm each
time, exchanging its previous squareness for something more
svelte, aided by the dainty trochaic steps of "missing" degrees
between beats, anticipated in Fugue 3. With this renewal, the
inverted subject (in the pedantic sense) is followed by the subject
(in the tonic) before the normal answer. A further repartee of
answer and subject in reversed voices frames a counter-exposition
(S.T., B.A.; T. and A. being inaudible).

The closer canonic possibilities may be readily calculated by
comparing the notes of subject and inversion on the two main
beats and observing the harmonic incidences of typical canons at
the octave. (The actual direction of the melody below is determined by the fact that the musical alphabet in any octave begins
at C. An adjustment of octave above or below, at musical discretion, is assumed for each canon)—

BARS	1	2	3	4
(1) *Subject*	| D A |	F(E) D |	C sharp D(E) |	F
(2) *Subject in canon at*				
two beats		| D A |	F(E) D |	C sharp D |
(3) *Inversion*	| A D |	F A	B flat A(G) |	F |
(4) *Inversion in canon at*				
one beat		A | D F |	A B flat |	A |

The third and fourth bars are the crucial ones. In the subject, C
sharp can take A, B flat, or F if either note resolves by step, but
not D; and vice versa. In the inversion, B flat and A similarly
exclude each other. Accordingly for either subject or its inversion
direct canon (e.g. (1) and (2) or (3) and (4) above) is possible at

intervals of *two* and *three* beats. Canon by inversion ((1) and (4), (3) and (2)) is possible at *one* beat, and at *zero* (rhythmic unison); awkward at two beats, it occurs so only at a later stage of diminution (Fugue 7, bar 20).

Bach furnishes seven different canons on these lines, and he begins with canon at *one* beat, for its clear rhythmic impact. The rest are distributed to make alternative harmonic points. The game of cross-*rhythm* at 1–3 beats soon palls. While canon is at the octave, no interest of cross-*tonality* can arise. What can be done is to vary a pivotal chord. All canons to the *subject* are bound to promote a chord of the dominant for the fifth beat, most trenchant when the canon is direct and at two beats (no. (2) above). Canon by inversion (no. (4)) adds a piquant subdominant chord on the next beat. Canons to the inverted subject must recognize the submediant on the fifth beat, with more choice of chord. (The flick of keyboard tone is vital to the harmonic drive.) A major key tones down these changes of colour, and putting the follower entry in an inner part after one canon softens the cross-rhythm. With these nuances, two close canons by inversion in middle keys (bar 33, etc.) are followed by four direct canons (cf. Ex. 37B). Finally, subject and inversion are combined, the C sharp and B flat harmonizing (as part of a dominant ninth) but dreamily regardless of an extra bass part which drums steadily on the tonic. These seven canons carry the three-bar subject along in varying emphasis, with more polyphony than canonry to meet the outer ear, yet succeeding in orderly rejoinder as stated. Short sequences and impromptus, and plausible *stretti maestrali* or all-in entries of a fragment of the subject (bars 53, 65), fill in gaps.

Bach's fugues can rarely be distinguished by class. Fugue 5 was written to succeed Fugue 2, which suggests a sober, pernickety style and a white collar. Of the eventual successors, Fugue 3 is comparatively precious and pathetic. Fugue 4, episodic to the last degree, develops, after a sticky start, into breezy and brusque informalities, reflecting open necks, blunt and uncensored dialogue, and meals at any time. A meticulous sequel would have signalled a shade too obviously the arrival of Canon Close to dignify the scene! With singular prescience (Fugue 4 not having yet entered Bach's head) Fugue 5, in spite of its limited tonality, never betrays the clerk by any stiffness of manner. As unpredictable as Fugue 4 and more concentrated, it conveys a sense of travel and spaciousness in just continuation of the previous fugue's noble vagabondage. The metaphor is optional, but the smooth flow of free delivery remains.

In FUGUE 6, to which Bach came at first from the wider sphere of Fugues 9 and 10, he virtually resumed Fugue 5, by making close canon a point of style, but pertinently coloured it afresh by deriving his canons from the subject (now restored to four bars) at double speed. The comparative strands are typically as follows—

(1) *Subject*	| D : A	| F : D	| C sharp : D(E) | F
(5) *Inversion in canon at 2 beats, diminished*		| A . D : F . A	| B flat . A : F
(2) *Inversion*	| A : D	| F : A	| B flat : A(G) | F
(6) *Subject in canon at 1 beat, diminished*		D . A | F . D : C sharp . DE | F :

Canons are now invariably by inversion. They occur at *two* beats and then once at *one*, first for the subject (bar 1, cf. 25, 31; 16), then for the inverted subject (35, cf. 47, 64, 75; 58). Canons at *two* beats move to a poignant dominant ninth chord on the fifth beat. The first canon at *one* beat moves, again, from the submediant chord to a trenchant dominant on the fifth beat; the second canon reverses these chords. Each set begins with clear entries (B.S.: S.B.) and then becomes more involved. The rhythmic process is also adroitly reversed, by canon in normal rhythm, and thus in apparent extension, to the diminished theme (the inversion in bars 7, 15, the subject in 57, 74, cf. VII. 1, 13). This mainly organic counterpoint—free entries, both in a casual major, occur in bars 20, 42—makes a show of exposition, clustered round three normal entries (B.A.T.), each the centre of a chain of sub-entries in the same key. It passes to middle keys and consolidates in the tonic.

But Bach realized that the sum of the harmonic gains of the new cross-rhythm was not nearly enough to keep a second fugue going. Mere diminution of theme can only be an accessory, whose repetition easily becomes, as Mozart usually made it, a joke. But if it can be moderately maintained in a wider context, it will begin to establish its own half-beats as substantive rhythm. Moreover, when the diminished theme takes the initiative, with the normal subject in its train (bars 7, etc.), the attentive ear is becoming conditioned for a double metrical stretch in canon. Further, the insistent trochaic step of the diminished subject (filled in as in Fugue 5) was a recognized token of majesty whose decorative and sequential associations Bach could not resist developing (bars 11, 29, 51, 69). He brings them eventually to the inevitable "stately halt," which supplies a *point d'appui* for the last accumulation of diminished and "normal" entries (Bach's order). These are in the subdominant, making a supremely dilatory "A – – men," once more in a rapt mood regardless of the tonic held in the bass. (Each quaver-dot should sound as if doubled.)

It is no use hoping to enjoy this fugue without observing the interplay of the established two steps and the new four steps a bar. But as the advance of the latter to priority of impact is appreciated, the composer's acrobatic feat in keeping the fugue going for seventy-nine full bars, without any fresh basic material or any general variant on canon by inversion as shown, compels admiration. It is as hard to *base* a fugue on close canon as to write without using its convenient reverberations, as in Fugues 1–3. Somehow, as Bach was engaged on Fugues 9 and 10, a vague call to continue the reverberations of Fugue 5 in fresh contexts became concrete, perhaps after the sweep of Fugue 10.

In Fugue 7, the diminished subject secures the initiative, with the once normal subject in support. The upstart provides the inverted subject with a fresh direct canon at the fifth, which with an augmented entry formulates a fresh exposition (T.S., A.B.); it enters in its own right (bars 9, 17, 24, 55); and it forms its own canons (bars 20, 42) and half-canons (28, 45). But the now overworked majestic rhythm has lost its power. It must be enveloped in as liquescent counterpoint as possible. This will flood the ear in such a way as to make the drag of a long version of the subject act as a continuum of dry deposit. In this swiftly prepared context, paved by Fugue 6, the augmented subject, inverted, appears monstrously to complete exposition, four times the stretch of the alto answer, which it directly imitates at first, with a modulation to and from the dominant. This is inevitably in the bass. A further and capricious series of entries, canons and episodes, whirled along by the movement of finger in bass or top, promotes chorale-like appearances of the eight-bar theme in the other voices (T.A.S.), the first methodically normal but in the relative major, the second faintly recognizable as the inversion by its submediant touch in the fifth bar. The last entry is utterly exposed and confident; an episcopal figure led in by minor canons in duly rehearsed sequence. Hence—for this ceremonial admits of a human touch—the final accession to the centre-point must be diverted by a spontaneous interruption and adjustment before it is accomplished. (The rare chord of the augmented sixth intensifies the cadence, on top of the supertonic ninth.)

Fugal augmentation is a process about which one is inclined to ask not "how" but "why." By a contrivance of context which no precedent could have shown him, Bach, without the advantage of the organ, brings off a long subject and its inversion twice, each without obstructing, but rather disposing in four broad turns of stream-bed, the flow of the sixty-one bars of music; a unique feat, more acceptable to my ears than the lingering augmentations of the first E flat minor fugue. Here, not for the last time, a theoretic device, almost dead against the natural impulses to multiply steps, threatens to obscure the proper demands of music. Yet the listener passes on, satisfied that compression of theme *per se* has not only met its match in a spare series of extensions without grotesque strains but gained fresh music and incidentally a memorable cadence. Fugue and theme have found a new lease of life.

From there Bach might in revision have proceeded with the counter-subject rhetoric of Fugues 9 and 10, but he decided to place these as demonstrative diversions between two nominally triple fugues. More than some of his later critics, Bach realized that Fugue 11, in immediate succession to another triple fugue on very similar but stronger material, would be quite unacceptable to an alert ear. FUGUE 8, then, originally following Nos. 9–10, 6–7, assumes that a new basic harmony for the subject must be found in its accompaniment by fresh motives whose identity has previously been established. At this sub-climactic moment Bach declared his essentially keyboard intentions, and left a sword of justice swinging over the heads of all who presume to know better, by writing in three parts, manifestly for greater freedom of manual expression, as in the double and triple fugues in the "Forty-eight," and possibly with a view to a four-part fugue later, or from sheer satisfaction with the basic combination.

It is not hard to follow the almost patent stages by which Bach arrived at this combination. First, he chose the *inversion* of the motto-subject, as more poised than the subject. It had to be one or the other; no genuine combination would fit both (i.e. a part in which degrees 1–5, 2–4, 6–7 exchange later). It is noticeable that Bach prefers the inversion, probably for the stronger pre-dominant or pro-dominant chord in the third bar, in his finest fugues (4, 8, 10 and mainly 5). Let us call this *a*, the new subject *b* and a complementary counter-subject *c*. Theme *b* must start on the tonic, on a preliminary beat. A plain descent to the pivotal note where, as observed in earlier fugues, a submediant chord is highly expedient, produces the right kind of compulsive outline.

Example 26

It remains to break *b* up with an intrusive semitone, with harmonizing and decorative notes, and by pitting *a* against it in blunt syncopation. Yet this good contentious counterpoint lacks grit.

Example 27

An inner part can provide this simply by falling in thirds with the outline of *b*, as in Ex. 26, but with each note overlapping the next beat discordantly and resolving within it. Ornamental resolution, with sharpened and flattened notes in keeping with the piquant semitones of *b*, will be more characteristic and infectious. The discretionary third bar is given as for the combination; it appears earlier a fourth or fifth lower, in another part. The harmonic rhythm is now definitely four beats, even if the time-signature (originally $\frac{2}{4}$ with identical barring) gives two. This positive

Example 28

combination can be regarded as the planned objective of the fugue, the vitalizing harmonic turn which must be contrapuntally justified as the convergence of three themes which have already made their own life. Bach must have settled this before he worked out anything else, possibly by the steps indicated. He may have contemplated another fugue, in which *a* would be in the ascendant. (De-inverted, *a* must always be "real"; hence *a* as here.)

The main problem, then, was to deploy the new motives and reintroduce *a*, without a patent exposure of *b*, *c* and *a* in turn. Theme *b*, melodically compulsive, can stand a good deal; theme *c* is only an accessory to *b*, which is an advantage, but this cannot be called fugue on three subjects. Theme *a* must not at first dominate this fugue on *b*; it must appear episodic. Five stages of delivery may be distinguished. Episodes total more than half the fugue, but they are organic throughout.

1. Bars 1–39   Exposition of *b*.
2.   „   40–93   Counter-exposition and development of *b*, with *c* as counter-subject.
3.   „   94–108   Exposition of *a*.
4.   „   109–47   Further development of *b* and *c*.
5.   „   148–88   Combination of *b* and *c* with *a*.

The technical difficulty is to keep *b* on the musical side of exhaustiveness, to make the first appearance of *a* relevant, and to render the final combination conclusive, but repeatable. This may be remembered as we observe each stage.

1. In exposition *b*, longer than three bars at first (cf. bars 129, 151), readily acquires sequential features to accompany its descent down the scale, including *b* itself in close canon in the first of two extra entries. To spread these out, a hard-working figure with descending thirds (*x*) promotes episodes and combines with the first bar of *b* in a piquant descending sequence. (Cf. Ex. 39B.)

2. A fresh start (S.B.A.) with *c* as counter-subject must not be too formal. A new balance of primary keys leads on to major and other keys swiftly enough to make an early recovery (bar 82) possible. In the set counterpoint, *c* is completed by a descending figure in another part (*y* in Ex. 28), which promotes diversion in episodes by imitation, sequence and inversion, along with sequences arising from *c*. A false anticipation confuses the entry of recovery and a further false entry breaks into impatient bravura (S.A.B.).

3. The ground thus energetically turned but not reaped, *a* strikes up unobtrusively (A.B.S.), gradually identifiable as the chief figure of the series in fresh accents. The casual presence of former accessories (the original counter-subject, *x* and *c*) renders the context familiar, but the declamation is new.

4. Further development of *b*, *c* and *y* is at first automatic and almost uncontrolled (bar 114), but it concentrates in a double entry of *b*, with a descant of *c* and *y*, each half a bar or more earlier than usual (!). An entry in the dominant is confirmed capriciously by *y*, doubled by inversion in headlong sequence outwards.

5. In this disturbed atmosphere a pronouncement, combining *b* with *a*, is a moral certainty. But the *a priori* decisive combination of Ex. 28 would after all be an anti-climax after all the keen-edged counterpoint. The ascending fourth of *b* appears to have given Bach his cue. An entry of *b* as for F major could begin in A minor, with the right bass and with an adjustment of the third and fourth notes of *b* from D–D flat (bar 62) to D sharp–D. The combination thus begins (Ex. 29) trenchantly in the key offered, the dominant, and then reduces to the mediant major. Not to leave this in singularity, the answer offers an identical relation one degree sharpward with *a* now on top. By such releases of tension the blend of theme penetrates first in two casual major keys. This

leaves the primary keys for smoother, normal entries in varied voicing. To be on the safe side, *cy*, the least characteristic strand, is placed on top in a subdominant entry, while the tonic entries find their level with *a* and *b* on the outside of the harmony, freshened by a "Neapolitan" diminished second in the second bar of *c*, a compensating C sharp in *b* (soprano entry), and an ornamental but well-pointed cadence. A syncopated falling

Example 29

figure which follows the first entry of *b* in this section (S.) provokes extensions before each of the last two entries. These last five entries appear in riveting succession.

Through this consummate double-fugue and agile triple counterpoint, the main subject has been roused to a finer issue than before. It has been left comfortably where an old theme belongs, in the bass. It is devoutly to be wished that Bach had left it there, in principle. What further conclusions he tried will be considered in the due course of the revised order.

FUGUE 9, which first followed Fugue 5 as a gymnastic display of invertible counterpoint, now finds its place as a demonstrative fugue on two subjects, the first fresh and the second a plain version of the main subject, which needs no exposition. In the autograph the latter is in the usual minims, making clear the quarter-beat movement of the first subject. The engraving makes minims into semibreves, with double the number of bars, but the quarter-beats must not on that account become half-beats in performance. The change may well have been for convenience in engraving, and in any case the subject is of the supersonic type.

In this whirling style, then, the new subject (*d*) is exhibited in all four voices. An extra entry (T.) acquires the main subject in combination, as a stable Point or series of notes, to which *d* is revealed increasingly as the proper counterpoint. Six combined entries follow in bland succession, mainly at short intervals. In two entries the basic harmony is the same as at first, with a fresh upper part each time. In the other four, *d* is put up a twelfth, so that the harmony is quite different; the resolved discords in the second and fifth bars have become stray concords and fresh discords. This easier harmony, enriched by free polyphony—*a* is kept below after the first time—is heard partly in outside keys. In these alternative settings, the flying phrases recur in the stilted manner occasioned by the "plainchant" background. Connecting links are resourcefully derived from a sequential treatment of the falling figure of the sixth bar (bar 29, etc.), or of the ascent of the third bar (bars 81, 114). The two are opposed with some intensity in the last episode. The contrapuntal eloquence is steady, but the acrobatic style is strained. There are too many entries on so set a contrapuntal basis.

It is amazing to pass on to another double fugue, in which the main subject (inverted) is the second subject, so different is the outcome. FUGUE 10, headed *alla Decima*, actually exhibits inversion of the counter-subject at the tenth and twelfth (never at the octave), and apart from these variants the recurrent combination of seven entries again punctuates and informs a wider polyphonic expression, with considerable episodes, all in a decorative style. There the resemblance to Fugue 9 ends.

The earlier version of Fugue 10, superfluously but revealingly inserted by Emanuel into the engraving after Fugue 13*b*, begins, as at bar 23 (S.) of the revision, with a fresh exposition of the main subject, inverted, and shaped in three-bar rhythm as in Fugue 5. In the counter-exposition a fresh counter-subject is introduced, to combine with the subject at various intervals, thus reversing the order of old and new themes in Fugue 9. Let us call these *a* and *e*. The remainder of the fugue spreads out the patent or underlying delivery of *a* and *e* in combination at changing intervals. Bach later decided that to *start* a fugue with an exposition of *a* was otiose, on top of Fugues 3–8 and after the wittier treatment in Fugue 5. Instead, *e* must be made a subject in its own right, and piquantly enough to call for the simpler statement of *a*. No. 10 thus became a double-fugue, replacing the rich preliminaries of

Fugue 8 by modest expositions but balancing these by a long procession of combined entries and interludes, in which freshness of harmonic colour is a prime concern.

Further examination of the earlier version suggests the steps by which Bach arrived at the exposition of *e*, which as first combined with *a* (bar 44 of the revised fugue with F *naturals*) takes a modal

Example 30

turn quite out of keeping with a fugal lead of 1749. (In 1909 it would have been different.) Bach's first step was bluntly to sharpen the Fs there and thus make G a key-centre, from which the tonic is recovered a bar later.* But since a fugue cannot begin by establishing the subdominant without ambiguity, *e* must be announced a fifth higher, in D minor, but avoid going into A minor in the second bar. This might have had a normal answer,

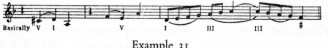

Example 31

but Bach's inclination with such a curve was to give a tonal, sub-dominant answer (see p. 166), and the prospect of Ex. 30 ahead settled it. In rejoinder, the other voices appear (as in Fugue 5) with an inversion of the subject (at the second) in tonic and dominant. This is amplified by a close canon-by-inversion, in the midst of the polyphony (A.T.), but a sequential episode loosens the weave, in preparation for the second fugue. Meanwhile an awkward subject has been mastered so as to produce a sense, not of grammatical struggle but of a singularly absorbed and unquenchable mood, which it will be the concern of the second fughetta to

* He made similar alterations, and a few others, in bars 33, 71, 73, 83 (S.); 60, 85, 92, 103 (A.); 36–7, 74, 86 (T.); 71, 73 (B.). (Cf. p. 242.)

qualify by its more direct rhythm. It remains to provide some connecting link by using an extemporary *basso continuo* to cover the first entry of *a*, and to add an extra half-answer to fill in the acoustic gap, thus avoiding a too conscious second start. It is not expedient for the latter to begin in the dominant, as in earlier double-fugues. The clear tonic is rejoinder enough to a trend frequently subdominant. Context overrules precedent in matters of structure, for a musician.

In the new fughetta free counterpoint and a facile sequential episode (ever-ready agenda for the idle moment) leave room for a generous counter-exposition, and also indicate that it should be characteristic. In the next entry, the double theme is well concealed; and not till three entries later are both subjects in outer parts. However, gradually it dawns on the listener that a combination of motive informs every entry from this point. Alert harmonic hearing will also distinguish the appearances of *e* at new intervals (inversion at tenth and twelfth is a safe guess), and some doubling of *a* and *e* in turn. The basic modal harmony, as previously indicated, called for redress, and so does the more sophisticated modulation above, which is mealy-mouthed. Thus the combined themes become transparent in perpetual inversion, with major keys to relieve the somewhat didactic tone of minor entries. Let us call the initial entry of the first subject in the combination *e*1, and its ascensions at tenth and twelfth *e*2 and *e*3, each with modifications for the answer type of entry. The differences of the seven entries (heard downwards) include the following "conjugations" of subject, besides *a*: *e*1, *e*2, *e*2 (counter-exposition), *e*1 with *a* doubled a sixth higher (major), *e*3 and *e*2, *e*2 and *e*1 (major), *e*3 and *e*2. It may be added that *e*1 is always below *a*, *e*2 above it when not doubling *e*1, and *e*3 always above. The outcome is that while the bass contains *a* three times—where it is most effective, as in Fugue 8—the soprano never repeats exactly the same phrase. Even in close succession these entries would never sound tautologous. Actually they are spaced out by episodes of 4–14 bars, some being impromptu sequences, others based on an ascending scale figure, which suggests pivotal dominant harmony for an established or imminent key note (bar 28, cf. 50, 56, 107).

In short, Fugue 10 is a creative advance for the inverted subject, challenging Fugue 4 on episodic spontaneity, confirming the double-fugue of Fugue 8 without any essential repetition of

Example 32

style, and incidentally defying the second G minor fugue (W.K.) as a document in invertible counterpoint. It is monstrous that the fugue is so little known, even to connoisseurs.

After writing Fugue 8, Bach could not resist working out a fugue on inversions of its themes, of which only *a* was made to reverse. He proceeded to write two totally invertible fugues, i.e. fugues of which the component parts are then inverted (at the fifth) and put together, in fresh voices (and octaves), to make a nominally independent fugue; he brought the canons, embodying the subject in an ornamental style, up to four; he composed the greater part of an enormous fugue "on three subjects" to which the main subject must have been contemplated as a fourth, since it can combine with the three already together in the fugue as left; and he contemplated an invertible fugue on four subjects. The exploitation of intellectual or rather arithmetical devices becomes much more conscious, and the musical touch more uncertain, during this last stage. It may be estimated that from Fugue 11 begins the second and more experimental stage of fugue-writing *per se*. Leaving well alone, we may consider this in detail in the next chapter.

NOTE

(*Page* 117) Sales having proved discouraging, a further and cheaper but still fine issue was brought out at the Leipzig Book Fair, 1752, with a preface by F. W. Marpurg, fugal theorist, witheringly comparing "manly" counterpoint with "the destructive rubbish of womanish song." Forkel's copy is in the British Museum.

Chapter XIV

"THE ART OF FUGUE"

II. THE FINAL STRUGGLE

FUGUE 11 (four voices) is a double-fugue on the lines of Fugue 8. We may re-name the subjects *a*, *b* and *c*, in reference to the themes of which they are the reverse, but in their own right. Translated as they are, they are all *idées fixes* from the start in some sense. There is no need for ceremony in introducing them, and none can emerge here with the full stimulus of a thought in reserve. Further, while *a* has still formal significance as the original curve in the newer rhythm of Fugue 8, the laboured progress of *b up* an octave cannot carry the spontaneity of the descent which, as noted earlier, is its natural and vocal trend; and the upward movement of *c* has the same disadvantage, and the strained resolution of its discordant overlapping

Example 33

notes limits its usefulness. Thus the new combination will have less cumulative drive behind it, and be less compulsive in itself. Hence fresh polyphony is needed and possibly a new countersubject; and somehow *a*, *b* and *c* must take time off unobtrusively, the better to return. There is now a voice to spare, but no theme could make a satisfactory fourth, melodically, with so studied a combination. On the contrary, the extra voice must be used as decoratively and freely as possible to fill in gaps in the harmonic impulse. The main hope of the fugue is to be probing, by exploiting semitonal sonorities in the direction of an absorbing impressionism, aided by an ambiguous tonality, from which the original centre is patiently picked out. Some such calculations

directed Bach's always realistic attack on the material he had given
himself. The plan of this fugue is so similar to that of Fugue 8
that it may usefully be tabulated in parallel with it. (The *a, b, c* of
Fugue 11 are the inversions of the previous *a, b, c*)—

	Bars	Fugue 8	Bars	Fugue 11
(i)	1– 39	Exposition of *b*	1– 27	Exposition of *a*
(ii)	40– 93	Development of *b, c*	28– 70	Exposition of *b*, with *x* as new counter-subject
(iii)	94–108	Exposition of *a*	71– 89	Counter-exposition of *a* by inversion
(iv)	109– 47	Development of *b, c*	90–145	Development of *b, c* and their inversions
(v)	148– 88	*a, b* and *c*	146– 84	*a, b* and *c*; also *a* and its inversion

Some details of the new régime may be noted—

(i) The revival of *a* (beginning A.S.B.T. as in Fugue 1) is
effected in a leisurely vocal style. The two-minims-a-bar of the
engraving replaces an original two-crotchets, which implies an
anxiety to prevent too brusque a performance, and the searching
harmonic tread on each half-beat implies four beats rather than
two. An extension of the fourth entry by imitation, and an
extra, halting entry, draw out sweet night.

(ii) *b* is covered at once by its semitonal companion (*x*) and
remains underneath (A.T.B.) until it is due for a soprano entry,
when it de-inverts! (The natural, musical fall of the original *b* of
Fugue 8 demands a term of restoration.) General semitonal progression, in one or more voices, and an ascending fragment which
later shapes in the soprano (bars 31, 40–41, cf. Fugue 3, bar 19)
space out these rather desultory entries sufficiently to call for a new
incident. (Cf. Ex. 42C, 45A.)

(iii) The clear step of *a* in a plainer rhythm and less semitonal
harmony provides stability after the nervous trend of *b*, and its
contrast with section (i) is aided not only by the poise of the
inverted subject and the answer-subject order, with keys to match,
but an unusually disparate voicing (T.S.B.A.). Yet restlessness
afflicts *a* as well, and the last entry slips into the relative major.

(iv) This is the opportunity for *b* and *c* to insinuate their
worried, worrying sequence, approaching the tonic via the

submediant major. Theme *c*, affected in any extended treatment, is soon de-inverted, for purposes of imitation, followed by *b* at the third entry (T.) in a reminiscent passage (cf. Fugue 8, 125). However, normal *b* returns (S. and later T.). Meanwhile a restored *a*, no longer in dignified reserve, cleans up the harmony from time to time, with a de-inverted *c* in cheerful attendance (bars 101, 132). An intensified chase of theme suggests a peroration, but a sudden turn of chord diverts the key into the leading-note minor. However, *b* treats this tonic (as earlier) as the submediant of a fresh key, and so the entry is braced up to the supertonic minor.

(v) This proves to be the first of the combined entries, appearing, as in Fugue 8, as a chance "find" in a foreign key. Bach judged that the present product of multiple thematic economy, with each component already exhaustively drawn upon, could stretch only to two final repeats, one with *b* comfortably in the bass, the other with *a* triumphant and almost defiant in the soprano. The present entry, then, puts *b* over the top under cover of a surprise attack. Intermediately, the obvious choice of a combined entry in the dominant having been rejected, some reinforcement of *a* is desirable. Bach effects this through entries

Example 34

of *a* and its varied inversion together (S.A., T.B.). Thus *a* emerges finally and commandingly, beginning warmly in the submediant major (Mendelssohn intensified this approach in the

"Elijah" overture) and then acquiring a firm dominant bass for the first clean cadence since the exposition. The "masculine" final chord is striking, anticipated only in Fugue 9.

By his long art Bach has disposed his intractable, "unwanted" subjects and well-worn principal so that the weaknesses appear at the right places, and the nearly atonal texture is often strikingly enveloping. Yet here is a fugue of masterly syntax and fertile repartee, not a truly monumental finish to the double-fugue series. There is a struggle for expression, and surely a straining after the ample proportions of Fugue 8. To subject such a piece of agile diplomacy to the pomp of orchestral lead and climax is to impart a *folie de grandeur* the fugue does not deserve. It is neither majestic nor rhythmically of the sort that calls for the varied sonority of an orchestra of 1850. If in recent times it has contrived to be impressive in spite of such a sumptuous rendering, that has been due to the awful personality of the composer, and perhaps national fugal superstition, but not to the liquidation of the keyboard.

That Bach was not abandoning the struggle is shown by his subsequent serious work at invertible fugue. Yet his willingness to attempt invertible fugue at all is the sign of a singular absorption in the technical potentialities of a non-musical method. Let us summarize the formal facts about the first pair. Fugue 12a, as we may conveniently call Fugue 12 (the last numbered piece in the engraving), has a normal exposition, middle entries in the subdominant and submediant, and final entries in the tonic (Fugue 13a has the same key-scheme). Fugue 12b is constructed from the inversion at the fifth of the entire S.A.T.B. parts of 12a to form the new B.T.A.S. Gravitation and levitation exchange in two senses. Under steady control such an acoustic reversal is common enough in fugue. But no *entire* bass part of a normal fugue would be satisfactory as top, or top as bass. Hence the texture here is either limited to neutral ground, or surprises occur, as when the soaring fifth entry takes to burrowing at the roots.

Meanwhile in pitch degrees 1 and 5, 2 and 4, 6 and 7, change round. The common triad or fifth on the tonic remains, but those on the dominant and mediant change (flatward) to subdominant

and submediant, and vice versa, and only the tonic entries retain
their centre of gravity. All the cadences will reverse similarly;
for example, the bracing sequence of V–I becomes the "wetter"
IV–I, and on the other hand I–V turns to I–IV, stronger in its key.
All these automatic variants of pitch and chord, adjustable only in
choice of semitone, call equally for neutral progressions (recalling
the unusual sergeant-major who remarked, "I said *right*-turn, but
the left will be O.K."), or else for shocks. Among commonly
needed discords, the diminished seventh (♯7 2 4 6) retains its
identity, if complete, but the Neapolitan-sixth sequence (4–6–♭2
2–4–♯7) reverses, which is absurd. Discords by suspension (e.g.
D held against a harmonic E) resolve down a step; inverted, they
must resolve up (as A against G). This, too, is generally workable
but compromising.

In short, it is not a terrific problem to compose a fugue whose
total inversion makes bare *sense*, but that sense, being arithmetic-
ally determined and musically in the nature of a perpetual
reversal of chord and cadential quality, will challenge the reason
as much as the looking-glass room which has the window on the
inner side of the fire-place. Here, above all, one questions not
how but that. Looking-glass fugue provides its slight and mechanical nuances of fresh expression; the cross-rhythm and textural
weave remain identical, apart from voicing. Orpheus with his
lute made the mountains bow, but not, I think, by inversion.
Bach carries out his academic experiment faithfully, without
arousing any special admiration for his ingenuity or method;
and he may not have intended publication.

Dismissing the *a priori* judgments which such a method prompts,
we may observe that FUGUE 12 is a demure pursuit of the subject
in a new triple metre on vocal and decorative lines, with willingly
sequential episodes. It is astonishing that Rust, the editor of many
volumes of the Bach Society's monumental issue of Bach's works,
should have regarded this slick composition as the crown of the
whole series. The CONTRAPUNTUS INVERSUS is a heavy jest; one
is too frequently conscious of a thick left-hand part and lamed
sequences (e.g. bars 46–9), and the final levitation of the soprano
is as queer as any other gravitation to the moon. The three-voice

FUGUE 13a, on a free, acrobatic inversion of the subject, has a strong triplet rhythm and a new upward curve to replace the usual fall to the tonic. As in Fugue 5, the answer is by inversion, and the third entry is the normal answer; thus alternative answers are ensured, one of which will avoid that awkward subdominant touch in the looking-glass. A full recapitulation includes a vividly halted episode, which exploits the set colour of one diminished seventh. The first episode (Ex. 39C) promotes the others. FUGUE 13b, putting the top line of 13a below the two others, inevitably exchanges subject and inversion, which is scarcely noticeable at first after 13a. The alto of 13a makes a vigorous top part, the soprano makes a reasonably springy and not too voluble bass, and the bracing up of the tonality from the (wangled) submediant to the dominant for the second middle entry is an improvement. But who wants to discover this? The price of this centrifugal polyphony is that it is not quite playable by two hands. Bach accordingly later re-wrote 13a and 13b for two keyboards, with an extra free part in each, inserted as a manifest afterthought. He was always making keyboard music out of violin parts in this way.

Before this pair in the engraving, and in stray succession in the autograph and supplementary sheets, come the four canons. These are at a tangent to the main structural development, but they may be summarized here, as a "control" group of one long, fanciful line placed in a two-part setting by a canon or rule of endless imitation, as against the select imitation of a fugal entry. The canons here are prolonged pieces of strict, honest canon in at least two stages, each beginning with witty or decorative versions of the main subject and exploiting their schedule. They are the *jeux d'esprit* of a masterful mentality in a state of ominous equilibrium, or at best preparing for a much more ambitious design. They do not invite continuation, had there been opportunity. They combine different schemes of interval with widely different degrees of canonic urgency. In CANON I, "the most poignant expression existing of spiritual loneliness in tones" (E. H. W. Meyerstein), the *dux* part is in an exquisitely dreamy mood, and the *comes*, translating twenty-four bars of it at half-speed, soon becomes no more than a shapely background to the upper coloratura, a quite unconscious turn of consistent (inverted) curve, in the definition of which it pleased Bach to work to rule, with musically selected semitones. But to repeat the combination with the graceful sprawl on top was gross abuse of contrapuntal liberty. Very like a whale, as Polonius said of the moon (cf. bars 66–70). The original autograph version, freer from absurd incident, is preferable. CANON No. 2 is a lively Invention, showing canon at the octave in four crisp stages. The sense of rejoinder is kept up to the end, and also of the basic subject. CANON 3 frames a twofold canon: *comes* is first a tenth up and then, lowered a tenth, pursues *dux* at the octave. A leisurely interplay in each line of flowing and more incisive styles nearly loses a sense of imitation, but recovers it for the melodically more assonant second canon. CANON 4 similarly treats canon at the twelfth in florid manner, with a still slight sense of canon, thinly recovered halfway. This contrapuntal agility is chiefly a matter of patience and gumption, but it pleased Bach to show it in canon at each common interval, and in the process to abandon the main subject in extended interlude. He was now constructively *rid of the subject* as an obsession, in favour of two or more stages of ornamental variation. These wilful canons are as necessary to the later master-fugues planned as Wagnerian recitative is to the reverberation of *Leitmotive*.

We come to the last and UNFINISHED FUGUE "on three subjects," found separately and included by Emanuel Bach in the engraving without a clue to its relevance. (Rust mistakenly rejected this fugue from the series; hence his peculiar *penchant* for Fugue 12.) Three fresh subjects are treated fugally and exhaustively in turn: a plain *a* in vocal style, apt for inversion and close canon; a volatile but comprehensive keyboard motive, *b*, with which *a* combines loosely in counter-exposition (in two ways—bars 148, 169); and a chromatic and just invertible *c* (BACH in sound) to form a reinforcing inner Point to *b*, with *a* as bass and a free part on top. This is no sooner done than Bach's pen (or at least the surviving script, for Emanuel is untrustworthy) stops, at bar 239. Tovey, adjusting a trail laid by Nottebohm, completed the fugue

in seventy-eight bars, by developing Bach's essential triple
counterpoint by inversion and by adding the motto-subject to it
in four ways, of which the last returns effectively to Bach's scheme
as modified by the main subject as fourth voice (T., then S.). We
do not know what scale Bach contemplated, but Tovey's scheme
is exhaustive and at the same time ultimately (if not intermediately)
comfortable enough to be a credible summary of what the fugue
might have contained. Yet it all implies a belief in quadruple
fugue, as better than triple. This is most questionable, not least on
the evidence of Bach's earlier works. In all his "triple" fugues,
one theme is always subsidiary and is absorbed sooner or later by
another; and a set counterpoint for four "voices" has no aesthetic
advantage over one for three. So far Fugue 14 must be put down
with a firm query, rather than a firm regret that it appears
unfinished.* Fugue 15, the unwritten invertible fugue on four
subjects, need not be regretted at all. Tovey has demonstrated, in
a compressed style, what the schedule would have involved, and
how the themes and their combination might have been so
emotionally charged (he writes for strings) as to extend tolerably
in a total inversion. Yet what music can survive the exacting
routine of quadruple fugue of this cumulative sort and still be
invertible? The structure has become a form without the
animating spirit. As the first fiddle of Tovey's brilliantly steered
phantom Fugue 15b stoops to its final bow on the g string, we
are reminded of the Countess curtseying to her reflection in the
mirror in Strauss's *Capriccio*.

While, then, it would be more heartening and romantic to
contemplate the ageing composer advancing towards wider
horizons, and tragically halted less than a day's journey from the
top of Mount Pisgah, the evidence of alert listening from Fugue 11
onwards does not bear out such a *coup d'œil*. A truer estimate is
of fresh and tireless experiment without the achievement of
Fugues 4, 5, 8 and 10—

What I cannot e'er express, yet cannot all conceal.

The superlative standards of those earlier fugues remain, as a final

* See Note on p. 145.

testimony to the peculiar glamour with which fugue not only enhances the plainest melodic formula but also seeks and discovers new ranges and orders of imagery. Bach could recall a body of music in which, given the chosen theme, fugue had again and again been shown to be the right texture and structure, unexhausted by hard and continuous use. It may be asked why it was necessary to keep so monotonously to fugue. The answer is plain: method is the composer's business. If he can nourish a work of art by fugue on one main subject, it will have the advantage of a persistent symbol and a broadly consistent structure. And if it is a work of art, it is not the composer who is on trial. It seems necessary to make these statements in an equalitarian age, in which the listener (by the hundred, by the thousand, by the million, even) is assumed to be right. Candidly, then, there is a region of high pressure before which some travellers drop behind. The ultimate quality of experience there is not less real. As Holst once observed, thinking of pioneer musical weekends with his singers, the only way to become used to mountain air is to have more and more and more. If this account of Bach's journey has made some observers more at home in those still remote heights—"The Art of Fugue" being almost entirely neglected by public and private pianists—it will have conveyed something of the historic experience of pure thinking in sound which comes to modern ears and minds, for reception or indifference, in that final and eventful work.

It remains to consider the place of fugue in the choruses which so richly begin many of Bach's Gospel Pieces (now generically entitled cantatas) and form the main pillars of his greatest monument of belief and cumulative musical experience, the B minor Mass.

NOTE

(*Page* 144) With characteristic skill Busoni developed Bach's 238 bars (intact) into an independent and larger work, the "Fantasia Contrappuntistica." He did not finish Bach's fugue in any true sense, unless it is a grim, destructive one, of a grotesquely eclectic treatment of its plain "text." On Tovey's schedule, see p. 192.

Chapter XV

CHORAL FUGUE

IN the composition of the church music which occupied Bach on and off for about twenty-five years, the imitational side of choral polyphony drew him from time to time to fugue on one subject. He began early and ended with certain choruses of the B minor Mass, after which his fugal adventures in later cantatas are of less consequence. Certain features, arising from a more vernacular medium, strike the attention. A recurring counterpoint of subject and counter-subject is commoner, since it is more audible and effectively variable (and enjoyable) in groups of contrasting voices, with free additional parts and possibly an independent instrumental bass. Choral fugue may also be a fragment of a larger movement, and the fugal number is never more than one of several movements in a cantata, motet or Mass. The blending of fugue with sweeping instrumental refrains and dramatic affirmations in the Mass is at once an architectonic triumph and a supreme point of textual revelation, paralleled later by the harnessing of fugue to symphonic expression and vocal declamation on the part of Beethoven and Brahms. It is of some interest to trace the steps by which Bach reached this overwhelming point of musical expansion.

It will be convenient to distinguish two types of choral fugue, complete and incidental.

(i) *Complete fugue.* The earliest examples show little more than a procession of tonic and dominant entries. Such are the second chorus of the Mühlhausen cantata, "God is my king" (71),* and the epilogue of the funeral cantata, "God's time is the best" (106), where the chain of twofold entries ends with *one* partial delivery of the augmented subject, symbolic, no doubt, of the solemn entry into God's presence after death, but none the less peculiar in

---

* A numbered list of the cantatas here mentioned, with their German titles, will be found in the index. For other examples, and types, see Thiele and Neumann.

itself. In the first chorus of the Weimar cantata, "My spirit was
in heaviness" (21), the erratic detail of the S.T.A.B. entries brings
home the advantages of a consistent subject; the second chorus
brings orchestra and singers into an endless juxtaposition of
subject and answer. But the fourth chorus breaks into a balanced
fugue with a dominantward subject, middle entries exploiting
this bitonality and a trumpet answer giving the *coup de grâce* to
the trebles. The weaknesses, a pompous subject and a ubiquitous
and vapid counter-subject, scarcely have time to reduce the
counterpoint to absurdity; but the persistence of the counter-
subject shows a lack of control which the keyboard fugues avoid.

Example 35

Of the early Leipzig cantatas "Verily I say to you" (86) begins
with a curious bass air, in which a fugal plan is attempted, not
without confusion of purpose, in terms of the conventional
repartee of vocal solo and orchestral phrase. The chorus of "Jesus
took to him the twelve" (22) submits a slight two-bar phrase to an
unending succession of fugal entries in the changing polyphony
of three basic strands, prodigal sequential treatment and close
canon. Glib but erratic imitation reflects an uncomprehending
discipleship for a cantata hastily written to replace another
(No. 23) for a trial Sunday at Leipzig. In the above fugal chorus
of "Lord, enter not into judgment" (105), which emerges from a

tense picture of guilty man facing trial, the recurrent four-strand weave is more substantial, durable and vocally interesting. The turn into the major at the twelfth entry of thirteen is unbalanced, but the vigorous polyphony and independent instrumental bass make this an unjustly neglected fugue.

Of later fugal choruses, in "Who offers me thanks" (17), afterwards used (in affectionate haste) for the Mass in G, an elaborate refrain blends with fugal entry in two balanced stages. In "God goeth up" (43) the orchestra lead the chorus in a vivacious five-part fugue with a dominantward subject whose vagrant tonality is put to good use in minor keys, with conclusive entries and a triumphant, almost sensational, coda. The two-choir motet, "Sing ye to the Lord," almost a choral symphony, contains fugues at the end of two movements. The first ("Let Zion's children") is a balanced four-part fugue, bursting forth from the first cadence and accompanied by free polyphony or chorally reinforced. In "All breathing life" the choirs finally unite in four-part fugue. The subtleties of subject and answer are discussed in Chapter XVI. For the rest, first join in and sing! No pen can tell more.

(ii) *Incidental fugue.* In "Come, Redeemer" (61) a free fugal interlude divides a solemn opening and close in the manner of a French Overture. In the early Leipzig cantata, "To this end appeared" (40), a long line of concentrated fugue similarly moves at right angles to the opening matter, but without a change of tempo, so that, when the fugue finally gravitates to the key of the subdominant, primary but other, the original refrain phrases complete the movement without any ado. "Sing to the Lord a new song" (190) contains a similar fugal excursion; here a stronger and more impetuous theme modulates comfortably down to the dominant from further sharpward, and in this more commanding position a resounding flourish lets in the equally powerful refrain, now with chorus, in the tonic. Thus conviction, guided by a firm centre of reference, greets with steady trend the New Year and the opportunity for trumpets and drums and, one may guess, for writing dazzling choral parts under that cover. The fugue in the chorus of the late "All wait upon thee"

(187) moves broadly on similar lines to the dominant (minor), but with the elaborate finish of a more mature style, exploiting the sharpward turn of the answer in the final entries and leaving the second part of the refrain to restore poise. The chorus was used, with incredible insouciance, to end the Mass in G minor.

In "Thou guide of Israel" (104) refrain and fugue blend in two facile stages, the second of which starts with provocative monotony on top of the pronounced fugal entry in the same key. In "The Sages of Sheba" (65) the ceremonial entry in rural, wood-horn style prepares for more courtesies, and the fugue wastes no time in providing B.T.A.S. entries, close canon at the octave and twelfth in various keys, and altogether such an irresistible flow of Wisdom's salaams that the reverberating orchestral refrain is at first no more than extra group counterpoint. There is no reduction of texture. If the touch of these fugues is uncertain, the Bachian control of detail is constantly in evidence.

These fugal movements form a noticeable minority in the 150 odd choruses extant, beside the inevitably unfugal chorale-movements.

In the early-Leipzig setting of "Magnificat" for the customary Mystery play on Christmas Day, three of the five choruses employ fugal method. "Omnes generationes" is a tremendous emphasis of the predicative subject of Mary's *beatam me dicent* (treble) by means of a fully accompanied succession of close entries at effectively varied intervals of pitch and time, culminating in a lightning fourfold canon at the *unison*, hurled at the ear by thundering orchestral chords. A simple vision of pressing multitudes prompted Bach to write this brilliant pictorial Chase (to use the older term), conveying five-part double exposition, middle entries and full restatement in twenty-seven bars. "Fecit potentiam" is also essentially descriptive. Fugal exposition and a majestic, recurring four-bar period of harmonized bass combine in a steadily rising edifice of expression, only to be broken up by intensive cross-rhythm and a subversive bass of irresistibly descending fourths. The proud (of all classes) irrevocably scattered, it remains to symbolize the shock of adjustment to fresh and more realistic values in a plain but strained cadence. With like humour, the promise to the founders of Israel gains a solid, pedantic exposition—even with two similar answers running (S2, S1), an odd fixation—with more entries and a sequence "out of Genesis" to follow. Evidently the text did not move Bach to the urgent fugue he developed elsewhere, or he was more concerned with the fading daylight of a December afternoon, and the consequent need to compress. (On another setting, see p. 18.)

These were the stages, some valuable in themselves, by which Bach came to the fugal mastery that attended his greatest creative impulse. Whatever social ambition and professional discontent contributed to the writing of Mass music for the Dresden (Roman Catholic) court to which he hoped to be appointed composer,* no ordinary call of employment or exercise of workmanship carried Bach along in the "Kyrie" and "Gloria" which he sent to that court. Still less expedient was it to go on to "Credo," "Sanctus" and "Osanna" settings, totalling the now familiar twenty-four movements. The completion of this body of work or works, known invariably but loosely as the Mass in B minor, is of that creative quality for which there is no category known in advance. One of the signs of this unprecedented expression is the presence of eleven fugal movements in the fifteen choruses, constituting a fresh document in fugue but also a coherent range of expressive delivery altogether on a different level from the chance and indefinable emotional outcome of a keyboard collection. Seven numbers are substantially fugues, four use fugue in a wider scheme, but in this series of riveting compositions, each on a complete stage in the ritual text, it is essential to observe each fugal chorus in its proper order and context.

After four stupendous bars of personal summons, then, the FIRST KYRIE develops into an extended chorus, in which stages of fugal refrain and vocal fugue are joined and combine. The subtlety is that the refrain returns (in the dominant) under the guise of choral-orchestral counter-exposition, yet moving irrevocably to *its* answer, a supertonic entry for trebles.† Once in, it goes

* Cf. K. Geiringer, *The Bach Family*, p. 184.
† I shall write of trebles, because this was the setting, but continue to use S, S1 and S2 for short allusions to specific top voicing, to avoid a departure from previous usage.

on to the end of its twenty-four bars, with an eloquent choral reinforcement. In a symmetrical second stage of supplicant humanity, the answering voices rise from "publican" depths of self-reproach. The fifth entry (S2) is in the subdominant, but two impressive extra bars screw up the pitch to admit the returning refrain in the tonic, rhythmically predestined to the last bar but texturally variable, trebles and inner voices respectively exchanging parts in the main. This long and calculated procession of twenty-one entries is made significant by the finest of subjects, which binds *ritornello* and *fugato* alike in haunting periods. It usually overlaps the next entry for a bar, but the crucial diminished second of the fourth half-bar is accompanied freely, not burdened with counter-subject; a passing hint of a more particular fugal art.

The SECOND KYRIE is an essentially compact four-part fugue on a concentrated subject whose twisted intervals penetrate throughout, driven on steadily by the instrumental bass and supporting harmony.* Here the orchestra doubles the voices throughout. A descending line in falling or rising sequence, with other features, spaces out seven entries in free polyphony, and a syncopated phrase in close ascending canon forms a disturbing *codetta*. The subject responds with close canon in pairs (A.T., S.B.), but the *codetta* returns, along with a sequential phrase, and ends by adopting the flattened second of the subject in a piercing treble lead to a descending canon, moving subdominantwards. The subject's more solid canon (B.S.) restores the opening mood with intensity to spare. For the reverent listener—and by "reverence" is meant no bending of knees but an elementary effort to understand the symbolic recollection of the life of God as it broke upon the world by the innocent endurance of a criminal's death —the "Kyrie" music has created a compulsive sense of disturbance, as against the mundane background of voices and instruments raised in constant, conventional repartee, in possibly strange and distracting surroundings of magnificence or discomfort. The music-drama is what matters. The Church

---

* This harmony is left to be extemporized, plainly or decoratively, on the chords indicated by figures over the bass.

cantatas are the Gospel music of this ritual, peculiar to the
Lutheran service, and their choruses, too, must be conceived
inwardly in this context. Mere listening will not make sense.
This is not "concert" music.

The problem of "Gloria" music is to maintain a fundamental
ecstasy of praise without forced vitality or monotonous texture.
In GLORIA IN EXCELSIS DEO, then, a spacious refrain frames an
exultant Vivace of formal pattern, but ET IN TERRA PAX at once
voices human longings—for the message of peace depends on an
act of faith—in an urgent and impromptu antiphony of voices
and instruments. The soothing central phrase expands dynamic-
ally in a straight fugue; a fresh *roulade* for bringing home
bonae voluntatis is overlapped by the next entry and thus forms a
steady and exuberant counter-subject, the vocal counterpart of
Janacek's bells!* Watchful string chords safeguard the New
Order of untiring goodwill here announced, but the polyphony
is discreetly and patently vocal. This exposition closes in the
minor. It is balanced by a complete counter-exposition for
chorus with orchestra, with trumpet proclamation masterfully
supporting the last entry at the natural heights of a *clarino princi-
pale*. Further antiphony and direct entry complete the fugal
circle with a singular sense of restraint, yet with the agelong ideal
of a Christian civilization heartened afresh with determined
and infectious phrases.

GRATIAS AGIMUS TIBI PROPTER MAGNAM GLORIAM TUAM, completing the first paragraph musically as the return to D shows,
suggests a more formal movement. In the dignified choral fugue
Bach had written (on top of an orchestral prelude) for a setting of
similar German words, "Wir danken Dir" (Psalm 75), for an
earlier council-election cantata (29), he found the direct polyphony and compact interlude he needed. It remained to replace
the declamatory setting of the second sentence, *und verkündigen
deine Wunder*, by a simpler phrase, reserving the ornamentation
for *gloriam*. "Gratias agimus" thus at once announces fugally two
subjects for its compound sentence, each in close canon, the second
developing succinctly in lieu of an episode; almost a humorous

* "Glagolitic" Mass.

sublimation of earnest councilmanship, including Mr. Second Subject's vain attempts to address the chairman (bars 13 and, more urgent, 28). Whatever the metaphor, the blunter and fresh canon of deliveries in pairs (S.B., A.T. with trumpets) readily absorbs the more desultory imitation, supported by a strong supertonic seventh to promote cadence. (The recurrence of this chord in "Dona nobis pacem" seals unforgettably the concluding summons of the Mass.) The plain vocal ascent of municipal pride achieves sublimity in the end. By a convention of the period the solemn (funeral) trombone could not be introduced in direct support of the last bass entry (bar 35), but it is not therefore quite certain that if this had been usual, Bach would have been glad—here or in "Dona nobis pacem"—to add or substitute a trombone for the entry of the drum (and third trumpet) that he has written! He was not so deaf as he is sometimes made out to be by his admirers.

Qui tollis, following "Domine Deus" (duet) without a break, resumes the *eleison* strain with painful intensity. Once more, in the choral opening of the prophetic "Behold and see" (cantata 46), cutting out prelude and second fugue, Bach observed the nucleus of a true setting for "the hardest part" (G. A. Studdert Kennedy). It remained to re-shape the now opening subject, from tiresome declamation to a simpler and more pointed phrase, and later to make *suscipe* ascend (B.T.). "Qui tollis" thus displays the conventional supplication of fugal entries, with an impressively irregular answer. The second set of entries, in finer detail, is twice absorbed in refrain-phrases, in which a flute canon adumbrates the divine grief with developing coherence, over the choral utterance (bars 20–27, 34–50). Fugal ceremonial is set in relation to a cumulatively riveting appeal, a little more compelling here for *not* being anticipated by an earlier *ritornello*, and because its final half-cadence leads to entirely fresh matter, rejecting the complementary chorus of Cantata 46, a just but hard sacrifice.

"Qui tollis" having been completed, then, by the profound solo-obeisance of "Qui sedes," "Quoniam tu solus" establishes a new calm with its courtly assurance of honest devotion and imperturbable refrain. Into this Cum Sancto Spiritu bursts with vague fanfare-polyphony, consolidated in a gorgeous sequential cadence. Fugal exposition of a new theme continues the thought, with overlapping entries as in "Et in terra pax," and again a turn into the minor at the last entry. Refrain material, previously presented so casually as to posit an earlier, perkier *ritornello*—an earlier (lost) cantata-movement is the obvious explanation— sweeps this development decisively aside and launches further fugue in keys dropping steadily flatward from the mediant minor, with prodigal half-entries and polyphony surrounding the five official entries. The tonic thus gained, the cadential-phrases, re-shaped—bars 117–21 now follow 111–16—hurl the music to its vibrating close, led by a glamorous first-trumpet. Thus sheer counter-exposition (for the tonic is the ultimate key as surely as the fifth term of 17, 13, 9, 5 (interval above keynote) is 1) reaches ecstatic heights with unfaltering energy. For the observer of the pioneering keyboard fugues, choral fugue has hardly begun to expand!

At some point or other Bach realized that, although to a Lutheran composer a Missa ended with the "Gloria," this Mass-music must go on, in settings of "Credo" and the rest in connexion with the Mass, possibly for a (Roman Catholic) coronation ceremony, but Lutheran in interpretative spirit. Revealing exper-ience had aroused wider revelation. So he passed on to the creed.

For CREDO IN UNUM DEUM the "Credo" Tone was possibly the inevitable "subject," though rare in other than plain settings. A curve rather than a theme, it carries little rhythm. With the aid of a tramping, militant instrumental bass and a counter-subject (T.) Bach developed a short but expansive seven-part fugue (voices and violins), with middle entries, double-entries and, rejoinder to tradition itself, the Tone at half speed. The music matches the unrelenting march of the centuries from Nicaea, disputing and enlarging, but always going on. For PATREM OMNIPOTENTEM Bach picked on a fugue of clarification, derived from "God, as is thy name" (cantata 171, Psalm 48, 10), with a re-pointed subject, an extra "answer" opening for continuity, and some amplification of texture. A vigorous exposition and shortened counter-exposition, with overlapping and so far contrapuntal entries, reaches a triumphant "endless" coda, originally set to "unto the world's end" and not unworthy of the mysterious universe now hymned. Bach then set the second paragraph up to "Crucifixus" for soloists, but eventually wrote a fresh choral setting for "Et incarnatus est." Here, over throbbing string chords and figures, the chorus pursues an imitational style in two firm stages, each unpredictable in detail, visionary in quality; the musical thought gropes to the end. In "Crucifixus" a steady ground-bass of dragging semitones marks the moments of endurance throughout, with incidental choral imitation. This is no place for the pressing entries of the Passions. Again, "Et resurrexit" develops refrain-phrases in a spacious, scarcely pertinent chorus in D, almost "rounding off" the piercing edges of its predecessors; and "Et in Spiritum Sanctum" makes a pastoral bass solo of its doctrinal sentences in music suspiciously free of its text.

After these two ample *ritornello* numbers, balancing impromptu vocal repartee and orchestral refrain, CONFITEOR calls for a fugal pronouncement. Reserving the very jejune "Confiteor" Tone for later contrapuntal incident, Bach writes a fugue for chorus, with instrumental bass, on two original but formal subjects. Each is delivered in more or less close canon, and most resourcefully developed in direct canon at various intervals, in itself and in

(S1: anticipation of bass. S2 and A: *a* at twelfth
and tenth. B : *b*)

Example 36

combination. (Cf. bars 2, 55 and 4, 42, 53 for the variants of *a*; 48, 63, 93 and 105 for *b*; 31, 37, 88, 98 for *a* with *b*). Presumably Bach worked out such a fugue *per se* in the absence of a more

relevant commentary on Baptism and the remission of sins. But a
tramping bass carries the elaborate cross-rhythm along in the
imperative manner of "Credo," and as a major interlude in this
F sharp minor chorus—or more strictly, as a fresh counter-
subject—the whole "Confiteor" Tone appears briskly in a close
canon at the fifth (B.A.) and later at half speed, almost rhythm-
less. This intensive and finally almost automatic vocal Point
counter Point of 120 bars keeps going till the end of the tenor
Tone, but it is heading, not for a close, but for the great transition
of the coming text. As the polyphony dissolves miraculously, a
vibrant Adagio contemplates general resurrection in probing
harmony, peering over the abyss of first experience.

Fresh inspiration treats this as a darkness from which the escape
is the vision splendid. The rest is triumphant, trumpeting refrain
(having missed the opportunity at *iudicare*, Bach could not keep
out the Last Trump here), vivid declamation and simple imitation;
a token of joyful, transfigured homecoming, deliberately vernacular (and in fact derivative) in texture, and inevitably in D, but
trenchant in corroborative detail and unpredictable in issue. In
this, the most dazzling moment of the Mass, for those who can
see further than television, fugue has no place. The final release is
conditioned partly by that searching fugue on two subjects and a
Tone, as in Beethoven's coda in the same context. But for Bach
the life to come could never be rendered in the set elaborations of
fugue. He, most fugal of them all, left that to the Viennese School.

SANCTUS (a separate score but in D) develops in powerful
periods of declamatory bass and harmony (especially bar 5).
When the latter has plunged suddenly into the mediant minor,
the fabric collapses to admit a fugue for the six-part chorus and
orchestra. A strenuous and enduring subject is attended by a
counter-subject (T.) throughout. Doubling of the subject a third
higher (avoiding the separate entry of the sixth-voice), and of the
counter-subject likewise, enriches the sonority of many entries
and avoids a set progression. Slight episodes, minor keys, the
trumpet doubling the bass at its own melodic register and then in
canon with the treble, vary the course of a flowing and balanced
fugue; so flowing and balanced, indeed, that it is hard to sing

smoothly and well, without strain or false accent. The art of this serene music is never transparent, and so it avoids the self-consciousness a fugue might have had after the unquenchable phrases of "Sanctus." It is almost Mozartian in its sheer delight in its texture, but it may be noted that the subject ends as a bass.

With an unusual perception of the rift in the text, Bach begins "Osanna" as a separate section. He uses an earlier chorus of spreading birthday congratulation, in D. After solo-settings of "Benedictus" and "Agnus Dei," the latter piercing new depths of the divine suffering, he returns to "Gratias" for the music of "Dona nobis pacem," lacking now the verbal justification for a second subject.* Whatever the inadequacy of this literal repetition with a little fresh detail (bars 18–19), the move to the most logical thematic development of the vocal consort is an intelligible stroke of penmanship, and the choral-orchestral double-fugue is sufficiently significant in itself to be a worthy setting for a final testimony to the civilizing influence of true religion. There is no question that, as a climax to the twenty-fourth movement of this unparalleled work, the last canon and trumpet ascent to D, harnessed to G sharp, confirm a final sense of having risen to the height of a great argument, of which no improvement can now be conceived. In the context, the music consecrates the will for reconciliation with God by justice towards men at all times.

In these salient moments in the various stages of the Mass, then, Bach showed once and for all his power to dedicate fugue to fresh issues. As Byrd had found before him, wrestling with the text drew from Bach a hidden force which he could not recover, and which no purely musical theme could ever evoke. In later collections he explored fugal pattern more and more for its own sake, but one concludes this serial survey of Bach's fugal works here with a lively sense of ultimate quality, not of transition towards a maturer experience. The most treasured household sounds in fugal form may still come from the Mass. The voice can speak as no instrument can, and Bach's orchestra is a vital complement to vocal intonation and polyphony, both for its penetrating and varied sonority and for its own irreplaceable

* See Note on p. 158.

images of splendour and strain. The Mass choruses are so far
sui generis. To belief and unbelief alike they offer a message of
intense humanity and confidence in the furthest future. One
cannot say whether it is due to the revealing technical experience
behind it or (as Byrd would have maintained) to the faithful
pursuit of subject and refrain in steady meditation upon the text
which, in hundreds of languages besides Latin, still punctuates
devotional parish life.

NOTE

(*Page* 157) In common with a great many other readers, I cannot accept
the virtually and oddly *a priori* contention of Mr. F. Rothschild (*The
Lost Tradition in Music*, p. 25, contradicted—owing to a misprint?—in
the table on p. 286) that, when Bach marked the four-minim bars of
"Gratias" and "Dona nobis pacem" with the same time-signature of a
barred semi-circle (or C) but added *Alla breve* (in the original parts and
later score) in "Gratias" and omitted it (in the score) in "Dona," he
wished to convey radically different tempi of two beats a bar in the
former case, and four in the latter. (The signature of a barred 2 for the
two-minim bars of the original chorus in "Wir danken dir" (cantata 29)
is pronounced by Mr. Rothschild to mean *one* beat a bar and thus to
agree with "Gratias.") There are no solid reasons for accepting Mr.
Rothschild's arbitrary deduction, from certain selected theoretical
statements of various periods, that there was an accepted *tempo ordi-
nario* (40–60 beats to the minute), or for maintaining that Bach was consistent and meticulous about time-signatures, including the pivotal
alla breve. In this case, since the 2 of the cantata-chorus must mean two
beats in some sense (fast or slow), the common-sense harmonization of
it and "Gratias" (rhythmically the same music apart from figural detail)
is that the former observes two minim beats, the latter four for its bars
of double length; and there are plenty of precedents for regarding $\frac{4}{2}$
(or $\frac{4}{4}$) and not $\frac{2}{2}$ as the obvious sense of the barred semi-circle. But the
tempo at which the music is to be taken must be determined, not by any
metronomic hypothesis (unless indicated by the composer as a guide),
but by a comparison of the rhetorical effect of the given polyphonic
and harmonic rhythm, in its musical context, and in the actual density
of the original performance in its probable acoustic environment (and
of actual performance in relation to this estimate), at faster or slower
rates of speed. By this test, two-beats in "Gratias"—making the harmony on the second and fourth minim subsidiary, and the symbols of
the glory of God in mortal ken an increasingly noisy clatter of eights
—makes difficult, at best virtuoso movement, and the faster, the more

difficult. On the other hand, a brusque four-beats which (with quarter-beat figures tidily decorating the minim pulse) sounds right after the exaltation of "Laudamus te," must needs take on a deliberate splendour to follow the burden of "Agnus Dei"; and *a fortiori* it takes a more pondering tempo to complete the inspiration of the whole B minor Mass in the brief orbit of the same music.

We now reach the point at issue. Mr. Rothschild insists that Bach's omission of *alla breve* in "Dona nobis" means four beats, and hence a tempo more or less twice as slow. In other words, forty-six bars of coherent harmony and cumulative instrumental texture (up to the full orchestra) are now to be identically repeated, to a shorter and more recurrent verbal phrase, at half speed; not, perhaps, literally, but recognizably enough to prompt a feeling of doubled pulses throughout. Such a *fuga per totam augmentationem* would be the last stage in the grotesque use of a slide-rule method. Indeed, that a distinguished practising musician should enjoin such a method of calculating a nice decision, and draw such a fantastic deduction from it, can only be understood in terms of the documentary obsessions of a writer not trained to think critically or honest enough to abandon a fallacious dialectic. The notion of halved tempo does not bear serious discussion, and it has only been considered at length here because the book gives a deceptive appearance of documentary backing and logic. Regrettably, we are forced to contemplate Mr. Rothschild banging his head against the wall of musical common sense with the same pertinacity as he uses in knocking down Bach's actual signatures in the "Forty-eight" as if they were unable to spring back to their place in the London autograph. On the real problem of "Dona nobis," as repeat-music, we remain as we were, dependent on a sense of the acoustic dramatic.

Chapter XVI

BACH'S FUGAL CRAFTSMANSHIP

WITHIN the constantly chosen framework of a fugal movement, Bach was one of the most consistent of composers, and a progressive craftsman. In "The Art of Fugue" he tabulated in live examples the refinements and corollaries of a technique he had begun to crystallize in the more mature organ fugues, the later collections being the product of a sparer or more exhaustive invention, rather than of a complete change of methods. There is plenty of ground for bringing together the 150 odd fugues which have so far been considered separately or as part of an integral series. In this chapter I propose to examine at "walking" speed the cumulative evidence of Bach's choice and handling of material, at each stage of fugal structure. Except in the most formal and general aspects, mainly of key and texture, there is very little that is automatic in Bach's fugal style, but his practice is sufficiently solid and intelligible to be codified, and many apparently capricious decisions can be referred to an underlying rationale, embracing both the musically logical and the rhetorically impressive. Much more often than not, the use of a particular fugal device can be attributed to musical principles. This is not a matter of abstruse and arbitrary analysis, but simply of classifying impressions received and remembered from integral experience. "Freedom depends on law"—and the kind of law.

Concerns for a syntax correct by rule have occupied all too much attention in most manuals on fugue. (Prout gives 50 pages out of 200 to the Answer.) The present consideration of the wider relationships of counter-exposition, developments of various kinds, and episodic construction, seeks to restore a balance much overdue in the study of the scope of fugue, and of Bach's long art in particular. It has been my aim to bring out the common purpose of the contrapuntal features, whether economic or prodigal, and something will be said about the harmonic interest which underlies or supplements these. The cumulative impact of nice choices and structural-textural initiative is something of what Bach's fugal art means in practice; something not to be lightly imitated, as in a week-end competition or examination question, but to be noted as a token of those precise intimations, and of a generally disturbed state of mind, by which good living comes to a sense of achievement.

The various collections will be denoted as follows: organ works, O.; the "Forty-eight," W.K.i and W.K.ii; "The Art of Fugue," A.F. References to Mass-music will mean the B minor Mass, and all general Latin references will be to the text of this. The sol-fa notation will be employed here, as the simplest and clearest for the purpose, for the indication of the related degrees of the scale, namely: (i) for the major scale **d–r–m–f–s–l–t–d^1**, with lower-octave extensions of **d$_1$–d**, and upper of **d^1–d^2**; (ii) **ma, la** and **ta** for the flattened degrees of the minor scale (the **doh**-minor notation is essential for showing common features in different keys, minor or major), and **fe**, etc., for sharpened degrees in a modulating line. I have also occasionally used a colon and full-stop to indicate the third and even beats of the common quadruple metre.

EXPOSITION

SUBJECT

The integrity of Bach's subjects is a constant factor. "Not too short or too long" is a meaningless injunction. A subject can be long if it is balanced but not a self-contained eight-bar phrase, and if it is not over-used (O., D minor *and late G minor; W.K.ii, E flat, E minor; the Chromatic). W.K. prefers up to four bars. Two down-beats are the least to preserve integrity. When they are reduced to one (W.K.i, D, E, A flat, A, B flat minor; ii, C minor) the subject becomes, rather, a salient feature of the poly-phony, and the music achieves rhythmic span by other means. Apart from the metre, rhythmic thrust is given by the natural stress of longer after shorter notes, figures grouped round one

---

* Where not otherwise stated, this will refer to the "Dorian," the late Weimar fugue which begins with an ascent to the mediant.

note, or by syncopation, direct or implied (W.K.i, C minor; ii, C). Harmonic rhythm may support the metre, or at least a two-bar period, by implying chords of the tonic and dominant, etc., in given half-bars or longer periods (O., early G minor (**d, d, s,** etc.); W.K.ii, D (**f | s, d**), G (**d, t, l, s**), B (**d, f, s, d**); A.F. *passim*). Cross-accentuation may add character (W.K.ii, C sharp minor, F minor: **d . s : . d**). If the answer changes **r** to **d** at first, it will break up this harmonic rhythm slightly, and in any case additional parts will modify the texture, but a firmly harmonic subject will retain its stimulus.

The melodic *curve* similarly varies in integrity, and may be direct or interlaced with decoration and implied harmony, but the essential curve will show a firm path. With negligible exceptions, **d** or **s** is the starting-point. Curves beginning on **d** commonly ascend (in general direction) at a certain gradient and then return "downhill" and so more rapidly (O., B minor); **s** is the usual climax (W.K.i, F sharp minor), and **d**ˡ fanciful (W.K.ii, F). A fall from **d**ˡ to **s** or **f** or further is less common (W.K.i, C minor; ii, D; A.F. 8, 9), and a twist from the **d**ˡ–**s** traverse upwards rare (O., F). Curves beginning on **s** almost invariably descend, sometimes after touching **l** (**la**), **d**ˡ or even **m**ˡ. It is quite striking, in a wide survey, how constantly this quasi-vocal stretch up from the tonic, or a gravitation from the dominant, or a balance of the two, provides a compulsive, repeatable inflexion. The release of energy for ascent and descent constitutes the active and passive moods of melody: summons and appeal. Semitonal touches arise occasionally (W.K.i, B minor; ii, F sharp; A.F. 8; the Chromatic), and may contemplate a fresh scale and key, but a too mannered subject soon becomes a nuisance. It was not Bach who wrote whole fugues round B–A–C–H.

Plastic or tough, the subject is never negligible and often the doyen of the development. The evidence of Forkel and others, that Bach developed a theme or bass quickly but invented it slowly, is abundantly confirmed in the select quality of the fugal subjects, which many readers (and not only players) will be able to recall by tens with some precision, without the aid of "comic" words.

ANSWER

The rationalization of unruly variants in answer seems to have been the chief object of many writers and teachers, for whom one consistent rule is worth ten acceptable but less regular relationships. However, answers are an interesting miniature study in the problems of achieving an artful continuity of expression, and Bach's principles may be stated without a disarming array of exceptions, and without more recourse to degree-number than a statement of pitch-interval makes necessary.

The obvious blunt response to the announcement of a phrase is the same at the unison or at a fifth or a fourth higher, at one octave or another as determined by actual or imagined voices. (Alternatives of lower octave may now be assumed in any allusion to an interval measured, as is customary, above pitch of reference.) The rhetorical conditions of Bach's North German milieu, namely an argumentative mood and a quickly developed tonality, excluded a unison reply as stagnant, and a fourth higher as either equivocal or in the inexpedient subdominant. The virtuoso organ fugue in D minor is a warning against this flatward tilt. Exceptionally, the inexorable ascending fourths (i.e. falling *keys*) of St. Matthew Passion 33 (fugue) help to define with grim vivacity the headlong fall into the pit invoked. Otherwise Bach takes an answer at the fifth for granted, so observing in one way the standard contrast of earlier music. Long choral experience had tabulated, for a given pair of voices in an imitative style, two basic stretches round a final or centre-note, the "authentic" octave or mode beginning with it ($\mathbf{d}$–$\mathbf{d^l}$) and the "plagal" octave or mode including it, a fifth higher ($\mathbf{s}$–$\mathbf{s^l}$).

What is more pertinent, either octave divides naturally into two unequal halves ($\mathbf{ds}$, $\mathbf{sd^l}$; $\mathbf{sd^l}$, $\mathbf{d^ls^l}$), and these two modes or registers of typical vocal movement must needs answer each other in their respective halves. In particular an initial $\mathbf{ds}$ is answered with $\mathbf{sd^l}$, and $\mathbf{sd^l}$ with $\mathbf{ds}$ (not with the literal $\mathbf{sr^l}$ and $\mathbf{rs}$), for those are the most natural pairs of sounds in either case, as observed in the second, third and fourth overtones of a vibrating column of air. A bugler answers the rising fifths of Reveille by a rising fourth, not a fifth, which would not only be harder to lip but sound a disturbance of the expected sequence. Similarly, **sd** ("Get back to bed") is answered **d**ⁱ**s**; conversely **sd**ⁱ is answered with **ds**, and **d**ⁱ**s** with **sd**. The demonstration of the acoustic facts on the oldest wind-instruments, accepted by the perceptive ear, inevitably made a hard core of the relationship of the three primary sounds, **d**, **s** and **d**ⁱ, in symmetrical pairs, the actual octave being determined by the voice desired.

In common with his period, long imitated later, Bach on these principles answers **ds** with **sd**ⁱ, and vice versa, *where these pivotal sounds are at once in evidence* in a subject. But once the pivotal pair has been recognized—and being pertinent in the first key, it will be less definite for purposes of the next key—the particular curve of the subject asserts itself as the binding relation, in the proper degrees of the new scale, not merely observing the right intervals from the last pivotal note. The variations of typical response hang on the question when or how far **d**, **s** and related degrees should or may be regarded as pivotal. We may distinguish four kinds of opening, presenting single, double and ambiguous pivots, and modulation. The advantages of confining a subject to one half of the octave will now be apparent.

(a) Single Pivots

(i) Phrases that begin on **d** or **d**ⁱ and do not lean on any early **s** are answered readily at **s–r**ⁱ or **s–r** level (W.K.i, E). The curious term of a *real* answer for this exact reply will be accepted here. Hitches are rare. W.K.ii, G sharp minor, with a **d, r–s** cast of subject, tempers the point of its real answer by non-committal harmony; **s, l–d**ⁱ would sound absurd, and **s, s–d**ⁱ tedious.

(ii) Phrases that begin with **s** and do not emphasize **d** will usually be answered with **d** at first, with **r** later (W.K.i, C sharp, F (**s ls, d . mr***); ii, A flat (**sm, d**ⁱ **. t**); the Chromatic (**s la, dr . ma**) and cantata 187 (**s**ₗ **s s f r, d d**ⁱ **d**ⁱ **. d**ⁱ **l**) but not the chromatic fugue in C minor, which is bound to remain real: **s f s la, . r d r ma**, not **d . d r ma**. In general, the minor is avoided for this group).

---

* The point after which an answer is permanently exact and predictable will be indicated by a dot.

(b) Double Pivots

(i) Where **ds** or **sd** shape the initial curve, they are answered by their natural complements of **sd**ᴵ or **d**ᴵ**s**. This avoids the abruptness of an immediate **r**ᴵ but leaves **r**ᴵ to fall into place at once later. The term *tonal*, denoting musical rather than literal imitation, may be accepted. In most cases a real answer would have been a possible alternative, but Bach liked to keep the jog of "reality" in reserve, thus half-establishing **s d**ᴵ (**d f** in terms of the new key) as an alternative for later keys as well. W.K.i, E flat minor (**d s la s, s d**ᴵ **. ma**ᴵ **r**ᴵ) and ii, E flat (**d s f m, s d**ᴵ **. d**ᴵ **t**) show at once the euphonious anomalies of the ascending fifth, and W.K.i, G minor (**s la d, d**ᴵ **. ma**ᴵ **s**) and ii, C minor (**s ma f s d, d**ᴵ **. ta d**ᴵ **r**ᴵ **s**) of the descending fifth. But in W.K.ii, C sharp, **d m d s f m** avoids the pedantic answer, **s t s d**ᴵ **. d**ᴵ **t**, for the more musical **s t s d**ᴵ **. ta l**.

(ii) Conversely, where **s d**ᴵ or **d**ᴵ **s** shape the curve, they are answered with **d s** or **s d**. The easier turn can be observed in the ascending subject of cantata 105 (**s s d**ᴵ **s d**ᴵ **s, d d . s r s r**) and O., E flat (**s m l s d**ᴵ, **d t**₁ **m d . s**). The descent appears in W.K.i, B flat minor (**d**ᴵ **s la**ᴵ **s**ᴵ **f**ᴵ, **s d . ma**ᴵ **r**ᴵ **d**ᴵ); ii, B flat **r**ᴵ **d**ᴵ **s m, l s d . t**₁).

(c) Ambiguous Pivots

(i) Phrases which present a close association of **d m(ma)s** or **s m(ma) d** may point either way, according as **s** is regarded as pivotal in its own right, as in Group (*b*) (i), or as an offshoot of **d**, as in (*a*) (i). Bach's treatment seems at first capricious, and shocking to the men of rules; but less so on close comparison. His inclination is to consider **s** as pivotal as usual, as in O., late G minor, and the keyboard Toccata in C minor (**s ma d, d**ᴵ **. ta s**), W.K.ii, G, A.F. 4, the finale of the two-keyboard concerto in C (**d m d s m l s, s t s d**ᴵ **. t m**ᴵ **r**ᴵ), and cantata 21, finale (**d m s d**ᴵ, **s t d**ᴵ **. s**ᴵ). The exceptions to this nearly all prove their case easily. O., early G minor (**d s ma r d**), has a five-bar subject, after which the caution of a tonal answer would be misplaced; so with the long keyboard fugue in A minor ($\frac{3}{4}$). *A fortiori*, in the final fugues, in an established key, to "God's time is the best" (106), the organ

Passacaglia and A.F. 1–11, a tonal answer would be incredible. In W.K.i, E minor, the rapid **d ma s d**ˡ admits of no variant. All these have real answers. (See also p. 130.)

(ii) A similar problem arises over the **d**ˡ **t r**ˡ **s** type of subject. Bach's practice is, and must be to avoid angularity, that **d**ˡ with a **s**-group is to be answered tonally by **s** with a **d**-group; a **r**-group is too far-flying at this stage. Hence the procedure in W.K.i, B (**d**ˡ **t** (**d**ˡ) **r**ˡ **s** (**l**) **t d**ˡ, **s m** (**f**) **s d . m** (**fe**) **s**)—on which more ink has been spilt than if Bach had had twenty *wives*—is quite acceptable. So in the fugue in E flat (Peters, 214), "Patrem omnipotentem" (here an extra "answer" maintains continuity with "Credo"), and in W.K.i, A. In "Pleni sunt coeli et terra," a **s t r**ˡ group follows a **s**-group. In reply, **s m**ˡ **l, t r**ˡ **f** ˡ **r**ˡ **t s, d**ˡ becomes **d l r, m s t s m d . s.** Writing "in the spirit," Bach disdains the lore of nicely calculated less or more (though he originally began **s s**ˡ **l**). He goes for the fundamental start, an uncommon ascending major sixth (not seventh), a responsive but not contentious continuation, and the necessary modulation-up at the end. Elsewhere a blunt **t** is answered by **fe,** in a tense, almost painful context (second "Kyrie"); but often this slips in a later answer down to **m** (sharpened mediant), pointing subdominantwards (W.K.i, C sharp minor, cf. G sharp minor and "Let him be crucified"; ii, D sharp minor). W.K.i, E, was listed under group (*a*) (i). The off-beat **s** and **t** of its **d**ˡ **r**ˡ **s** (**l t**) **d**ˡ are negligible, indicating a real answer, the tonal answers (**s s d . m fe s** or **s l d . m fe s**) being grotesque. Hence this is not musically inconsistent with W.K.i, B. Accent is vital.

Any variant curve entailed by the answer may be considered available in later entries in the tonic or foreign key. The answer will tend to establish the dominant, supported by the harmony, but this is sometimes avoided (W.K.i, E flat minor, A flat; ii, G sharp minor). In the wider schemes of choruses which break into fugue, subject and answer may sometimes reverse order. In the fugue in the early "God is my king" (71) the eight tonic-subdominant, alias (as it proves) dominant-tonic, entries are confusing. In the first fugue of the motet "Sing ye to the Lord" a similar answer-start sounds right. The third entry is tonal (**d s d,** not **r s r**), and the uniting of the basses for the fourth entry establishes *it* as the subject. The second fugue ("All breathing life"), arising from the dominant chord but not key, simply begins at dominant level. Again the third entry is tonal (**s d¹**, not **s r¹**). It then becomes apparent to any key-conscious ear that the fourth entry is the real subject, modulating to the dominant, the third its answer; the contrast is duly exploited in other keys. "Cum Sancto Spiritu" (tonal in third entry) is equally clear. Thus a fresh type of accessory fugal opening is carefully manœuvred into a smooth exposition. A.F. 3 applies inversion of subject likewise.

(d) Modulation

Subjects which modulate to the dominant will contain two features: (i) a phrase or note in the main key; (ii) a transition to the dominant. The first is answered pivotally, as in Groups (a)–(c), but otherwise in or towards the key of the dominant. The second calls, not for a "real" move to the new dominant, i.e. the original supertonic, but rather for a "tonal" redress by lowering the pitch a step and thus returning to tonic level. Thus a **d–s** assertion of *key* is normally answered with **s–d**, as with implied *chords* in Group (c) (ii). If after the pivot notes there is not enough space for modulation to and from the dominant, this must be effected later (W.K.i, E flat). If modulation back to the tonic would be too much of a decline, the remedy is the same (Ib. E minor). The recovery of the tonic level may begin early—another point where musicianship challenges rulemanship—in the interest of retaining in its original shape the second and more typical turn in the subject (Ib. G sharp minor and B minor), or it may follow a convenient rhythmic cæsura, but in any case it is in the nature of a reaction, instead of the usual jog sharpward. Useful, then, as a counter-twist in foreign keys ("Sing ye," *fin.*), the answer to such a subject is too corrective or enervating for constant use in the original keys, except semi-humorously or quizzically (W.K.i, G sharp minor). In a long fugue its inevitable adjustments rarely escape tedium (O., "Legrenzi" fugue).

Prout asks (seriously) whether a subject can be modified at the end. If a tail-phrase, at first necessary as a link, becomes a hindrance, it must be dropped (W.K. ii, B; A.F. 8); *a fortiori*, a tailnote can be sharpened at once (**ma, t**) if the kink makes for emotional release. The aim of a fugue is not to "X-ray" the subject but to use it as a salient image of a growing thought. Subjects are for fugues.

The "exceptions," then, to Bach's principles of rejoinder can be relied on to prove the rule in a wider consideration of tonic and dominant features in their rhythmic or broader structural context. His musicianship at these often awkward and exposed turns is an assurance that what fugal ritual there is, is being performed with intelligence, not for the sake of keeping to a "ruling."

COUNTER-SUBJECT

The answer receives a bass or, by an extension of use, becomes a bass. In either case the general function of the counterpoint is to punctuate the subject without an excess of tonic and dominant, and to provide contrary melodic movement, rather than reinforcement of the subject in thirds and sixths, which cannot last (W.K.ii, C, A flat, B). Counterpoint means also a resilient counter-stress and contrast of detail, without the steady friction of a close canon. A specific line may stay only for the exposition, or be a permanent labour-saving device, as indispensable for rekindling as a gas-poker. Bach uses the latter type rather more often than not, and in my estimate regrettably often. The fugues without appreciable counter-subject are as noteworthy as the respectable majority. However, some counter-subjects seem almost the making of a fugue (W.K.i, C minor, F sharp minor; ii, C, G minor, A flat, A minor, B flat minor; the Chromatic). For such, the differences of subject and answer are a stimulus to adapt the concomitant detail (not a warning to postpone forming the counter-subject till after the pivotal notes, as some coaches seriously suggest, lest there be a Success the less). Sometimes the essential counter-subject arises later (W.K.i, C sharp minor; ii, B).

EPISODE

The answer may extend in what is commonly called a *codetta*. Some of these interim phrases prove their independence later (O., D minor; W.K.i, C minor, G, A flat, B flat minor, B minor;

ii, D sharp minor, F, A flat, G sharp minor). Bach's art lies in the casual delivery which leaves the exposition to continue undisturbed. Utterly incidental extensions of the answer are also common enough.

FURTHER ENTRIES

Entries, usually at least as many as there are voices desired, complete the exposition in an alternation of subject and answer, of varying top and bass, in a cumulative weaving process. The stretch of ten fingers makes three "voices" the most convenient for a true keyboard style, four practicable, and five exceptional; the feet can add one real part. In vocal fugue, more than four or five entries may be tedious, and this excess is avoided in "Cum Sancto Spiritu" and "Pleni." Monotony is evaded by different harmonizations. Rarely, the subject recurs for the fourth entry *after* an answer or replacing it (W.K.i, C(!), F minor, F sharp minor). The last entry of minimum expositions in three (or five) parts will normally end in or near the tonic; those in four (or two) parts, in the dominant. This is common in volatile, succinct three-part fugues, less so in four-part fugues (W.K.ii, C, D). An extra entry may reverse either type of trend or confirm it (Ib., F, B; F sharp minor). Thus a dominantward issue is, to borrow a definition from honest Prout (Rule 112), "though frequently expedient, and even preferable, never absolutely necessary." Accession to the dominant favours a step into the relative minor by rising sequence (bass: **r s, m l**), but there is no need to abandon the tonic, as in a sonata first-subject. Hence "redundant" is a rather egregious text-book term for such optional "overtime."

ORDER OF VOICES

Bach's preferences yield some interesting trends. Let us again call the voices for rough comparison S., A. and B., with T. for a fourth part when required.

(a) Three-part Fugue

In thirty fugues (W.K., A.F., etc.): (i) 14 begin S.A.B.; (ii) 11, A.S.B.; (iii) 5, B.S.A., B.A.S. or A.B.S. Miscellaneous fugues favour A.S.B.

(i) Descending voices mark the more subtle fugue, the subject escaping notice but ending on the outside (W.K.i, 6–7 and ii, 10–12 are interesting coincidences).

(ii) Ascending upper voices are a convenient variant, the alto bridging the gulf between S. and B. entries. Coincidences include W.K.i, 8–9 and ii, 13–14.

(iii) The initial interval of a twelfth between entries makes B.S.A. a special textural effect, but the overtones of the bass fill in gaps (W.K.ii, 3–4). B.A.S. is confined to W.K.ii, 19–20; Bach avoids melodic subjects in three-voice fugue. A.B.S., the inverse of A.S.B., is found in A.F. 8, where the darkening of texture is notable. S.B. is not a practical start.

(b) Four-part and Five-part Fugues

These may be grouped together because, once the texture has the secure sonority of three parts, the additional voicing matters little. In over sixty fugues examined (Ib., O. and Mass): (i) 17 begin B.T.A.S.(S.); (ii) 10, T.A.S.B.; (iii) 6–8 each, A.S.B.T., S.A.T.B.(B.) or A.T.B.S.; (iv) 1–3 each, A.S.T.B., T.A.B.S., T.B.S.A. or T.B.A.S.(S.).

(i) B.T.A.S. is an eminently word-intoning accumulation of corresponding pairs of voices, a challenge to labyrynthine polyphony ("Sing ye," second fugue), and suited to any dignified subject that can bear exposure to the end.

(ii) T.A.S.B. rises more lightly for the minimum three voices and adds a disruptive but fundamental answer.

(iii) In A.S.B.T. lower voices answer upper. For the tidy-minded who prefer a clear outside entry to close the exposition, this group, which includes test examples (A.F. 1 and 11), must be remembered against the forty-eight of the present sixty (and forty-two of the "Forty-eight") which encourage a working rule in their favour. Insouciance has its qualities. S.A.T.B., a popular vocal order, demands a light or plastic subject (W.K.i, B flat minor; ii, none). A.T.B.S. (reversing T.A.S.B.) balances falling entries by a clear soprano lead.

(iv) A.S.T.B. is strangely neglected (O., D minor; W.K.i, C; ii, A flat). T.A.B.S. suits austere music (W.K.i, F minor, F sharp minor). T.B.S.A. brings T.B. up to support S. (Ib., A flat and O., E flat). Like A.B.S., T.B.A.S. is rare. In "Credo" it is grounded on instrumental bass. The other fifteen alternatives of four-voice fugue are avoided, apart from the acrobatics of A.F. 5-7. S.A.B.T. demands two answers running. S.T., S.B., A.B. and their opposites are "impossible" starts; four examples are in A.F. 5-7 and 10 (original version). A.T.S.B. and B.T.S.A. are both awkward to pair off with subject and answer.

This empirical survey is enough to show Bach's preference in every period and *métier* for five or six orders of voice, with occasional and controlled experiments with other and less readily bound successions, but a constant exclusion of all combinations that do not begin with the cohesion of conjunct voices. Vocal analogies are kept steadily in mind, and the compulsive quality of a constant ascent or descent. If any unsolicited confirmation is desired, listen to the fugues in "Messiah" and the Mass in D. On the other hand, three-voice keyboard fugue is more subtle and calls less for conjunct textures.

COUNTER-EXPOSITION

A durable subject will stand a second set of entries, keeping rigidly or sometimes eventually to the tonic-dominant orbit. Entries may be consecutive or freely spaced out, but retain cohesion of some kind (W.K.ii, G sharp minor and the Chromatic). There is now no need for each voice to enter, or to enter once only. The consort of voices is an analogy which ceases to be pertinent, once the weave is entire. The process may stop at two entries. Counter-expositions are found in most of the big organ fugues. In W.K.i there are thirteen examples, in W.K.ii, ten. A.F. boldly puts up six in the eight normal fugues (1-5, 8-10). From the crudities of the early organ fugue in C minor to the richness of A.F. 10, counter-exposition is a constant feature in Bach's larger designs, and awareness of its in-part conservative transitions has clarified many fugues for one listener. The following are the common means of renewal—

(i) There is only a partial reduction of voices, or none at all.

(ii) The order of subject (S) and answer (A) is modified, with key to match, either type being repeated if desired. In at least two examples the SAS of exposition recurs, but SAA, AAS, AS and SA are equally common; four-voice fugues equally vary between SASA, SASS, SAAS, SAS and SA, as well as between the more tartly responsive ASAS, AASA, ASA and AS. There are also the exceptional key-detours of W.K.i, A minor, and O., B minor, impatient of conventional rejoinder. The answer will usually be real and uncompromising, if it was tonal before. It may be observed how invariably the ASA and ASAS of academic favour appear, and also opening with the answer, assumed the regular thing by the distinguished authority in *Grove's Dictionary* (5th edition, III. 517). He should be grateful to O., D minor, and W.K.ii, E flat and E, for pukka ASAS examples. But what are they among so many that have not observed the code?

(iii) The order of *voices* in charge of the subject may change round, and in particular change melodic direction (up or down), entirely or at first. This is a subtle and not invariable alteration of the exposition. Of thirty-six fugues, in sixteen there is no noticeable change, in fifteen there is a general reversal of direction, in five each entry changes. However, where the exposition bares the subject in B.T.A.S. order, counter-exposition is either avoided, as in three-voice fugues, or is rare and diversified by close canon (W.K.ii, E flat, E) or counter-subject (Ib., B). A.F. 2 is monotonous on this score, with eight outside entries.

(iv) Some or all of the voices may exchange subject and answer! This "prime variant" (Prout) may make for variety, but no one would be conscious of the exchange, or miss it, in a medium where the "voices" have no abiding personality or contrasted registers. By this stage it is no longer even of antiphonal interest whether subject or answer appears at the top or elsewhere. One rule of common sense, however, may be mentioned. If the counter-exposition begins in the same voice as the last entry, it must be with its melodic opposite (W.K.ii, A flat, B flat; *a fortori*, the actual recurrent voice of cantata 40).

(v) The subject may be inverted in some or all entries (W.K.i, F sharp minor, G, A minor, B; A.F. 5), or treated in close canon (W.K.ii, E flat, E).

(vi) A fresh counter-subject (O., Weimar C; W.K.i, C sharp minor; ii, B; A.F. 10, original version) or fresh counterpoint (*passim*) may renew the feel of the subject.

(vii) The tonality may rarely take in other accessible and suitable keys, such as the subdominant or relative major (keyboard A minor, $\frac{12}{16}$), or go further afield but return to tonic or dominant (O., B minor; W.K.i, A minor; ii, B).

(viii) A third set of entries may follow, varied by close canon or a new counter-subject (W.K.i, A minor; ii, E; A.F. 8).

(ix) Episodes may proliferate (Chromatic).

These various degrees of counter-statement may range from the almost automatic extensions of W.K.i, E and F, to those counter-expositions which are either completions or preliminaries in a larger scheme (W.K.i, F sharp minor; O., E flat, fugue 1). The spacious organ fugues in F, D minor and G minor make patent the spread-out process devised for long interludes in long Services; in W.K. and A.F. this becomes swift and succinct. In either style the counter-expositions are at least as deserving of modern study and imitation (if any) as close canon.

DEVELOPMENT

MIDDLE AND LATER ENTRIES

The exposition may vary, then, from the most perfunctory or punctilious routine to a positive expansion in a developing and capricious context, confined in key. But sooner or later there is a greater sense of release and development, followed occasionally by a gesture of recovery. These phrases must not be read in terms of sonata-form. The subject may appear in full again and again, and sometimes in tonic or dominant at random, without redundance. But a chain of quasi-vocal entry is first joined in concise or profuse measure, and then single entries may be judged to have the general impulse of the full exposition behind them. They can thus move more easily from key to key, assisted by growing episodes. Finally, the main key returns and the fugue winds up in a close ranging from a single entry of pat rejoinder, or even a free coda, to the insistent tread of the closing bars of O., B minor.

Pronounced gestures of recovery pointed by key, on a fugue's own proportions, are thus entirely occasional. Further instances include O., D minor; the Chromatic and the long keyboard A minor ($\frac{3}{4}$); W.K.i, C, C minor, C sharp, D minor, E flat, G minor; ii, C, E flat, E, F, F sharp, G minor, B; A.F. 2, 3, 13. Contrapuntal devices may enhance the sense of climax, but they will have invariably appeared earlier. We may speak of middle entries, then, but rarely of a middle section.

The orders of variation after the exposition may be classified as follows—

I. KEY-SCHEME

The key develops in proportion to the subject-matter to be disposed. In major fugues, an entry in the relative minor may be expected; it is rarely avoided (W.K.i, B; ii, E flat, F, F sharp, A flat). The supertonic minor replaces it in the first and last of these, and with the mediant minor forms a recurrent support of minor-key variation, with the leading-note minor a less common variant. The subdominant is a primary key which, excluded from the exposition, is inevitably a frequent resort on the way to recovery later. Rarely, the minor keys of the dominant, tonic or subdominant are used (W.K.ii, A flat). But the supertonic major of O., D, is a very isolated extension on the sharp side.* In minor keys, the relative major is missed in O., "Elgar" C minor, E minor, and A.F. 1 and 3. The submediant and leading-note major provide occasional support, especially in replenishing A.F. The Chromatic Fugue reaches the sharp submediant minor. The subdominant is again frequent, and also a passing tonic or dominant. These changes of mode (major-minor) either sharpen the edges of a contrapuntal combination against the conflicting detail of the minor key, or conversely relax the conflict for the smoother course of a major entry.

In general a key-scheme simply regulates the flow of entry and fresh counterpoint, so that an element of renewal may enter unobtrusively in an off-hand key and consolidate later. Key-contrast is rarely exploited for its own sake. Indeed, the positive

---

* See Note 1 on page 192.

rut within which key-development normally moves in these 150 fugues is at first disconcerting. Fresh planes of expression are not the concern of fugue as Bach practised it. When he wanted them, he broke away from fugue into instrumental refrain and declamation. But at least Bach did not expose the motto-theme of A.F. to the D major assurance which Mendelssohn, Tchaikovsky, Liszt, Franck or Karg-Elert might have found for it. For that alone, an extra trumpet should have sounded for him on the other side. And the opposite applies to those who try to extract orchestral grandeur from Bach's researches instead. In Bach tonality is for fugue, not fugue for tonality.

2. FRESH COUNTERPOINT

Many fugues rely on the exhibition of a subject with changing counterpoint and voicing, disposed on a key-plan; the counterpoint being free or partly dependent on a set counter-subject. O., G minor, is an admirable instance of this constant re-weaving, apart from the final fixation (see Ex. 10). Consistently fresh counterpoint is rare in the organ works (F minor, both C minor fugues of the Weimar period, the late G and the E flat). It is commoner in the shorter fugues of W.K. Apart from close canon, long fugues which maintain a consistent contrapuntal flow include W.K.i, B flat minor; ii, E flat, F, F minor, G, G sharp minor, B flat; A.F. 1, 2, 4, 12, and the C minor Toccata. These should be placed against the more conscious craft of organic development in the next group.

3A. STRETTO, ETC.

The subject may be treated *stretto*, i.e. in noticeably close canon, incidentally or more characteristically. This device is rare, because inaudible in inner parts, in the organ works. It appears perfunctorily in the late G and E flat fugues, and trenchantly in the D minor (Ex. 7, 13). In the last, it is introduced in the relative major, a favourite "calm" point for new developments (cf. W.K.i, G minor, and ii, B flat minor). In W.K., *stretto* is noticeable in seventeen fugues, in varying degrees but always at least twice, avoiding singularity. It is the making of W.K.i, C, and ii,

D and in part E. In A.F., *stretto* is the prime stimulus in No. 5, prodigal in 6–7. In the Mass, it distinguishes every turn of "Gratias" and "Confiteor," and special turns of the second "Kyrie" and "Qui tollis."

Inversion

Melodic inversion aids *stretto* in eight fugues in W.K. and in A.F. 5–7. Its contrary motion aids the counterpoint, while preserving a sense of organic feature. Inversion is used *per se* but incidentally in W.K.i, F sharp minor and B; ii, C sharp minor and D sharp minor; and constantly in the Toccata in G minor. In the vocal fugues inversion is conspicuously absent. Bach did not try to exchange taut stretches upward and compulsive descent where it was against nature. He left that to Mozart, Beethoven and lesser fugal writers.

Diminution and Augmentation

Diminution aids *stretto* in A.F. 6–7 and fills a gap in W.K.ii, E. Augmentation marks the final and pedal stage of the "Magnificat" and late C major organ fugues, transforms the last stage of W.K.i E flat minor, and punctuates the polyphony in A.F. 7.

Before discussing *stretto*, it will be convenient to sift the musical possibilities of inversion. The term is misleading. It means reversing ascent and descent, not putting the music upside down, a trick of double *notation* which it amused Bach to develop into a "crab" canon for King Frederick, *inter alia*, in the mock-erudite manner of the period. Inversion with the key-note placed at the fifth degree* is the commonest process. Melodically, the two halves of the scale remain intact, except for minor-key variants, and apart from the transformed shape of the theme the pitch-relationships only begin to point in opposite directions when the implied or actual harmony is considered. Here, while **d m s** remains **s m d,** as a whole, **s t r**$^\text{l}$ and **d**$^\text{l}$ **l f** interchange, and thus any dominant implications become subdominant or submediant. Subjects built round **d–s–d** are thus the smoothest for inversion, and W.K.i, B, and ii, C sharp minor (**d–r s**$_\text{l}$**–d, s–f d**$^\text{l}$**–s**) become

* See Note 2 on p. 192.

preciously subdominant, which gains a precise context to justify it. In A.F. 11 the chromatic turn of the original **d¹ ta l la s** of Fugue 8 makes the inversion, **s la ta t d¹**, tolerable; it is the force of descent which is missing. Inversion from zero is sometimes workable. Dominant and subdominant now interchange directly, **d m s d¹** becoming **d¹ l f d**. The chromatic **d–s–d** subject of W.K.i, F sharp minor inverts easily at the fifth, and later at zero, when the gravitation to the subdominant is in place. W.K.i, G, with a **d r m f** outline, brightens counter-exposition by a jaunty inversion at the fifth (**s f m r**), and later adds inversion at the third (**m r d t₁**) in the minor. The D minor fugue (Ib.) inverts its **d ma d la** at the second (**r¹ t r¹ f**) with inversion at the third in canon later (bars 14, 22). A.F. 10 inverts its first subject at the second in the exposition; A.F. 14, its B–A–C–H at the seventh (forming E–F–D–S!).

Close canon may be distinguished by (*a*) a harmonic, (*b*) a melodic, type of subject, or by both elements in turn. The former amplifies an absorption in a chord (usually the tonic) with cross-rhythm and diverting incident. The other type thickens a curve *per se* in a convenient succession of thirds and sixths, at least two notes deep and possibly also two keys thick. This may be overlapped and extended by further entries, forming a *stretto maestrale* of continuous cross-rhythm, but such an automatic series can only be a sign of harmonic release. For repetition, imitation by one part, cemented by free polyphony, is more durable. Bach seems to have regarded *stretto maestrale* as frivolous virtuosity, useful for an interlude (A.F. 5 and even "Gratias" in its original pomp of councillors-elect), or, as in W.K. ii, D, to dispose of an awkward theme, or as in W.K.i, C, for consistency of style. He put it in to *save* mental energy. It remains to distinguish the two types in the concrete.

(*a*) *Harmonic Outline.* A subject whose outline is based (entirely or at first) on a tonic or other chord can be amplified by a direct canon at the octave or fifth. It entails adjustments of **ds, sd¹** to **sd¹, d¹s¹** or exact intervals as may be convenient, harmonization of coincident **s** notes to form "relief" chords of the dominant, and similarly of coincident **d** notes for chords of the subdominant or

submediant, and exploitation of coincident passing and originally
non-harmonic notes to form intermediate and positive other
chords. Canon by inversion will suit equally in general, is a
stronger contrast melodically, and may make better harmony.
Exploitation of this casuistry of close imitation can be found in
W.K.i, E flat minor, A minor and B flat minor; ii, D, D minor;
A.F. 5; the soldiers' chorus in the St. John Passion, and cantata 65.

(Canons with the *subject* (outline counterpoint); cohesive
harmonic groups are bracketed)

Example 37

Two sets of examples may be quoted with skeleton harmony.
The bearing of the available canons on the harmonic rhythm has
been examined in detail for A.F. 5, where Bach starts with the
closest cross-rhythm (by inversion) and turns to direct canon at
further removes later. Alternatives are canons at double or half
speed, and of normal speed to either of these. They can be observed in W.K.i, E flat minor, and, more wittily, in A.F. 6 and 7.

Bach's singular achievement in A.F. 5–7, all the more impressive after four episodic fugues and as a stimulus to the production of fresh contrapuntal matter later, calls for brief notice here. The essential variety of close canonic entry may be summarized as follows, the details of context being in Chapter XIII—

Canons 1–2. *Fugue* 4. Two late entries at sixth and third.

Canons 3–9. *Fugue* 5. Seven entries, direct or inverse, beginning in middle keys; with two accumulations of half-entry elsewhere.

Canons 10–15. *Fugue* 6. Six types of inverse entry: four at double speed, two at half speed (normal following diminution), the latter being overlapped by the former in a tense weave of diminished, normal and diminished theme (bars 16, 58, 75). The repetition of Canons 10, 13 and 14 (bars 1, 35, 57) in fresh detail brings the total to thirteen (not counting entries at more than a bar's distance from the *leader*, e.g. bars 3, 10, 37). At the end "double speed" approaches the normal, and normal a condition of half-speed. (This manipulation of the basic rhythm is commonly under-heard.)

Canons 16–21. *Fugue* 7. At least six fresh canons: five presenting the diminished theme, in canon in turn with the now rarer normal rhythm, the equally diminished theme, and the augmented subject (bars 3, 20 cf. 42, 23 cf. 50); one following the augmented theme with the normal. In contrast, Canons 14 and 6 re-assert the normal rhythm (bars 1 and 13, 36).

Canon 22. *Fugue* 11. Of two late entries the first is basically No. 9, and the second a fresh canon by inversion at the third, at zero-interval in time.

These thirty odd entries constitute fifteen harmonizations each for the normal and inverted subject, as leader-entry, and three for the themes in simultaneous impact. The five successive bars of the theme (or half or double these) will be found to combine variously the following patterns of changing harmonic bass for the two main beats of each bar, which may be taken to cover the placing of a fresh harmony off the beat. A chord in brackets is occasional. The position of a chord (root or inversion) is not shown, except for the second inversion, shown by the addition of a c.

Bars	1	2	3	4	5
To Subject	I : V	III(II) : I	#VII : (I)II	III	I
	II :			(II)	
Direct canon	(II) : V	I : IV	V(9) : I	I.IV : V	IV
		III(V9) : I	: VI(V9)	VI.IV : #VII	I
Inverse canon	I : V	I :	V : IVc	Ic : I	I (major)
By diminution	(IV) :	Ic(V7) : VI	V9 : I	I(III) : #VII	I
	V : Ic . V		III :	I.IV : V	I7
				III : VI	
By augmentation	(V9) : I	I : (VI)	V : (I)V	I.III : (VI)	VI
	VI.IV : V	I . VI : . I	V9 : VI(II)	I.III : I	VI (major)
To Inverted Subject	V : I(II)	III : V	VI : V(IV)	III	V
	IV . :			(IV)	
Direct canon	V : I . VI	I : (Ic . V7)	VI : Ic	I : VIc	Ic . V (major)
	IV :		: V	I7 : IIIc . VII	III = I
By diminution	V : I	I :	VII(IV7) : V9	IV7 :	V
	I : IV	Ic :	III :	I :	
Inverse canon	IV7 . VII : I(VII)	I :	IV7 : V7	I : IV7 . VII	III = I
By diminution	V :		V9 : I . VII	: VI	
	VI		Ic . V		
By augmentation	V . I : IV7 . V	I . VI : V . I	IV :	I . III : VI	I7 = V7
	V . Ic :			I . IV7 :	
	IV :				

(b) Melodic Outline. Where a melodic outline proceeds in groups of conjunct degrees or other regular sequences, a close entry may reinforce it in thirds or sixths (W.K.i, C, F: ii, B flat minor; Mass, "Gratias," "Confiteor"). It remains to avoid weak unisonal or semi-unisonal movement in the audible detail of the harmony. Canon by inversion is possible here, if the outline is conjunct, since for any scalic phrase an inversion at the fifth makes concords for four notes (e.g. for C D E F G, (G) F E D C below). Further, any conjunct phrase is potentially part of a chain of sevenths and thus admits the harmony of (i) conjunct phrases in similar motion at two exclusive pitches (1 *or* 2, Ex. 38A); (ii) phrases in contrary motion as explained above; (iii) phrases that fall a fifth inside a beat and rise a step, or rise a fifth and fall a step (contrary motion), or fall a third and a step (similar). On these lines Bach brings off a canon by inversion, doubled in thirds, to a subject doubled in sixths and then thirds, as rousing *release* after a long series of direct and inverse canons (W.K.ii, B flat minor). The simpler weave but thicker resonance of the polyphony are impressive. But Bach was seldom satisfied with this blunt kind of rhetoric.

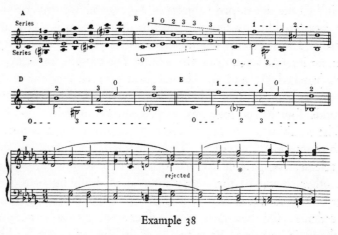

Example 38

3B. ALTERATIONS OF SUBJECT

Apart from formal variations by inversion, etc., the subject may be altered incidentally but poignantly by semitonal changes, ornamental figures, a fresh position in the scale, or rhythmic treatment. Semitonal traits arise in W.K.i, E flat and G; ii, C minor, D minor, F, A flat; A.F. 1, 8 (bar 148). Decorations, in W.K.i, F; ii, E; and A.F. 12. Changes of curve or degree appear in W.K.i, A flat, B flat, B; ii, C sharp minor (*fin.*); A.F. 1 and, most strikingly, 4. Re-accentuation, in W.K. ii, A flat, A.F. 2–3, and the Chromatic. Rhythmic extension by sequence replaces the subject in W.K.ii, C and F. All these fine points meet a need for fresh stimulus. They mark a composer who learns his fugue from his musical judgment, not from rules. It is only necessary to follow Bach's habit of playing over a book of W.K. to realize how subtle his apparently strait-laced themes are. After them, many of the piquant transformations of Beethoven, Franck, Liszt, Wagner, seem very conscious art.

3C. SPECIAL COUNTERPOINT

In marked contrast with all this ingrowth of the subject upon itself, counter-subjects may be developed with special versatility, from the decorative or trenchant counter-phrases of O., Weimar C, W.K.ii, C sharp minor, G minor and B, and "Pleni sunt coeli," to the developed subjects of A.F. 9 and 10. Inversion of the counter-subject a tenth or twelfth up or down is a common variant. Harmonic implications are tabled opposite. Restrictions are: an interval *repeated* in No. 1 must not become an octave or fifth (marked †); and an interval must proceed conjunctly if it inverts as a seventh or other dissonance (marked *). In No. 1 seconds, fourths and sevenths are presumed resolved.

The combination of Nos. 2 and 3, 3 and 4, 1 and 5, is common, if the components construe. The outcome is, once more, a sense of release, comparable to that of an effective *stretto*, but here smoother owing to the steady interval of doubling in a given entry. The common motive is harmonic relief, especially from a set cadence. On these lines, from a discreet observation or control of the basic harmony, Bach produces the similarly contrived but widely differing counterpoint of the examples given, as a nucleus or prevailing content of later entries, disposed conveniently in contrasting key and held apart by relevant episodes. W.K.ii, G minor, and A.F. 10 seem to stress the argumentative side,

W.K.ii, B, a state of greater absorption, of which "Pleni sunt coeli" is the technically *legato* anticipation, promoted by the material tedium of the sixfold entry of a long subject but delivered

Nature of Variation	Contrapuntal Content	Comparative Intervals in the Essential Harmony above the Bass Stated							
1. Original	a/b	1	2	3	4	5	6	7	8
2. Inversion at the 8ve	b up an 8ve/a	8	7	6	5	4*	3	2	1
3. Inversion at the 10th	b up a 10th / a or b / a down a 10th	10	9	8†	7*	6	5†	4	3
4. Inversion at the 12th	b up a 12th / a or b / a down a 12th	12†	11	10	9	8†	7*	6	5
5. Doubling	a a 3rd below / b or a / b a 3rd up	6	7	8†	2*	3	4*	5†	6

in a context of sublime discovery and following, incidentally, a studiously canonic fugue ("Confiteor"). Such is Double Counter-point at the creative stage.

3D. TWO OR THREE SUBJECTS

Occasionally two subjects are developed at once, as in the fugal finale of the organ Passacaglia. Alternatively, one or more counter-subjects of a conclusive set of entries appear first as independent subjects, whose development begins as episode but proves organic sooner or later. O., F, and W.K.ii, G sharp minor, and "Confiteor" exhibit two subjects. So does A.F. 10, but here the first subject is so soon subordinate, and its contrapuntal variations so marked, that it remains much nearer the previous group, to which it originally belonged. W.K.ii, F sharp minor, exhibits a subject, a counter-phrase and another subject; A.F. 8, a subject, a counter-subject and another subject; A.F. 11, inversions of these; O., E flat, three subjects (or two subjects and a counter-phrase) of which the first, twice transformed, combines with the others in turn and forms an integrating factor; A.F. 14 (unfinished) and 15 (unwritten), four subjects. The most success-ful number of subjects is two or two and a half! The best of these examples take the initial pulse furthest beyond its initial exhibited range. The central *Affekt* remains. In some fugues the subjects are no more than contrapuntally suited (O., F). In W.K.ii, F sharp minor, the linking of character is closer. In A.F. 8 the main subject of the series vitalizes the first combination of subject and counter-subject, and the gradual resolution of the final tension of the three-strand weave, at first screwed up an extra turn by harmonic adjustment, is one of the discoveries of fugue. A.F. 11 is a fatal attempt to repeat the process with inverted motives. A.F. 14 is a studious exordium to a presumably quadruple fugue, which would have added a new facet to the main subject in the final combination (Tovey manages with a struggle to exhibit the subjects and their inversions in two variants each), but I miss the sweeping cogency of A.F. 8.* An invertible quadruple fugue (A.F. 15) could not have added much more, and would have been cramped, thoroughly as Tovey's reconstruction conceals this by his inversionary skill, which lightens the burden of 15*b*. If Beethoven (op. 133) is anyone to go by, Bach's E flat organ fugue proved the most prophetic of wider developments, preserving a central melodic curve in distinct movements, transformed yet identical.

4. EPISODES

Entries of the full subject have inevitably gained first attention. But the intervening matter shows equally a mind at work, and here, too, Bach is a pilot "with few whistles" (of conscious re-direction). Among writers Prout, Gédalge and Oldroyd have illustrated fully certain ways of development in particular instances, but they leave an impression of *ad hoc* methods. Apart from the impromptu character of episodes in a number of organ fugues, Bach's habits are recurrent enough to be classifiable into at least six types of production. Four show organic development, two depend on improvisation or free harmonic progressions.

(a) Extension of Entry

The last bar of the subject develops sequentially, especially in bass: O., Weimar C—to which all other mention of O., C, will

* See Note 3 on page 192.

refer—bars 64, 119; W.K.i, B flat (17);* ii, C (43), E minor (18, 35, 47), E (32), F (24), F minor (15, 45), F sharp (24), G minor (8), A flat (26, 39), A, B (24), B minor (76); A.F. 1 (60), 2 (65).

(b) Sequence

An integral part of the subject develops on its own—

(i) by *false entry*, i.e. entire enough to suggest an entry (*passim*);

(ii) with a fresh contrapuntal figure or chordal progression: W.K.i, C sharp (23), E flat (22), E, A flat, G sharp minor, B flat; ii, C, C sharp minor (8, 39), F, F sharp (24), G, B flat (67); A.F. 8 (28, 114), 9 (29, 81), 13 (13, 24, 41);

Example 39

(iii) with a vibrating chordal figure oscillating round a fixed point in Alberti style (W.K.i, C sharp, 37, 39).

* The figures in brackets refer to bars.

(c) Development of First Episode

O., C (49); W.K.i, C minor, C sharp, E flat, F minor, F sharp, F sharp minor, G, A flat (inversion at the twelfth), B flat minor, B minor; ii, C, D (30), D sharp minor (36), F, F minor, G minor, G sharp minor (49, 119); A.F. 1, 3, 4, 8 (25, 135); and the long A minor for keyboard.

Example 40

(d) Counter-subject Development

Chromatic; W.K.i, C minor, D minor, F sharp minor (23, 35), A, B minor (34); ii, C, G minor, G sharp minor (75); A.F. 3 (19), 8 (74, 114), 11 (52, 60, 97, 118, 168).

Example 41

(e) Extemporization

(i) A rising phrase of conjunct notes, especially in the bass: W.K.i, E flat (24), F (56); ii, E minor (55), G sharp minor (84); A.F. 5 (62), 11 (49).

(ii) A similar descending phrase: O., C (48, 77); W.K.i, B flat minor; ii, E; A.F. 6 (43), 8 (74), 11 (155).

(iii) Ascending fourths or falling fifths in sequence: O., C (56); W.K.ii, C sharp minor (62), B (69); A.F. 4 (123), 12 (46).

(iv) Harmonic and melodic figures in combination (W.K.i, E minor, G).

(v) Miscellaneous: W.K.i, D, G (Alberti); ii, C sharp minor (13), D minor (8), F (8), F minor (47), F sharp minor (57), A minor (11, 19), B flat minor (62), B (71, 89); A.F. 1 (17), 3 (19, 46), 4 (*passim*), 6, 7 (31), 8 (15, 53), 10 (50, 70, 79, 89, 98), 11 (38, 49), 12 (36); the long fugue in A minor (108–21, 156–end).

Descending fifths in rising sequence, fastidiously harmonized

New figure in alto with   Quick inversions of polyphony, developing this chord
characteristic chord

(Neapolitan cadence deflected by slow soprano descent to tonic, halted by diminished sevenths, on augmented sixth, etc.)

Example 42

(*f*) *Harmonic Sequences*

Usually with a falling line in the foreground or background to prompt the chordal movement.

(i) *Leading to an Entry:* O., C (96); W.K.i, A flat (31), A minor (78), B flat minor; ii, E (21, 32), F (55, 72), G (60), G minor (63, 77); A.F. 8 (91, 165, 178), 11 (48, 122, 144, 172), 13 (58).

(ii) *Arising from an Entry,* after some tension by discord or semitonal movement: O., C (30, 92); W.K.ii, D sharp minor (34), A flat (44); A.F. 4 (81), 11 (17).

Example 43

These selected references, heard in their context, convey cumulatively a powerful impression of versatility, aptness and relevance over and above the expressiveness of the entries.

5. HARMONY

The motive of most contrapuntal processes is to freshen the harmony of entries. Certain by-products enrich the established progressions of the major and minor scales. (Bach's experiments

with the older modes are mentioned at the end of Chapter VI.)
The following combination blends double and irregular suspensions and resolutions in close succession, by exploiting the conno-
tation of each note of the basic phrase as harmonic, suspended,

Example 44

non-harmonic or ornamental. Bars 33, 42 and 91 of the same
fugue (p. 28) are also unconventional resolutions. Another document in uncompromising treatment is O., F (27, 33, 69, 120, 126,
138, 162). The added-sixth chord of bar 7, etc., reappears in
W.K.i, C (12, etc.). The augmented fifth appears in O., C (53),
W.K.i, F sharp minor (37) and elsewhere, but the texture of the
organ fugues is usually uneventful.

Semitonal writing becomes characteristic from time to time,
from O., "Elgar" C minor *med.*, and W.K.i, F minor, to A.F.,
3, 4, 8, 11, 14. But the Chromatic Fugue itself demonstrates the
control of oscillating tonality by a pivotal dominant chord of
adjustment up or down. Three characteristic pre-dominant or
pro-dominant chords, not yet *vieux jeu* at the time, may be mentioned; the diminished seventh, the augmented sixth and the
Neapolitan or Phrygian sixth. As a variant of the dominant
minor ninth, of which it will here be considered the equivalent,
the diminished seventh is decisive in W.K.ii, A minor and B flat
minor, A.F. 8 and 11, and the Chromatic, straightening the key
after a diversion. W.K.i, C minor *fin.*, subtends the chord over a
sustained tonic. The supertonic ninth appears similarly over the
dominant, trenchantly in O., late G (71), insouciantly in the
impromptu addition of W.K. ii, G (61). The same chord is constantly used by itself as a final mental stretch, released in a dominant chord and so homeward (II_9–V–I): O., B minor; W.K.i,
C sharp, C sharp minor (109), E flat, A minor (80), B flat minor;
ii, C minor, C sharp minor, E flat, F (82), G minor (79), B flat,

B; A.F. 1, 4 (131), 7. A supertonic major ninth is used similarly at the end of "Dona nobis pacem" (repeating "Gratias"), as a final stab of resolve in a world of uncontrolled violence: the supertonic sublime. Bach was well aware of the power of the ninth and seventh, but he restrained it rigidly, and confined it to select fugues.

Rarely, the subdominant chord of a minor key is strained, with the third in the bass, from normal to augmented sixth (**la d¹ f¹**, **la d¹ fe¹**), thus forming a piquant pre-dominant element. The position with **fe** in the bass is favoured. Among insouciant uses are O., F (127, Italian version), A.F. 4 (133) and 5 (85) (German) and 11 (181–2) (French). Context throws the chord into greater relief in A.F. 7 (59, after II$_9$) and 9 (76). A.F. 11 uses the chord with bold informality (69, 114, 146) over the flattened supertonic

Example 45

as a pro-dominant and thus pre-*tonic* chord, after which the return to the dominant minor ninth (175, 180) is effective. These chords are exploited to match the stress of the painfully climbing second subject here, but in general they are controlled.

The most piquant pre-dominant is the chord of the flattened supertonic, associated with the operatic style of A. Scarlatti and other Naples composers. Bukovzer traces the chord back to the Phrygian mode. This seems mistaken, for in any case more than half the thrust of the present progression lies in the dominant (or dominant-seventh) chord that follows. It colours the second "Kyrie," and in part the first, and it appears with an arresting pause on the issuing dominant chord in O., late G, W.K.i, A minor, and ii, A flat; A.F. 8 (172, 178, 184) glances pathetically at Naples thrice before it expires. But in the cadence of the fugal chorus of St. Matthew Passion No. 33, the Neapolitan sixth seals for all time the resolution of men of good will (without Picander's smug theatricality) to pursue with ruthless justice the persecutors of the innocent. The cadence of "Qui tollis" is also the last link in an unparalleled chain of tense expression.

These, then, are the most trenchant harmonic points. In engaging contrast, a bass stops on dominant or tonic and lets the polyphony run on till it is spent. It is a conservative craftsmanship, like Handel's. Yet when memory turns a page ahead and comes upon Schumann's B–A–C–H and would-be Bachian fugues, one finds so much colour as to blur the original image; and while Mephistopheles-Liszt and Liszt (sonata) had their sharp-tongued excursions with fugue, neither could keep it up. Bach could not be bothered with such luscious and crumbling subtleties! His harmony was to keep the contrapuntal fare fresh.

Harmony can be thin or thick, close or spreading, and the working contrast of three and a larger number of parts widens the range of a given combination. Moreover, if melody is mentally separated from its accompaniment in the same part, the resultant true polyphony may often exceed five parts. We remember the lightness of many three-voice fugues, but also the astonishing richness of W.K.i, C sharp, ii, F sharp minor, and, above all, the Chromatic. Bach adds extra parts when he requires them for emergency's sake (A.F. 5, 6, 7 *fin.*), but not otherwise. He has no need.

A long art carries the growth of the imagery or dialectic, or whatever the subject may suggest, to a sense of completion. "The Art of Fugue" tabulates treatment which Bach had often devised more fortuitously *ad rem*. His main formula is to break up the natural harmonic organization of a subject by another, and when in doubt to try a motive a third higher or lower. (Breaking organizations, as human and inefficient, is perhaps the mark of a dynamic force in industry; a harmonic sequence, too, can be too personal and turn sour.) That is the apparent aim of all this counter-exposition, key-roaming, double counterpoint, canon and, if urgent, a new movement or recurrent refrain. To perceive the latent exigencies of a "well-covered" subject is to gain closer contact with Bach's aesthetic consciousness. The technical mastery is less than the art, but it is the key to it. Under these circumstances the detailed study of Bach's concrete procedure, and the attempt to gauge his structural principles, need no defence, for those who seek to heighten the pitch of their existence in this limited and rarely Methusalean life. It is possible, indeed, to let these fugues flood the ear in turn for their sensuous impression, as some people take in "The Nibelung's Ring" or *Ulysses*—not with the approval of their creators—but it may be wondered how much remains, and what. However, I shall be beating at an open door at this stage, because no one except a reviewer is likely to have reached this page unless he is interested to discover why fugues make such different impressions and yet suggest the presence of a common dialectic, whether coherent or not.

NOTES

1 (*Page* 174) This fugue needs all its room for its key-balance of VI–III–VII minor and II–V–I major. So for VI–II–V–I. The reverse order, I–V–II–VI (or VII minor), equally demands space for return.

2 (*Page* 176) I have used the term "inversion at the fifth" in this book to mean this translation of the tonic, and similarly for its re-setting at other intervals or ("at zero") none.

3 (*Page* 184) Tovey makes Bach's combination of three subjects (his last seven bars), *plus* the main subject in place of a free fourth part, the "solvent" combination after three trenchant variants by inversion, etc., with the motto finally rising to soprano, and a poignant cadence (per *bach*) with the last note of the first subject, held, as bass. The ending is satisfactory, but I find certain progressions in the variants far-fetched (especially bars 242, 255, 267, 274–5), and the contrapuntal variations (than which no better could be devised as organically) correspondingly laboured, in the style of A.F. 11, not A.F. 8. Tovey's thematic acrobatics take the ear by surprise, with their logical but ungrateful twists of meaning. Bach might have been satisfied with a shorter and less ingenious penultimate stage. We do not know; and as I have said earlier, four themes are not much better than three, except for the integrating power of the motto. Tovey "corrects" Nottebohm by syncopating the motto at the sixth and seventh notes. (See Schwebsch.)

Chapter XVII

FUGUE BEFORE BACH

SYMPHONY did not begin with Mozart, and in the broad sense fugue has had a long history. Monothematic fugue can be traced back into the sixteenth century. As we step beyond this built-up area into the more isolated and fitful constructions of earlier periods, the route becomes desultory and disconnected, while the landmarks that survive are scattered in museums or are a matter for further search.* Yet not only can the tracks be found or presumed, but it becomes clear that as late as 1600 the future of fugue, as understood in Bach's time, was far from being assured. At this critical stage the island race can make some claim to have handed on a torch to foreign craftsmen. In the belief that in every piece of true history there is guiding power for the present, I shall attempt to summarize the contrapuntal development of phrases for their own sake, which spread to keyboard music and eventually settled down to certain types of fugue on one central subject, such as were distinguished in Chapter II. The more instrumental type presupposes the command of figures and rhythms suited to the keyboard. That command was acquired by gradual and then lavish experiment in fresh kinds of sound-clusters; often, indeed, at the expense of any continuous thought. It will be pertinent here to observe something of the pioneer work which enabled Bach's "Keyboard Practice" to move freely in the world of its own choice, without indulging too lightly in reminiscences of the keyboard's infancy in the I-knew-him-when tone of the family nurse.

Music seems to have entered organized life as a magical part of religious ritual. It stayed, rather defensively for many centuries and in later "Puritanist" periods, as a softener of hard mental crusts of hate and distrust and sheer boredom, and ultimately as

* See Note 1 on page 213.

entertainment in demand. Yet monks observed and praised its inner logic and its control of texture. In the twelfth century Alanus Anglicus commends "our Gregory" for his discovery of music neither too seductive nor too blunt, and describes the blend and overlapping of voices entering at the octave and fifth—

*Cum tribus una sonans vox litigat, immo iocatur.**

That forecasts well enough the growing and often conflicting associations of argument and amusement. Socially, minstrels were long classed, with jugglers and dancers, as undesirables, but in England at least in the twelfth century the Church, at the height of its power as feudal landowner, consented to a moderate recognition of the irrepressible, cheerful instrumental music that was delighting burghers and nobles alike, and the organ was adopted for services. The early opening of that door to harmony for its own sake, followed by the rise of organists from the educated classes, made possible many artistic advances in the future. The regular rhythm of the moving feet infected music more and more, in the absence of verbal sense, the sustained sounds promoted cadence and tonality, and the wandering finger drew ahead of voices in range, rapid movement and power of harmonic suggestion in a single part.

A still amazing blend of "litigation" and lyric may be observed in a musical setting on a page of a unique manuscript, Harley 978. The writing is that of a thirteenth century book-hand, and its clear connexion with the Reading Abbey calendar that follows it, and with other records, dates it 1250–1260.† The last of five "motets" in this collection, the famous "Sumer" Canon, is a remarkable production. It contains a melody with the racy spontaneity of folk-song, symmetrical and (as defined by visible additions in a later hand) rhythmic. Its slick recurring eight-bar pattern suggests, indeed, the influence of the French iso-rhythmic motet. But here the unequivocal tune is presented as the theme of a quadruple ROUND or perpetual canon (at the unison), supported by a two-part *pes* or pedestal in "drone" style, a

* See Note 2 on page 213.
† See Note 3 on page 213.

forecast of the later basic Tones and Grounds. No such manifold rhythm, or anything like it, is known earlier, and one wonders whether the canonry did not begin in devilment and then win unexpected approval. Further (which is also without precedent) this straight-and-again-from-the-shoulder music celebrates a rapturous and altogether Wessex dream of summer, in the first place, but at apparently the next remove a more conventional meditation, "Perspice Christicola," the words of which are written roughly below the English. (The absence of Latin words for the bass parts confirms a general impression of pious doggerel hastily added to bring the music into line with "Ave, gloriosa Mater" and the other three three-voice pieces, which are wordless but churchy.) The instructions in Latin about the canonic entries surely convey, not the learned composer, but a simple explanation to educated singers of a popular practice less known to the august and temperate. Either way, here is canon in wonderland. As the sounds of this timeless creation floated up the Royal Festival Hall, 1951, linked with like songs of spring, autumn and a Christianized December,* seven centuries of cultural evolution crowded into one glorious hour, defying barbarism, like the hall itself.

The script also includes three dances for two instruments in an equally jingling rhythm. The last, a *stantipes* or extension of the set dance called *ballata*, eventually shows what modern listeners might term an answer in the dominant to the subject repeated in

(In bar 6 the upper part has a B natural, through the absence of any B-flat signature, but it may be doubted if the antinomy would have been acceptable)

Example 46

the bass, now closing in the tonic. This is actually a later "verse" of a balanced melody of 8–8 bars, but the firm sense of rejoinder is there, like the sheer cross-rhythm of the canon.

Faute de mieux, the next landmark is from the early fourteenth

* See Note 4 on page 213.

century. It has little of the direct appeal of the Round or dances of the Reading collection, but it marks a beginning in the break-away from vocal style. It is contained in two leaves, closely written on each side and with one or more leaves missing at either end. The charter-hand of individual letters in the lower harmony (a very early example of letter-notation) identifies the music with a register of the Cistercian Abbey at Robertsbridge, Sussex, with which it is unquestionably bound (28,550). Three of the six pieces are in the nature of preludes in the sectional dance style known as Estampie, and three are keyboard versions (rather than parts) of motets. The unknown composer, who must be at least as English as any Robertsbridge monk,* confronts the listener with a keyboard style! Apart from the passing antiphony of the hocket or hiccough (a group of responsive notes to fill a vacuum), there is no imitation. But the texture is fresh. Besides the block harmony in 2-3 parts, there are hints of harmony and melody in one part (cf. Ex. 6, b2).

Example 47

What is more, the very pertinent transcriptions of choir-music herald a type of keyboard polyphony prevalent for over three centuries. The fourth and fifth pieces are figurations of motets found in the music inserted in the racy dramatic satire on the Church, the *Roman de Fauvel*; the second piece transposed (without precedent) up a tone. (Wolf thought that the position of the abbey favoured such a French contact.) The musical impression is not of an accompaniment but of genuine keyboard interludes, with a few scattered or guiding words. The instrument is

* See Note 5 on page 213.

commonly assumed to have been the organ, on the grounds of its long use for providing *organum* (pun not intended) or decorative accompaniment to a chant, and of the appearance here of a dual notation later typical (for economy's sake!) of German organ books. There were the *great* or fixed church organ, the *positive* and physically portable instrument immortalized by Van Eyck, and the *portative* (*organetto*) or regal held by the player. Pedals were added in France in the fourteenth century (in England in the eighteenth). The keyboard instrument, the *échiquier* or chessboard, jerking the hammer by a "check" against the strings, and described in 1388 by a distinguished patron, John I of Aragon, as "like an organ which sounds with strings," was current by 1350; but the same enthusiast is anxious to obtain the *estampies* in a book belonging to a well-known *organist*. Whatever was intended here—and no one can go into a passion about it—from now the chekker and organ types developed in parallel on common musical ground, and for over two centuries much keyboard music could have been written for either of them. With them advanced the viol family, in a losing race where soloists were concerned.

What happened in the next period remains a matter for bold guessing, not positive statement, but the evidence is increasingly decisive. The main provenance is now Italian, late fourteenth century German tablature (Breslau Friary) not being considerably beyond the Robertsbridge stage. In a group of "estampies" and "saltarelli," presumably for viol (29, 987), a "Lamento di Tristano" and another saltarello show the three-beat expansion, *in string idiom*, of a simpler two-beat refrain which follows. In the same script (No. 52) is a typical vocal CACCIA or Chase by Niccolo "del Proposto" (? son of the provost), Nicholas of Perugia, as a Florentine copy shows. This exhibits two-part canon with a full part below, in two developed stages of descriptive fantasia and lyrical refrain. What, then, of keyboard music? The historian has now to reckon with a considerable set of arrangements of French and Italian vocal pieces of the *trecento*, which are coming to light in a dual script with a strange history. Formerly in the keeping of the Carmelite monastery at Ferrara in North Italy, it was listed under the name of Go(o)dendach(Gutentag) or

Bonadies, its *later* contributor (1473-4), and was so mentioned by Ambros in his *History of Music*, vol. 3 (1868). Then it went underground. In fact, it wandered south and came down the Via Emilia to Faenza, where it was received into the District Library around 1889, for the Bonadies *Regulae Cantus* in that library are the subject of an article by A. Cicognani in a Milan journal in that year. This is decisively confirmed by Entry No. 117 in the printed catalogues of the library published in 1896 (and 1918), and by Schmidl's Dictionary, whose original edition (1888) contains no reference to Godendach, while the second edition (1927) has a definite entry. In 1929 the script appeared at an Exhibition at Bologna. Once at Faenza, however, Bonadies slept with his fathers another fifty years, till in an article in 1939 the script was identified as the missing Ferrara Codex. The writer, G. Roncaglia, was still mainly concerned with the later or Bonadies section of the script, which includes theoretical matter of some interest, but he noted (at last) the intermingling in an alien hand of "tablatures for instrument and bass," some with and some without initial text-titles, and he reproduced a page in facsimile.

A year later Professor C. Van den Borren skilfully identified from this single page an ornamental two-stave version of a Ballata by the late fourteenth-century organist, Landini, and other and notational signs of the Italian *ars nova*, and inferred that the volume must be unusually rich in such transcriptions; but he oddly assumed the piece to be a "fantasy for two instruments," although such duets are invariably given in separate parts elsewhere, and he accordingly rejected the term "tablature." Equally incredulous of the organ, Dr. Knud Jeppesen demanded a pair of wind instruments in his notice of the piece in his subsequent book, *Die italienische Orgelmusik am Anfang des Cinquecento* (1943). In 1948 Dr. D. Plamenac, having followed this singularly mobile and disguised evidence on the lines indicated, decided to redeem the sixty-year time-lag by probing first hand in a now damaged building. In 1951 he furnished a full and substantially decisive interim report, with twelve facsimile pages and four transcriptions, on what he rightly re-named (as being anonymous in the earlier pages) the Faenza script (No. 117), and especially on the twenty-nine earlier instrumental pieces which have text-titles and therefore admit of easier concordance. He promises "substantial publication" later. Of the earlier and larger part of the script (104 pages to 79 for the Bonadies additions), the titled pieces include French and Italian secular songs and one "Kyrie" (plainsong); two Machaut Ballades are balanced by known songs by Landini and the earlier Jacob of Bologna. Plamenac assumes, reasonably enough, that the two-stave "score" is in fact a setting for a keyboard instrument, and considers the positive organ a possible suggestion, but a spinet or clavichord more likely for the surprisingly agile bravura of, for example, "Biance flour" (almost a Toccata), or the decorative treatment in "Jour à jour la vie" of an original upper part known from another script (B.M., Cotton Titus 26); with two manuals for the crossing parts of Machaut's "De toutes flours." The "Kyrie" may be compared for style with two settings of the same Tone in the "Buxheim" book mentioned below and with a later paraphrase in Attaignant's *Tablature* of 1531 (cf. Y. Rokseth, *Deux Livres d'Orgue*). Through the agile hand of some W. T. Best of the period, transcription is bidding fair to become a way of expanding keyboard idiom on a steady vocal foundation; not, indeed, as surely or as gratefully as the valleys would one day be exalted (for English ears) with vocal virtuosity, but with much greater freedom than the plodding bravura of the hitherto isolated transcript of a Landini ballata (Paris, B.N. 6, 771). The R. H. part contains its own liquescent harmony and other features of a cultivated, rather irrepressible, keyboard idiom. The need to play part-songs from separate parts, mentioned below, becomes less cogent. The date might be the late fourteenth century, since the composers so far identified are the older generation, but the keyboard style is much nearer the fifteenth century.*

Without our going beyond the present stage of partial survey, then, this repertory of about fifty pieces, isolated as it is, strengthens the ground of fact in our approach to the main body of controversial evidence, an immense collection compiled by the

* See Note 6 on page 214.

fifteenth-century Florentine organist, A. Squarcialupi, of some apparently vocal pieces by Jacob of Bologna, the blind virtuoso Landini and other fourteenth-century figures (Laurentine Library, Florence, *Pal.* 87). Against the natural supposition that these are organ accompaniments, Prof. Otto Kinkeldey* has assembled evidence that the virtuoso organists in Italy and elsewhere exercised a new and later standard method of translating choral polyphony into keyboard idiom, reading from the choral score or even from parts. He argues that the texture, colour and (most cogent of all) the six-line notation of Squarcialupi's pieces, confirmed on the text by abundant illustrations of regals, are more eloquent of an instrument than of voices. Indeed, one of Landini's pieces, *Questa fanciulla* (*This maiden*), is itself found elsewhere in the above-cited organ arrangement, less polyphonic and more bravura. On this hypothesis, the organ was challenging the viol as the universal and omnivorous instrument; and like the words so much more industriously interwoven into piano versions of Wagner, the texts are for reference only. Certainly no other supposition explains the gap in our records better than such an "Operation Keyboard." It is reasonably well substantiated by the musical style and by literary references both to dazzling organ activity and to the performance of transcriptions with textual aid. Some kind of musical achievement must be predicated in keeping with a century of organist composers.

The fifteenth century was certainly occupied later with the expansion of keyboard style, as revealed in the collection made by Brother Adam Ileborgh of Stendal in 1448, and in the large assembly of over 250 pieces attributed (in a later hand) to the Carthusian monastery at Buxheim (near Munich), and pointing to the Great Organ in a final instruction about pedals, but mainly secular in content.† (The possible contributions of Dufay and Dunstable are shadowed only in arrangements of their vocal works in the Buxheim Book, which are paralleled by organ pieces in the same book. All that can be said is that the declamatory freedom, with plainsong or independent bass, of Dunstable's

* See Note 7 on page 215.
† See Note 8 on page 215.

motets and Dufay's crisper style, point to a release of the
ten fingers in the German way.) From the utterly pedagogic
descant exercises of Paumann's *Fundamentum organisandi* (*Teach
yourself organ accompaniment*) to the wantonly ornamental pieces of
Ileborgh, the restless finger seems ever on the move, the counterpart of the doodling on many illuminated manuscripts. Otherwise there is vocal polyphony, often literally so. But there is no
more Chase: the aim is one prevailing line, and that at the top.
The accent is on melodic extension, not on inner logic.

In the sixteenth century these tablatures or studies in development became general and extended to France, Spain, Italy and
Poland, and also to string and lute studies by Hans Gerle, Ganassi,
Judenkünig, d'Aquila, da Milano, and others. In Gerle's book
(1532) is a "fugue" that treats simple phrases in turn fugally, in
descending fifths. The fourteen organ pieces in ARNOLT SCHLICK's
TABLATURE of 1512, the first keyboard work to be published, at
once strike the ear equally by the smooth texture and by the ready

Maria Zart *(Mary Sweet)*

Example 48

imitations of their intimate chorale-prelude style, anticipating
Bach's "Little Organ Book." The more *Ricercar* or insistent
treatment arose in the work of the Venetian organists, the
Cavazzonis, Willaert, Buus; and later the Gabrielis and Merulo. At
least one of Buus's Ricercari (and only the toughest ears will face a
second) is basically monothematic. Yet the subjects cannot stand
up to it. Nor can I share the approval with which Mr. G. S.
Bedbrook, in his wide, fresh and enthusiastic survey, *Keyboard
Music from the Middle Ages*, quotes subjects by Giovanni Gabrieli.
They seem melodically aimless in outline.

Meanwhile, in Spain Bermudo ("Declaración de instrumentos
musicales") and de Sancta María ("Arte de tañer Fantasía") were

developing what we may call madrigal structures in the various Church modes, mainly in a vocal and imitational style. Sancta María aimed thus at spreading the craft of *fantasia*-making amongst the finger-tied. Like these, Antonio de Cabezón, organist and clavichordist to Charles V and Philip II, explored the modes in connexion with the eight psalm-Tones, in numerous short "Verses" (interludes to lighten the burden of "psalm droning") in imitational idiom, and in long "Tientos" or Ricercari for each Tone.* In the latter, fugue on one subject dissolves into madrigal structure, but occasionally this reliance on a succession of tuneful phrases is arrested by a final outburst of rhythmic impulses and keyboard bravura, as in the more bracing TIENTO FOR THE FIRST TONE. The last twenty bars are impressive. A plain falling phrase (D^I C^{I}D^I BG AB C^I) is developed (not too literally) three notes deep in descending sequence in Variation style, against triplets, a ♩ ♫♫ figure, sextuplets, and quarter-beats in turn. In such ornamented phrases Cabezón sounds happier and freer than in the fugal style. The TIENTO ON THE THIRD TONE, called *Fuga al contrario* (i.e. with answer by inversion) but no less madrigalian in plan, may impress Pedrell and other admirers, but if this be the genuine Cabezón, I should not blame the workaday monk who decided on such occasions "to retire to a deep cellar and wait for the All-clear," like a later member of the Drones' Club. In vol. 3 of his *Spanish School*, Pedrell quotes a letter from the critic, Karl Krebs, referring to Cabezón's "facility of creative technique," and Pedrell's own estimate of the composer as "the Spanish Bach" was later endorsed by Apel on account of his "exalted seriousness of purpose and complete contrapuntal mastery." "Complete" seems to me a definite misstatement, and while there is no doubt at all about the firm and advanced character of Cabezón's writing, especially in harmonic colour—Pedrell notes the augmented fifth (*passim*), a hint of the diminished seventh (bar 34 of the bravura Tiento discussed), and the constant integration of the modes over a common note—the diffuse structure of these fantasias of around 180 bars remains, and the much more spontaneous flow of the "Diferencias"

* See Note 9 on page 215.

or Variations on popular tunes (see the example in Apel, *Masters*) shows his truer métier, in a tradition peculiarly Spanish at first. Cabezón came to England in 1554, leaving behind him stray conjectures of "influence" on English music.

From sixteenth-century England itself an early, slight and barely legible or complete fantasia has survived (5, 465 *init.*), in which, after a repeated, meticulous scale-figure in jig rhythm, an abundant bravura at the top flourishes over a low bass in almost late-Beethoven manner. The first clear evidence of "Early Tudor" on the keyboard is the handful of eleven spinet pieces in a volume of miscellaneous music (Royal Appendix 58). In the most extended and distinctive, a Hornpipe by Aston (Apel, *Ib.*), the pervasive feature is a rhythmic bass of a few notes, over which the top part roams in symmetrical phrases or in a more bravura manner, or sometimes (as at first) in repartee, suggesting imitation. The texture is artificial and uncertain, but it is a genuine keyboard idiom, quite different from Schlick and not dependent on any Tone. The type of extension is Variation, not polyphony; the Spanish touch, perhaps (or another case of Cabbage Heads). The large collection of mainly organ pieces gradually compiled by Thomas Mulliner (30,513, transcribed for the *Musica Britannica* series) shows an equal fondness for using plainsong tunes as a mere pedestal (not necessarily in the bass) for musical acrobatics.

Example 49

Smaller collections of plainsong fantasias (15,233 and Royal Appendix 56) confirm this cultivation of virtuosity by Redford and others. But Mulliner's book also contains slight examples of the "vain voluntary"* that ignored plainsong for imitation's sake. Allwood's is a modest but coherent example of this pursuit of phrase, quoted by Hawkins amongst the admirably complete illustrations of his cumbersome *History* (Ex. 49).

* See Note 10 on page 215.

Mulliner gradually introduces his friends and posterity to Redford and the virtuoso Blitheman and Tallis, let loose on the keyboard. Then, in *My Lady Nevill's Book* (1591), published in 1924, the performer encounters the forcible personality of William Byrd. Later collections, 30,485 and *Forster's Virginal Book* (Royal Music), also favour Byrd. Numberless Pavans and Galliards, a few Grounds and many folk-song variations almost crowd out an occasional Fancy or Voluntary. In the mystical twenty-one pieces of *Parthenia*, or the virginals' maiden speech in print (selected and engraved by William Hole, 1612–13), the select "triumvirs" are Byrd, Bull and (introduced as the Orlando who "parallels di Lasso") young Gibbons, who provides the only fantasia. Yet there are further sizeable examples by Gibbons in *Cosyn's Virginal Book* (Royal Music), and a Flemish collection, dated 1628 and entitled "Tablature/Mr. Dr. John Bull" (23,623) is as rich in fantasia as in dance-pieces.*

But there are besides over twenty fantasias by various composers in the famous but rarely explored collection of virginal music in the Fitzwilliam Museum, Cambridge, published in 1899 and now known for a certainty to have been compiled (in the Fleet prison) by Francis Tregian (d. 1619), a Cornish Roman Catholic, as the editors sceptically conjectured on the score of internal evidence and their researches into the family history.† I shall refer to the book as T.V.B. It introduces the modern listener to the fantasias of Giles Farnaby, better known for his brief and polyphonic "Rest," and of Peter Philips, as well as of Byrd, Bull and Sweelinck. It is thus both comprehensive and *recherché*. The keyboard works of Gibbons and Weelkes (ed. M. H. Glyn) were published in 1925; of Byrd (ed. E. H. Fellowes) in 1950. Those of Bull (ed. Glyn) stopped at the second of four volumes, leaving nearly all his fantasias forlornly "under the counter." There they remain.

Putting together these stray surviving collections, we observe that the phrase-by-phrase ornamentation of Pavan and melodically derived Galliard, of folk-song and occasionally plainsong, has

* See Note 11 on page 215.
† See Note 12 on page 218.

become the main concern. It seemed as acceptable "argument" as the Toccatas of contemporary Italian music, not to mention the early devotion to Variation on the part of a later keyboard composer renowned for his discursive style, Ludwig van Beethoven. If the tune is at the top, it may be absorbed in figurative harmonic accompaniment in the same part, prophetic of Bach's G minor fugue, or mounted in free polyphony, with slight imitation. If the tune moves to lower voices, as in Byrd's "Walsingham" set, any rejoinder is at the octave, and still the tune. "Grounds" (Byrd, Cosyn) are commonly variations on themes composed to be bass; they, too, are occasionally invertible at the octave (*Nevill*, Second Ground); but their fixed rhythmic span precludes counterpoint. Only in FARNABY's "GROUND" (T.V.B. 240) is the pedestal elastic and movable and in fact half ground-bass and half polyphonic subject. The confusion is worth remembering for future developments. A similar sensation of a movable trapeze marks the development of hexachord formulae (*Ut re mi fa sol la, Ut mi re*, i.e. **d r m f s l, d m r**). Byrd's *Ut mi re* piece (Ib. 102) exploits close imitation at varying interval and augmentation, and in stiffer style Bull's almost notorious example (Ib. 51) explores a key-range that demands an "equal temperament" tuning commoner in later music. But these are too near the "Lesson" stage, in its most elementary sense, to be fruitful as wholes, or to be true fugue. They are held fast by process.

In this context of argument by ornamentation, the virtuoso stage of the translation of vocal line which has been observed since the Robertsbridge era, we gradually become aware—for the order of pieces in the Tregian and other collections is incredibly fortuitous—of the Voluntary-Fantasias, in which the subjects are totally optional in motive and mode, and original in their perfunctory style. The long FANTASIAS AND VOLUNTARIES OF BYRD show several extended examples of the type. The only common feature is an imitational start. There are three kinds of development*—

(i) The fugal style is replaced, sooner or later, by more homophonic sections in the manner of a Medley (T.V.B. 52,103).

* See Note 13 on page 218.

(ii) (*a*) A madrigal structure is maintained, quite often with capricious changes or decline of metre, up to a final sweeping dance-rhythm of six or nine beats, the after-stamp, so to speak, of the infectious "Carman's Whistle" or "Loth to depart" (Ib. 8 and the vast 261; Fellowes 8, from 30, 485);

(*b*) a similar dash of bravura makes an equally insouciant ending (*Nevill* 26 and 41; Fellowes 9, from Paris 1122).

(iii) Madrigals or string fantasies are ruthlessly transcribed (*Nevill* 29; Fellowes 6, from no. 15 of "Psalms, Songs & Sonnets" (1611); Fellowes 7 (R.C.M. 2093), of which, unnoticed by Fellowes, *half* is amongst the transcriptions from strings in B.M. 29, 996 and the equally odd other half is *Nevill* 42, in A minor and C, vain Voluntary, indeed, and by no means "rare"). If Byrd was aware of the Ricercar fantasia, it did not interest him. His satisfaction with these rambling and inconsequent pieces of counterpoint, six of 100–200 bars, is baffling, but the five or six copyists show connoisseur demand.

FARNABY'S eleven long FANTASIAS (T.V.B.) similarly halt between Medley, laboured transcript of Canzonets, and a wordless, aimless, madrigal-plan, with or without a final dash of rhythm or bravura. John Mundy (Ib. 2) and shorter examples by Nicholas

(The precise meaning of the ornament-sign appearing here can only be inferred from sundry and divers variants on record. Here an upper mordent seems indicated. See Thurston Dart, *The Interpretation of Music*, p. 120)

Example 50

Strogers (Ib. 89), John Lugge (Ch. Ch. 49) and "B–C" ("Cosyn" in a later hand: Ch. Ch. 1,113, Nos. 73 and the chromatic 62) go for a final bravura. Weelkes's two Voluntaries (Glyn) are negligible. Of the TOMKINS FANTASIAS I have seen (Ib. 59, 61 and *Bodl.*

Mus. Sch. C93), most employ an *Ut re mi* kind of theme, which they smother with notes. "Thomas Tomkins' offertory" amounts to over 300 bars on an almost equally trite one-bar "subject," which is later ironed out to AC¹ BC¹ D¹B A in Cabezón style. Compared with these extravagances, GIBBONS'S FANTASIES (Glyn, vols. 4 and 5) at least keep some proportion. Nos. 6, 7, 9 and 11 were evidently popular for some time. Gibbons's method varies between the madrigal type (nos. 8, 16 (*Parthenia*), 17, 18, and, more compact, 6 and 11), a blend of fugue and bravura (9) and Medley (7 and 19). In No. 9 imitation raises a learned head, Ex. 50, soon smothered in scales. The long six-phrase No. 16 has character, but remains inconsequential. The organ appears to be the instrument.

In all these works the keyboard either follows a line-upon-line course and cuts its losses in verbal articulation, or indulges in its own figurations *per se*. In nominal contrast, PETER PHILIPS'S FANTASIA IN G-Mixolydian (T.V.B. 84) repeats its plastic two-bar subject thirty-nine times (perhaps the Pauline "forty save one," as E. W. Naylor suggests) in a multiple repartee of subject and answer (15 to 24), with entries at double and half speed and in close canon. The subject is resourcefully used by Byrd in the twelve-fold opening (again numbered) of T.V.B. 261. Here it becomes a rhythmic measure, spasmodically polyphonic; fugued and grounded by turns, as it is major and modal by turns. (Cf. P. Cornet, *Fantasia 8 tuoni*, quoted by Ritter).

(*By kind permission of Breitkopf and Härtel, Wiesbaden*)

Example 51

Amongst this group BULL'S FANTASIAS (all but two or three remain unpublished) prove at once the most experimental and

the most historical. The Medley type appears in examples in
D minor,* A minor* and C (*Cosyn* 49; 23,623, nos. 22, 48).
The madrigal type is exhibited in two Ricercari (Ib., 51, 52) in
utterly vocal style, in the vast No. 45 in F with final bravura, and
in the D minor* (T.V.B. 108) with the second half dropping
impromptu and irrelevantly into Ground. But TWO FANTASIAS
IN A MINOR* (23,623, 15, 19) and TWO RICERCARI in F and D
minor* (47, 50) are nearer later fugue than any other English work.
In No. 15 the counterpoint, indeed, is bravura from bar 23, but

Example 52

the solemn, almost minatory subject persists, doubled a third
below in bars 33, 70. No. 19, a tribute to Sweelinck (d. 1621), is
described as "on," i.e. in expansion of, a fugue by that composer,
in whose *Works* (Seiffert) the fantasia can be found but not the
"fugue" (if any). Here an ascending semitonal subject dominates
the counterpoint, which is significantly imitative, florid and free
in turn, in Venetian style. A polar bear's cough makes a ripple
(they say) in the Sahara; but also in the Leipzig Fair! So, the
Bull digital movement can be discerned in the more orderly
proportions of an organ fugue in E flat of a century later. Bull
never entirely absorbed his showmanship in the fugal pattern,

* i.e. the Aeolian mode modified.

but his pursuit of a single contrapuntal theme has not yet received its true historical estimate (see also p. 216).

The Flemish provenance of these pieces is a reminder that Bull, like Philips, spent the end of his life abroad, partly in communication with Sweelinck. The movement towards Ricercar may so far be attributed to the influence of the distinguished Amsterdam organist

*Cuius fama Italos tetigit salsosque Britannos.**

He in turn shows a penchant for chromatic texture that may be due to Cabezón or Bull. Certainly, the FUGA CONTRARIA which Tregian's exceptional contacts enabled him to include as his No. 217, is as concentrated as it is dull. The method is confirmed in the fugal CHROMATIC FANTASIA of 196 bars in D minor. A nervous, semitonal subject and answer exploit a sequential counter-subject in ten entries, with close canon to follow; a fresh start produces a new counter-subject and secondary phrases which combine in turn with the subject at half speed, bravura, *stretto*, and feverish doubled speed over sustained dominant and tonic pedal-notes. The initial trenchancy wears thin halfway. This is followed in the Seiffert edition by a fantasia of 317 bars and six others on the same scale (nos. 3, 5, 8–11). The piling up of devices fails to convey a sense of musical purpose, but the cultivation of theme was an essential turn at right angles to the theme-as-you-go method, and proved far-reaching. Nos. 1–2 have dominant answers. They proved prophetic.

By some contact, not so far explained directly, Sweelinck brought his country's music to a terminal point in the Venetian style. In the same sense he gave the initiative to Germany. His pupils included the Halle composer, SAMUEL SCHEIDT. In the second Part of Scheidt's NEW TABLATURE, 1624, each number begins fugally, and then develops contrapuntal variants of the subject extended at half speed or less. No. 1, for example, harnesses exposition, counter-exposition with delivery at half and double speed, an interlude in triple metre with close canon, and further counterpoint of increasing vivacity. Fugue and variations

* Plemp, *Poemata;* quoted by Seiffert.

mingle in bland confusion. The second variation of No. 3 in G
thus forecasts A.F.2 in its bumpy rhythm. The third Part consists
of interludes on the "Magnificat" Tones, after the example of
Cabezón. These round off bouts of fugue and variation with a
melodious "Sicut erat" postlude with resounding cadences.
No. 5, on the fourth Tone, gives a noticeably semitonal version

Example 53

of the Phrygian mode (E to E, white notes). Perhaps the *Mater
Dolorosa* stands in the background. But the ear wearies of the
superfluous chromatics as much as of any Victorian pretence at
Passion music. The main feature of historical interest is the approach to harmony for its own sake. The cadence (Ex. 53B) anticipates Vaughan Williams's Mass. As fugue, Scheidt's openings
have a desperate way of sounding equally economic and increasingly alike and redundant. His re-creation of keyboard music is
demonstrative rather than aesthetically positive.

JOHANN PACHELBEL, from whose pupil, Johann Christoph
Bach, his younger brother Sebastian learnt the organ as a boy,
attacked the "Magnificat" Tones with equal persistence and a
more accomplished style.* His 94 POSTLUDES ON THESE TONES, as
we may call them, are each a fugue or fughetta, not a mixture of
methods. The harmonic texture is still in flux, the Mixolydian
and Phrygian modes being used in turn for the third (and in part
the eighth) and fourth Tones. But the major appears for the fifth
and sixth (and eighth) Tones, and the rest are more minor than
modal. In these "modern" groups the dominantward answer,
which launched at least a hundred good fugues later, is established.
Melodically, we can observe the awakening to life of a dry,

---

* See D.T.O. VIII, 2 (cf. B.M. 31,221) and D.T.B. IV, 1 for the organ fugues,
and D.T.B. II, 1 for the keyboard.

elongated, just human bone, in the progress of one subject.
No. 12 on the first Tone, and No. 1 on the sixth, are full double
fugues. Another double-fugue in the miscellaneous organ works,

Example 54

a RICERCAR IN F SHARP MINOR, arouses stronger conjectures of its
having jogged Bach. The second subject is not only doubly invertible but also strongly suggests to Bachian audiences the third
subject of W.K.ii, F sharp minor. The identity of key is decisive!
Pachelbel's keyboard works include seven fugues whose subjects
show more hand-mindedness, harmonic interest and rhythmic
shape than in the organ fugues. But the alternation of these
features is exhausting to the ear. The subject of No. 6 IN A, the

Example 55

only succinct subject, employs movement in thirds to keep it
alive, as in No. 5 IN G. Garrulity spoils the trenchancy of No. 7
in B minor. It is no surprise to learn that Pachelbel's last work,
"Hexachordum Apollinis"(!), comprises variation sets.
    The Pachelbel polish contrasts with the stiffer polyphony of
Froberger, court organist at Vienna, a pupil of Frescobaldi at
Rome, and later a striking visitor at the court of Charles II. In
his fantasias and Ricercari* the modal basis hardens all the transitions, and the division into sections in different tempi is disintegrating. The prevailing melodic curve cannot stand the wear and
tear of such triple fugue (e.g. in Fantasias 3 and 5). Yet it was
through this sectional fugue that BUXTEHUDE, for example,

* D.T.O. IV, 1 and X, 2.

expanded his craft. His ORGAN FUGUE IN G MINOR (No. 5 in Spitta's edition) embodies fugues on two subjects and a final fantasia in the modern "Medley" sense. In No. 7 (same key) one melodic line meagrely fertilizes three fugal movements. Buxtehude prefers fugues on separate subjects, sometimes joined by impromptu interludes and always "stirred well" by the whirling figures and massive harmony of a closing and often tedious rhapsody. The Buxtehude bravura attracted Bach, not the G minor and other dull fugues of Böhm, organist at Lüneburg. Böhm's métier was chorale-adornment.

In the "Fiori musicali" of FRESCOBALDI, which Bach copied out, the sectional method becomes set, in the Canzonas and Capriccios. Different metrical versions of a given curve suggest successive fugal stages. The second subject of a Canzona in G minor (Breitkopf edition, No. 42) was developed by Bach in his Canzona in D minor; but the main subject lacks character. In a more elaborate example in G (Ib. No. 58) a descending semitonal line appears in rhythms of four, three, four, six and four beats; but again the composer overdoes it. A similar *folie de grandeur* haunts the chromatic "Post il Credo" (Ib. No. 30) when it comes to augmentation. These lengthy ceremonial interludes were too much for Frescobaldi. A much-reprinted fugue in G minor (Torchi, *L'arte musicale in Italia*, vol. 3) is much more coherent, but Bukofzer has declared it spurious. Without information on the text, I should describe it as Handelian, advanced if of Frescobaldi's period, otherwise "passing in a crowd."* The double-fugue in E minor (Ib.), in multiple metre, has been ascribed to Georg Muffat.†

The actual environment of J. S. Bach's fugal approach, then, contains a barely established monothematic habit, and a modicum of decision not only in favour of major or minor but also of dominantward tonality, but scarcely a settled structural tradition, and no models of melodic character. Yet from this persistent economy German music took its strength, reaping the fruits in Bach, as later in Beethoven and Brahms. And without these

* See Note 14 on page 218.
† *Kirchenmusikalisches Jahrbuch*, 1893.

dogged ventures on rationed theme, fugue might have died out. It was not at all necessary to the fashionable pursuit of keyboard suite and variation. By the test of *galanterie*, Bach's fugues were out of date before they were written at all.

NOTES

1 (*Page* 193) Plain figures will indicate items in the Additional Manuscripts of the British Museum, where not otherwise stated; *Bodl.*, the Bodleian Library, Oxford. Facsimiles of early scripts can be found in J. Stainer, *Early Bodleian Music*, and more particularly in H. E. Wooldridge, *Early English Harmony* (vol. 1) and J. Wolf, *Geschichte der Mensural-Notation* (vol. 2), the last two offering modern transcriptions in further volumes. A few other relevant transcriptions can be found in A. Davison and W. Apel, *A Historical Anthology of Music* (vol. 1), Arnold Schering, *History of Music in Examples*, and, more particularly, W. Apel, *Masters of the Keyboard*. Dom Anselm Hughes, transcriber for Wooldridge, is invariably criticized for his rhythmic mistakes in translation, but the fact remains that *Early English Harmony* (vol. 2) has for over forty years been the only repository of commonly intelligible versions of most of the music of Harley 978 and all that of 28,550. It is a pity that it has not been reprinted with corrections.

2 (*Page* 194) One voice sounding with three argues or even jests (*Rerum Britannicarum medii aevi scriptores:* Satirical Poets, vol. 2, ed. T. Wright). So K. Kolb calls his collection of preludes and fugues for church use (1733) "*Lusus vocum inter se innocue concertantium.*"

3 (*Page* 194) See *Music Review*, IX, 2: article by Dr. B. Schofield, who has kindly advised me on the handwriting in this and the Robertsbridge scripts. "Sumer is i-cumen in" can be seen in coloured facsimile in *Grove's Dictionary*, 5th edition, vol. 7. The dances mentioned are in Wooldridge, and singly elsewhere. A similarly rhythmic tune, bursting into sudden and sheer harmony with equal revelry (*Bodl.* Douce 139), is quoted by E. Meyer in *English Chamber Music*. There are *hints* of canon in the earlier Notre Dame group. Available lists in Harley 978 and elsewhere suggest that there was far more music at Reading and its cell at Leominster than we know about.

4 (*Page* 195) In Vaughan Williams, "Folk-songs of the four Seasons," given as part of the Festival of Britain. The hall is built on what was ruined dockland.

5 (*Page* 196) In view of the constant *ou(v)ert* and *clos* indications of half and full closes, the title of the third piece appears to be "Retrove," not "Petrone," but neither shows any clear sense. The script test is dead against the growing theory started, I think, by Apel, that the "Italian" features in the mensural notation of the upper part point to a

foreign visitor (as such). The records at Penshurst Place show no Italian names.

There is no lack of evidence of continental contacts. Robertsbridge was a comparatively poor House, but wool contracts between it and the Frescobaldi of Florence date from the thirteenth century. All Cistercian abbots were under obligation to attend the annual Chapter General at Cîteaux in Burgundy. On Robertsbridge documents, see an appendix in Dr. R. A. Donkin's thesis on "The geographical significance of Cistercian Foundations in England" (Library of King's College, Newcastle-upon-Tyne). Nevertheless, it must be stressed that the Robertsbridge music (both sound and notation) remains solitary and insular evidence as it stands, under obligation to no foreign influence until earlier keyboard music of unequivocally foreign source is discovered. Pending this, the legitimate slogan is an unabashed "The nations not so blest," when it comes to music for its own sake. Not for nothing did the Abbey entertain Edward II in 1324! The script remains an isolated fragment in a historical void, probably typical but in the lack of other evidence unrelated and enigmatic.

6 (*Page* 199) See "Keyboard music of the 14th century in Codex Faenza 117" (D. Plamenac) in *The Journal of the American Musicological Society*, IV, 3 (1951). Cf. articles on Godendach/Bonadies in *Gazzetta Musicale di Milano* (1st September, 1889), *Atti e memori dell' Accademia di Scienze Lettere ed Arti di Modena*, serie V, vol. iv (1939), *Revue Belge d'Archéologie*, V (1940), p. 251, C. Schmidl's *Dizionario Universale dei Musicisti* (1888, 1927) and the new *Encyclopaedia, Die Musik in Geschichte und Gegenwart;* and the Faenza sections of *Inventari dei Manoscritti delle biblioteche d'Italia* (vols. 6, 26). Marpurg quotes the Bonadies "Kyrie" (nine bars) in his *Kritische Briefe*, II. 242. On that account this very plain "Kyrie" stole the academic limelight, not the wayward but historical plainsong setting.

In a further paper (I.M.S. Congress, Utrecht, 1952) Plamenac identifies *inter alia*—

(i) "Ballate" by Zacara, in one of which, "Un fior gentil," the opening section, repeated *da capo* later, may claim to be the first step towards keyboard fugue—

(*By kind permission of Dr. Plamenac*)

Example 56

(ii) Two "Masses," evidently for the Great organ, alternating with the choir, in contrast to the chekker likely elsewhere in the collection.

7 (*Page* 200) In his thesis, *Orgel und Klavier in der Musik des 16-Jahrhunderts* (1910). The letters of Nicolo Sagudino, secretary to the Venetian ambassador to Henry VIII, on the performances of Friar Dionisio, visiting and then resident organist, are interesting later confirmation of Italian prowess (Rawdon Brown, *Four Years at the Court of Henry VIII*).

8 (*Page* 200) See R. Eitner's pioneer article in *Monatshefte für Musikgeschichte*, 1887, and Mr. G. S. Bedbrook's new survey of the Buxheim book in *Music Review*, XIV, 4 (November, 1953).

9 (*Page* 202) *Obras de música*. See *Hispaniae Schola Musica Sacra*, vols. 4, 7 and incidentally 3, ed. F. Pedrell. The vast "Tiento" on the third Tone is quoted in full by Schering. Vol. 8 contains the Variations. A "Tiento a modo de canción" for the fourth Tone by Correa de Arauxo similarly combines a "madrigal" section in $\frac{4}{4}$, a slow interlude in triple metre, and a more rhythmic nine-beat exit. In the "Tientos" of Coelho (Lisbon, 1620; reprint, Schott) a similar waywardness of theme and step shows a more developed idiom.

10 (*Page* 203) See a 1555 entry under "Voluntary" in the *New English Dictionary*. The "Mean" (containing an ornamental middle part) by Blitheman, which Hawkins quotes with Allwood's Voluntary, is not "an ingenious Fugue" (*Grove*, 4th edition, s.v. "Mean") but a phrase by phrase setting of "Felix namque," twice as long as the Voluntary, in surprisingly vocal style, a contrast to the more typical "In nomine" in Tregian's book. A short Voluntary in vocal style by Redford is in Ch. Ch. 1034. Bull shows the influence of both composers.

11 (*Page* 204) Further and confirmatory fantasia-sources can be tapped in collections at Christ Church, Oxford (especially 1,113), the Bodleian (Tomkins), New York Public Library, the Paris Conservatoire of Music, and the National Library of Vienna (17,771).

The last collection, transferred from Venice in 1838 and consisting of pieces by Bull, except (quite certainly) for the first, is mainly in the "new German" tablature, with pitch-signs in letter-form and a wayward indication of octave and rhythm, marvellously economical of space (with a goose-quill) but communicatively ranging from the defiant to the utterly illegible or obscure. (The music department of the Library have obliged me with microfilms.) The first fantasia in the book, headed "Johan Bull 1621" is in fact an early copy—perhaps the first extant—of a fantasia which Eitner had published in 1871 as the work of Sweelinck, on the score of the composer's initials to be seen on the copy (c. 1625) he found, with two other Sweelinck fantasias, at the Grey Friary in Berlin. This was confirmed by the appearance of Sweelinck's full names in a collection made a decade later by "MW," i.e. Matthias Weckmann, who had studied under Jacob Praetorius, a

pupil of Sweelinck and the last person to think a Bull fantasia was by
Sweelinck. This chromatic fantasia has been discussed in its place
under its commonly assumed composer. The Vienna copy embodies
certain minor simplifications of the passage-work, which led the
Sweelinck editor, Max Seiffert, to declare the copyist a South German
(*Keyboard Works*, 1943 edition), but the essential counterpoint and most
of the figuration are there throughout. It is inconceivable that Bull
could have developed so closely constructed and closely woven a piece.
Somehow a confusion arose about authorship. Some clerical copyist
(the set is embossed for a prince of the church) was told that Bull was
the composer, possibly after a memorable performance by him after
Sweelinck's death—and believed it. As organist of Antwerp Cathedral,
Bull had become an established Dutch virtuoso, in the company of his
Amsterdam colleague in art, composed a fantasia described as "on a
fugue by Sweelinck" late in 1621, apparently as a memorial tribute,
and may well have played the chromatic fantasia in the same context,
with a resultant misunderstanding.

The next fantasia in the Vienna set shows clearly enough Bull's
habitual style, or rather manner. A semitonal subject, moving painfully up and hectically down half an octave, steadily appears at one
speed or another, but after ten bars of nervously insistent polyphonic
imitation, the texture collapses, as usual, in favour of the main Point,
set to a monotonous bravura accompaniment, the last word in jejune
illustration of what some text-books call the Third Order of Counterpoint and actually anything but contrapuntal; for example—

a a b c . d e f g : a¹ g f e . d c b a

against **f : f sharp**. This brief fantasia in A minor of under fifty bars is
cognate to the fantasia on a fugue by Sweelinck, noticed above. The
third fantasia (G minor) has a more rhythmic subject, curiously blending a dactylic monotone with a simple flourish. It is maintained for a
score of bars, only to stop. After "The King's Hunt" and a "Salve
Regina" setting comes a fourth fantasia, in D minor, much more
extended but expanding stiffly and distractedly, with quaint flimsy
cadences, Medley in pattern. Close imitation forms a reasonably
trenchant progression of discords by suspension, after the manner of
Bennet's "Weep, o mine eyes," but (after a fade-out in the third line of
the script) this dissolves into bravura, dominant pedal, etc., with
numerous stops, and a string of trite formulae to round off the fantasy.
After an immense set of canons comes a long fantasia in G modal-major
on *Ut re mi fa so la*, of which the beginning is evidently missing, for the
script starts in the middle of an ascent of the formula from C sharp. It
proves to be a copy, beginning at the twelfth bar, of Fantasia No. 51 in
T.V.B. (imitated later in A. Ferrabosco's string Fancies, one of which is

quoted by Walker from Christ Church MS 233 in *Musical Antiquary*, 1912). The notation is absurdly positional—e.g. G sharp appears as the minor third of F—but the text constantly corrects Tregian's script, reading, for instance, F natural (A. and B.) with the last A of the penultimate phrase, and restoring a missing B in the final, almost Parryish cadence, whose bass should end—

$$\mathbf{e\ d:c} \mid : b \mid \mathbf{c}: \mid : g \mid \mathbf{g}$$

The final choice of fantasia confirms the copyist's prophetic interest in the new "romantic" style for its own sake, long before Bach made it a vehicle for strained expression. (See *Monthly Musical Record*, Nov., 1954).

The set thus reveals Bull moving moodily and uncertainly towards monothematic fugue in his customary light-fingered manner, fugal and bravura by turns or in the two hands independently. That in one particular fantasia (the first of the set) Bull should have suddenly and exclusively disciplined his style, with the logical Ricercar now published (Novello) in Sweelinck's name, is beyond belief. Even the chromatic lute fantasias, such as Dowland's "Farewell" and an anonymous Fancy in D minor (*English Lute Music*, ed. D. Lumsden) show far more organization of contrapuntal figures, changing constantly in Dowland, more repetitive in the other piece. Bull is included in both the volumes that Weckmann compiled of music received, apparently, through his coach from Sweelinck, as "object-lessons"—others, beside Sweelinck himself, are Byrd, Farnaby, Philips and Gibbons—but not, I guess, as a master of fantasia. (An interim statement, based on microfilms, will follow; see p. 218.) English music counted abroad then.

A chromatic fantasia by another contributor, Erbach of Augsburg, recalls Sweelinck in spirit and in the letter (D.T.B. IV, 2). In part (57 bars) this, too, has been falsely and foolishly attributed, owing to mere proximity to numerous named pieces in a set of 364, to van den Kerckhoven, a composer of the next, more homophonic period (*Monumenta Musicae Belgicae*, Vol. 2, No. 126). Erbach was preceded by Lohet of Stuttgart (fughetta in C, cf. W.K. ii, E) and abroad by de Macque (three-subject fugue and a Capriccietto expanding Bull's Ricercar in F) and Luython, whose chromatic Ricercar in A rambles less than the "Fuga suavisima" of seductive title (M.M.B. Vol. 4). Erbach's pupil was Klemm (thirty-six short and formal fugues): Klemm taught Weckmann! Abroad, Guillet was writing fantasias in the twelve modes, on plain but persistent phrases. By 1650, fugue was just holding its own here and there. Cf. Seiffert-Fleischer, *Gesch. der Klavierm.*, I, 101 *et seq.*

Professor Joseph Muset's *Early Spanish Organ Music* (Schirmer) assembles nineteen pieces "from manuscripts found in various Spanish

churches," with an account of the organ in Barcelona Cathedral, whose
Great and Choir date back to 1540. There are Tientos by P. de Soto
and P. A. Vila, each in a jejune vocal style, and a physically vigorous
fugue in G minor by J. Oxinagas (eighteenth century). The plain
fantasias of Fuenllana (1554) for guitar forecast the Ricercar trend.

12 (*Page* 204) The identification of Tregian's signature (in his will)
is described by Elizabeth Cole in *Music and Letters*, October, 1951.
See also the July, 1951, number for an account of another and vaster
collection of vocal and instrumental ensemble-music, definitely in the
same script as the Virginal Book, but unearthed in 1950 and at that time
as conjectural in authorship as in 1899.

13 (*Page* 205) The Fantasias and Voluntaries can all be found together in the Fellowes edition of Byrd's keyboard works, somewhat
arbitrarily "edited." Failing this, in which the sources are clearly
stated, the readiest reference to another published version may be
useful to some readers, and is given in the text, where available.

14 (*Page* 212) A thorough, more sympathetic account of Frescobaldi's fuguemanship can be seen in an article by Dr. H. Redlich in
Music Review, XIV, 4 (November, 1953).

ADDITION TO NOTE 11

The four hundred pages (333–66) of the two Weckmann sets cited
above contain some ninety pieces by named or known composers, with
over a score of anonymous items. In the former class, Sweelinck and
Erbach account numerically for a good half, and for nearly all the
fantasias and ricercars. The remainder of these are: Cornet, D minor;
Gabrieli, 9th Tone, A minor and 4th Tone, E minor; Merula, chromatic capriccio in D minor, humorously described as 1st Tone, and
canzons in C from the 1615 set; and, at the very last in the collection,
Byrd with the redoubtable G major, T.V.B. 261, etc., and, as an odd
anti-climax, what must be a transcription from strings, *Nevill* 29. The
thirty-two English pieces consist chiefly of variations on popular song
and dance tunes by Bull, Giles and Richard Farnaby, Gibbons, and
Leonard Woodson, and some dance pieces. The French pieces are just
corantos by de la Barre and others. For documentary fugue, then,
Sweelinck preferred, after his worthy self, the dull but pursuant method
of Erbach, not the voluble false counterpoint of Doctor Bull, or the
smooth-flowing but thematically wayward fancies of Gibbons. Who,
after Bach, can doubt the Amsterdam composer's prophetic soul?

(I wish to thank the following: the Deutsches Musikgeschichtliches
Archiv, Kassel, for a microfilm of the two sets; Durham University
Library, for the use of an enlarger; Mr. O. W. Neighbour of the
British Museum, for referring me originally to Seiffert's account of the
first set; and Dr. F. Blume, for enabling me to locate the microfilm.)

Chapter XVIII

FUGUE AFTER BACH

WE have now summarily observed musical man's early rehearsal of keyboard fugue, from its first flickers in vocal canon and Chase and in ex-vocal keyboard adaptation. After near-extinction in the jejune subjects, endless phrases or overwhelming finger-work of Renaissance fantasia, and much confusion with variation at the next stage, fugue found orderly structure and consistent texture in Pachelbel and a more ambitious and rhapsodic development in Buxtehude. These and others were directive enough to set Bach on his unpredictable and unparalleled fugal career, first on the broader lines of freely episodic fugue on the organ, and then in pursuit of a more subtle and intimate creative impulse. Finally Bach gave himself up to fugue for its own sake. In Chapter XVI an account was given of the firm rationale which illuminates the varied stages of exposition and development, from early works to "The Art of Fugue." Much more often than not, Bach's craftsmanship transcends the level of composition by rule, and the only common feature of any importance is the replenishment of the basic harmony by means of fresh counterpoint, a new subject or the challenge of a diversionary episode; in other words, the achievement of variety in unity, the aim of all construction. The satisfaction of musical needs, alike in the choice of subject (and its periphery) and in the choice of treatment in sheer fugue or in reinforcement by fugue, is perpetually revealing, and our discernment of the composer's final resort to a more automatic and perfunctory choice of matter and structure in inversionary fugue is challenging. Could fugue go any further beyond such calculated processes and, if so, how far could Bach's patterns and methods be maintained without decadence or a note of parody?

Formally, fugue surprisingly continued in the background of the later eighteenth and nineteenth centuries, and beyond. An inevitable channel for vocal response in some choruses of Haydn and Mozart, of Schubert and Brahms and Verdi, it woke Beethoven's muse to fresh ecstasy in the Mass in D and in some piano sonatas and string quartets. Beethoven's coach for counterpoint was Albrechtsberger, an inveterate fugue-writer, and on the organ, especially, cumulative fugue has exercised a fascination to this day. But by Bach's standards of quality, all fugue after him was either occasional or artificial, and, when made the pattern of a complete keyboard piece, a conscious throw-back to a past period. His life-research into fugue revealed itself in the end as a historical imperative, as something that must happen sometime —in the discovery of the missing principle of unity—as a logical fulfilment of the first stroke of contrapuntal imitation which, at first almost accidentally (by late entry) but in the event inevitably, made Chase a musical habit for its own sake. But so complete an exposition could not be repeated! It could only be extended, tapering to a thin point of receding significance. Thus creative fugue became either an odd *jeu d'esprit*, or the accessory of a wider structure, or a precise and *recherché* process so stiff as to suggest the "rehearsals" of deliberate humour, or else to be downright homiletic. Sometimes the contrapuntal pressure is relaxed in favour of a melodic treatment of the subject, making fugue a lapse into Variation and Ground on earlier lines. It took Beethoven's powers of integration to break into sheer melody and harmonic progression and grand-piano sonority without jettisoning a fugal start. Most composers, having determined their subject, rely on elbow-grease to keep it polished, and so maintain their derivative impact. The nadir of this imitative process was reached and passed in some choruses of the Victorian oratorio that no one remembers. Indeed, to make a piece sound like a fugue is quite practicable, so that fugue-writing has long been a recurrent feature in the derivative composition which graces English college and diploma courses. The inner life of a fugue has been reduced to that of a puppet put through its paces.*

An apparently vast field of starters thus soon thins to a select few, with a number of "sport" variants that more or less cancel

* See Note 1 on page 249.

out, and a background of numberless efforts towards artificial respiration. The subject of this chapter can be condensed from the immense collection of often isolated and esoteric pieces, extant in print, to a critical issue, the mastery of which is patently rare. The unquestionable and historic aftermaths are common experience, and in the remainder it is unnecessary to mention every variant of pure fugue since Bach, for there is no prospect of its proving permanent. Fugue now survives as a way of developing texture. The old power of fugue to dispose entries in a coherent structure has gone with the collapse of tonality and of the hierarchy of key from tonic and dominant. But the spasms of fugal revival in the century after Bach are none the less interesting as a test of the survival-value of his musicianship and of some details of his thematic development. As such, they form an essential completion of our main subject. We may now consider the genuinely characteristic works concerned, with selected examples of the more indistinguishable but persistent output.

It is natural to compare, first, the fugal work of Handel. A master of many styles, a German by birth and once a candidate for Buxtehude's post, Handel was not likely to ignore fugue. Fugal choruses and incidents abound, some in immediate double-fugue, and there is a handful of keyboard fugues. But Handel used fugue chiefly as an economical, elastic plan for vocal entry, with or without orchestral refrain and further matter. He relied on a good subject and his fine vocal grasp, with a sense of the dramatic for climax, for an articulate chorus is not just a polyphonic medium but the voice of a participant in, or epic observer of, human affairs at varying range. (The prolonged pomposities of "He trusted in God" miss this dramatic touch.) Many choral answers are at the octave; the fresh texture is deemed contrast enough for the common listener expected. Handel rarely tried to argue in music. Nor did he pursue fugue noticeably for its own sake. He knew what he wanted, but he left fugue very much as he found it, apart from the epic contexts in which he immortalized the imitational style. Where these failed him, as in "Amen," he fell back on canonic commonplace and rhetorical close. It is significant that the resourceful "Let all the angels" is only thirty-seven bars, while the artificially extended "Amen" comes near bathos, after the concentration of "Hallelujah." Of the Six Fugues for harpsichord or organ (Peters, 4c), No. 1 in G minor (of which Beethoven copied out eight bars—MS 29,801) and No. 3 in B flat are loose double-fugues in near-vocal style, and No. 4 in B minor relies on a monotonous counter-phrase to revive its vocal subject halfway. Nos. 5 in A minor (*two* falling sevenths; later doubly reduced to a Plague, in *Israel*) and 6 in C minor compare naturally with Bach's more memorable fugues of half the size on similar subjects in these keys in W.K.ii. Here again, Handel's vocal texture wears thin. He writes (or plays) for a listener like Burney who is more interested in a re-echoing and *chantant* subject than in any polyphonic incident. His vocal counterpoint can be grotesque, as in "He led them" (*Israel*).

In 1747 J. E. EBERLIN, organist at Salzburg, published NINE TOCCATAS AND FUGUES. Fugue No. 1 in D minor is a reasonably

Example 57

well-worked expansion of its shapely subject. There is a reprint (Novello). Nos. 2, 5 and 7 are double-fugues. The eventual blend of arpeggio figure and conjunct ascent in No. 5 in C may be compared with Bach's Weimar C, plainer in main subject, as an example of the letter and the spirit. No. 2 in G minor has more

character. A common sequence of descending sevenths (l't, s'l)
in the subjects imparts a family resemblance to Nos. 6 in F, 7 in D
and 8 in G. No. 4 in E Phrygian minor keeps to the tonic and
dominant (A) throughout its eighteen entries. No. 9 in E minor
similarly wears its chromatic subject to the bone. How it once
found a place in vol. 9 of the Peters edition of Bach's organ works,
and why transposed down a semitone, I cannot say.* In England
Thomas Roseingrave published six double-fugues (1750) in loose
rhetorical style, and Philip Hart published three fugues for organ
or harpsichord (1704); one remains in manuscript (34,695, 42).
Hart wrote a song, "Simandra wears a grandeur in her mind,"
but, except for a rhythmically elaborate subject in No. 3 in F,
Simandra's spirit does not penetrate these fugues, apart from the
crude play of phrase. They seem to reflect the distrait nature of
English string fantasia in the seventeenth century. The promise of
Ward's freshness of phrase, for example, is not fulfilled, except by
the temperamental Purcell, and even in Purcell structure found
no abiding landmark, although fugue was recognized in Simpson's
Compendium of first-aid to composers (1557).

The later eighteenth century contains many other fugal ghosts,
some well-known for more general achievements. They can be
morbidly disinterred, with some earlier and later figures of similar
standing, in fugal sets eventually published together as *Auswahl
vorzüglicher Musik-werke* (*Selection of notable musical works*:
Berlin, 1835), henceforward V.M. here. This curious collection
contains a cross-section of fugue from Palestrina ("Tu es Petrus")
to Reissiger, taking in Haydn and Mozart. Here one may observe
the once famous HASSE in a CHRISTE ELEISON with a subject which
by a compromising answer (s la : fe s, d' ma' : t d') typically
avoids the spiritual stretch of Bach's comparable "Kyrie." Here,
also, are some HAMBURG FUGUES: a loose choral double-fugue
from a motet, "Kündlich gross," by "Kaiser," is not by Keiser
but Kayser (Zürich); but we find a long fugue in A minor on a
chromatic subject by Telemann; and a broad redemptive choral
double-fugue by C. P. E. Bach, whose combined themes unbend
after a taut minor start, as in A.F. 8.† A *Musikalisches Vielerley*

---

* See *Grove's Dictionary*, s.v. "Eberlin."   † See Note 2 on page 249.

(*Musical Miscellany*) edited by Emanuel contains a FANTASIA IN F BY J. E. BACH, which ends with a fluent, insouciant fugue in a sonorous style (Pauer, *Alte Claviermusik*, iii). V.M. introduces, besides, FUGUES BY J. C. BACH; and by the theorists, KIRNBERGER AND MARPURG,* one in B flat with a mannered, chromatic and invertible subject in vocal style, the other inevitably in D minor (see Ex. 59D) but not Ricercar; a fugue in B flat (op. 2) with a submediant start by Eberlin's pupil, P. G. PASTERWIZ, who published fugues in eights (op. 1, 2, 3) in an apparent search—especially in op. 3—for an original turn of subject; and a loose and academic double-fugue in D minor (op. 1, no. 2) by F. L. Gassmann, whose choice of medium in this and other fugal movements for string quartet provides a parallel to Mozart's arrangements of Bach's fugues, to be discussed later. In his quartets op. 1 Gassmann (d. 1774) derives his finale from a double fugue in the first two; in the other four, from the Minuet type not uncommon in Wagenseil and other symphonists. In six posthumous quartets Gassmann begins each with Adagio/Andante and Fugue, a likely jog for Mozart and, incidentally, Albrechtsberger. The prophetic fugue in Arne's fourth harpsichord sonata has a facile sequential subject (cf. Nos. 2 and 6 of his *Eight Overtures*).

In the world of fugue, Mozart is the composer that springs to mind from Alanus's prophetic phrase, *litigat immo iocatur* (argues or rather jests); not only in the "Musical Joke," an engaging fugal imposture on a spineless, inimitable subject. The piano fugues put the subject through its paces with a jaunty competence typical of Mozart at his most equivocal. The three-voice fugue which emerges, in an atmosphere of calculated suspense, in the keyboard FANTASIA IN C (K. 394) thus seems to toy with a symmetrical subject and pernickety (but sequential and useful) counter-subject, as Wagner treats Beckmesser's *coloratura*. In fugue Mozart favours four or five stages of swift primary-key statement and wider development in turn. Minor keys are thus "litigating" by bar 10. The first restatement includes a close canon (A.B.). The bass is at lazy, relaxing half-speed, not confirmed but instead springing back in automatic, amusing sequences

---

* See Note 2 on page 249.

at double speed, resembling a frightened parrot. These lend a certain aristocracy to the final entry of the bass with an extension of the initial figure in lieu of the full subject, recalling W.K.ii, C. Of the two fugues for four hands, the G MINOR FOR ONE PIANO (K. 401) relies almost entirely on its succinct subject, which, being tied to tonic and dominant harmony, invites translation. A taut E minor is reached in bar 40, the inverted subject colours a full restatement, and the possibilities of canonic and combined entry are exploited, as in A.F. 5, and indeed exhausted before the end. The FUGUE IN C MINOR FOR TWO PIANOS (K. 426) moves on similar lines, with a much more marked subject and many uncompromising turns. One would guess that the earlier fugue became an exercise for the later, with a correspondingly tough but no less invertible theme. In both the use of patent contrivances is in a vein more comic than serious, somewhat as in Shakespeare's tragi-comedy.* Mozart set K. 426 for strings (?), with fine adagio. Prince Radziwill used this (augmenting 14 bars) to usher in—Faust!

Mozart is more himself in the contrasted fugue of the finales of the G minor and C major symphonies (K. 550, 551): the first in a sudden, single and consistently tense development, the second in spasmodic bursts of high spirits—a cheerfully transitional exposition and restatement (bars 36, 189, 237), and penultimately a cumulatively quintuple combination, the abandon of which on a trifling but decisive signal for the terminus is one of fugue's best jokes at its expense. (The symbolic combination of tradition and temperament in "Meistersinger," on the other hand, is spoilt by its repetition as a routine jog to Sachs's last lecture. Apparently Wagner's experience of English oratorio served as a complete inoculation against any fugal writing, even to suggest Beckmesser. The parody is entirely of excessive melodic ornament and figure. Beckmesser thus recalls Pachelbel (fugue in F).)

Amongst other Mass music, the CUM SANCTO SPIRITU of Mozart's unfinished MASS IN C (K. 427) is an extended fugue. The subject, gravitating to the mediant (implying tonic chord) lends itself to canon at the octave, above or below, in an ultracadential

* See Mary Lascelles, *Shakespeare's "Measure for Measure."* (Cf. MS. 28,966.)

style. Mozart first lets the cadence reverberate against a wall of tonic sound (T.S.), and then suddenly diverts it to the key of the submediant (bar 29, cf. 106). At the later restatements he varies the issue by making the second note the keynote (**d f m** becoming **s d¹ t**) and then changing back, or by oscillating mid-

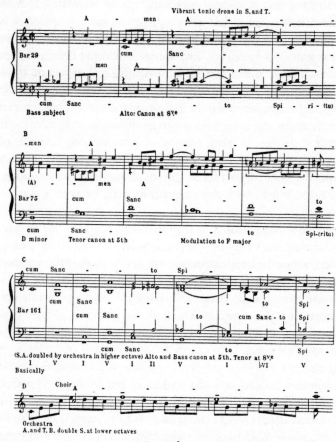

Example 58

way (bars 99, 121). A submediant entry similarly recovers the tonic at the end (bar 113). Thus the slump to the mediant never becomes a snare. Alternatively, the canon enters a bar earlier, at the fifth, making another chain of cadences available (bars 54, 75). The inverted subject, in canon at the octave, establishes a

firm point of penultimate suspense which turns to trenchant and
subversive harmony. It remains to recover the initial breadth
without being too literal, first by multiplying canon at the fifth
by canon at the octave and slithering out of the groove of
tonality (Ex. 58c); then by delivering the theme in manifold
canon at the octave at zero, with an equally unisonal orchestral
figure pointing fresh harmony. Thus Mozart, too, employs
canonic devices to avoid harmonic stagnation, filling the polyphony with vivacious counter-phrases (owing much to the
counter-subject) and indulging in more rhythmic repartee, choral
and orchestral, than Bach usually does. The combination of a
smooth-flowing fugue with an overwhelming sweep of basic
rhythm—rather than any structural advance—is Mozart's con-
tribution to fugal history. How "deep" the music is, in an old
College phrase, may be questioned, but after a bracing "Quoniam"
for interwoven solo-voices this fugue can sound at least brilliantly
conclusive, given the necessary vocal agility. Ecstatic it is not.

   The setting from earlier Mass music (K. 262) which usually
fills the gap at ET VITAM VENTURI forms another final fugue. Here
part of the subject in canon makes basic counterpoint at once
(T.B.). (This is practical because now **d f m** in the answer can be
made **s d¹ t** in the canon to it.) This canon below or above
entries is exploited in various keys, and increasingly shortened
canons in random sequence avoid tedium. The here single
restatement is amplified by new combinations—
       (i) reversed accent and double canon (B.A.S.T.);
      (ii) earlier canon and re-accented subject (B.T.A.S.).
The tail of the subject can now sweep the music home. The short,
probably early, OSANNA (K. 427) is a loose double-fugue in brilliant double-choir style. The final entry of the subject (A1, A2)
against another wall of tonic, and then of the extended counter-
subject against a more massive dominant pillar, strengthens the
close. The KYRIE of the REQUIEM MASS leads into a solid but
scarcely revealing double-fugue, with the counter-subject at two
intervals. With Handel's outline ("And with his stripes")
echoing throughout, I find this a confusing fugue. With it may
be grouped the partial double-fugue of Haydn's end-choruses in

The Creation and elsewhere, and of his quartet in F minor (op. 20, no. 5), anticipated by the triple fugue in the four-violin concerto by the Naples composer, Leo.

Haydn used fugue to start a chorus or section, but no more; the subject becomes a melodic motive, as in "The heavens are telling," magnificent but not fugue. Most of Haydn's fugue-endings are laboured.

Besides writing a small Gigue (K. 574) in a witty Bach-*galant* style at Leipzig, Mozart set FIVE BACH FUGUES FOR STRING QUARTET (K. 405): W.K.ii, C minor, E flat, E, D sharp minor and D. The fugues exchange the modest cut of the harpsichord for the individuality and sensual vibrance of four strings. The E major sounds particularly appalling so, i.e. with the unremitting vibrato of today. There are also arrangements of SIX FUGUES FOR STRING TRIO (K. 404A), which survive in two similar copies and must be attributed to Mozart in the complete absence of any credible alternative, for each fugue is supplied with a prelude. Two preludes are Bach's. The second and third movements of the second organ sonata become a prelude and (by courtesy!) a fugue in E flat–C minor; the second movement of the third organ sonata and A.F. 8 make another pair in F–D minor. But for J. S. Bach's fugues W.K.i, E flat minor and ii, F sharp major and minor (now in D, F and G), and W. F. Bach's double-fugue in F minor, there are graceful new preludes of 24–45 bars in the balanced stages of a miniature adagio. Thus curiously, at the bidding of a back-to-Bach patron, the Baron van Swieten, did the *galant* cavort with the *gelert*. Bach who himself had arranged the organ movement in F for a concerto (see p. 109) was now out-Bached. A minor interest of this incident is the fortuitous circumstances. Van Swieten, Court Librarian, had heard of Bach's fugal prowess from King Frederick II, and later from Marpurg and Kirnberger, and he ended by obtaining from Emanuel copies of his father's fugues in what must have then been rare abundance. Thus casually did Mozart come to know the intimate art of J. S. Bach, whose misconstrued renderings of polyphony he was only too ready to re-translate in glamorous string *timbres*. There is a parallel for the preludial accessions.

HAYDN wrote INTRODUCTIONS of 20–70 bars FOR SIX FUGUES FOR STRING TRIO by his predecessor at Esterhaz, G. T. Werner, arranged FOR QUARTET. The *Grave* for No. 4 in C minor is noteworthy, both for its fine and close texture, and for its treatment of a melodic curve (**d t₁ la s**) from which stemmed elements in Beethoven's op. 132, 133 and 131. But here the fugues (doublefugues in three cases) achieve greatness, if anything; it is not thrust upon them at the expense of the composer's intentions.

In his *Guide to Composition* (vol. 2, chapter 150) the Viennese organist, J. G. Albrechtsberger, to whom Beethoven came for counterpoint, commends fugue as most necessary to church music and productive of the most elevating impression in vocal and instrumental music. With the same humility as Haydn, who admitted he was "forced to become original," Albrechtsberger elsewhere remarked, "It is no merit of mine that I make good fugues, because I never have an idea that cannot be used in double counterpoint." Chapter 151 quotes W.K.ii, C minor and E as

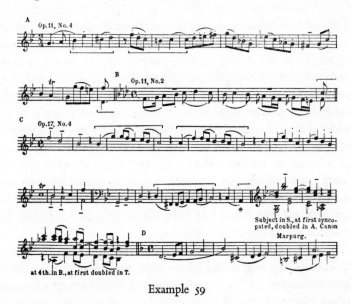

Example 59

examples of augmentation and diminution. But a little further appears a fugal subject of ascending sixths in the bass, falling sequentially (d¹ la¹ ta s¹ la f¹ s–ma¹ r¹ d¹) to the words "Et nar-ra-bo oper-a, o-pera Domi-ni." This echo of the psalms (from the offertory, "Dextera Domini") may serve as an ominous text for the over fifty fugues ALBRECHTSBERGER had published "for the harpsichord [later, piano] or organ"(!), in editions of mainly six apiece, and for the many Adagios and Fugues he produced, equally in sixes, for studiously varied string ensembles. Nothing, it seems, could stop this Master Hugues, though his fugues were not mountainous. Key-schemes were one stimulus (op. 1 in A, B flat, C, D, E flat, E, F, G, A, major or minor or both*; op. 6 and 11 respectively in G, D, A and F, G, A, major and minor; op. 16 in C, D, E♭, F, G, A major). Examples of short and long subjects from OP. 11 may be quoted, and then from OP. 17, the latest traceable. The F minor, a fugue of sixty bars, relies on free counterpoint, with a fresh bravura counter-subject in bar 46 ("pedal"). At the finish of the G minor the bass drops the subject after four bars, and the soprano entry (complete) acquires a tonic pedal; it is all easy-going. The congealing effect of the eight-bar subject of the B flat fugue can be readily imagined, but inversion and close canon in thirds (S.A., B.T.) add fresh touches. The next two fugues in op. 17 are on folk-song phrases in lilting four-bar symmetry, fatally and prophetically melodic, and a decline from Bach's G minor. The sets of chamber-music adagios and (usually) double-fugues, later with further movements to make a whole quartet (Op. 2, 13, 20, 21), bear out the composer's confidence in organic counterpoint, and confirm the fashion for strained adagio and a fugue of release. They offer the critic no seriously new matter. Albrechtsberger's prolific but derivative craft has been detailed here as an awful example of relying on a form which even in Bach's time had had hard wear. It is also a forbidding reminder that sincerity is not enough.

The spell of fugue was, indeed, still bewitching. In the first of SIX FUGUES for organ and piano Op. 29 (?1808), dedicated to Albrechtsberger, the Viennese composer JOSEPH LIPAVSKY expands a plain, rather pompous D major subject, aiming at a trenchant and pertinent coda (after pause) by means of close canon and

* See Note 3 on page 250.

chromatic harmony. The treatment is similar for grave No. 2 in D minor, light No. 3 in A, and solemn No. 5 in C. No. 4 in A minor obtains rather more from a chromatic descent, with a fresh counter-subject halfway and a rhetorical coda. CLEMENTI, who combined a wide interest in piano composition *per se* with a respect for Bach—he was the former owner of the London autograph of W.K.ii—wrote a FUGUE IN F (V.M.), and THREE OTHER FUGUES (Op. 6) for the harpsichord, all with shapely subjects, equipped both for episode and for Handelian exposure later. An elastic range of key, fudged *stretti* and plenty of casual bravura and cadence produce a feeling of ease and amusement, but not of argument. Clementi published "Musical Characteristics," a collection of preludes and cadences aping various styles. Here, it seems, is his unconscious parody of classical fugue, revelling in jejune sequences after more exuberant fancy, like the recurrent did-you-ever and I-mean-to-say of a professional humorist. The London recitalist, THOMAS ADAMS, known for a quarter of a century as the "Thalberg of the organ," wrote TWENTY-ONE FUGUES of varied character (34, 693). To make an end of this "also ran" list J. J. JONES, a pupil of Crotch and a London organist, published SIX FUGUES for organ or piano, of which No. 1 in D, with a rising conjunct subject, displays inversions (at fifth and third), close canons and half-speed entries. No. 2 in E flat, which Walter Parratt used to play at St. George's Chapel, Windsor, uses a more mannered subject with similar resource, but the part-writing is often obscure. No. 4 in C adds a second subject. Fugal composition has settled down to a state of rest, or movement in a straight line, pending a fresh motive-force. The derivative work of Attwood and Sebastian Wesley did not alter the outlook in the cathedral organ loft.

Beethoven almost possessed Albrechtsberger's mastery of double counterpoint, but he did not share his teacher's reverence for fugue in itself. For him fugue was always a *modus operandi* at a difficult moment, like sonata-form, never a self-contained orbit. (Discount the succinct and "romantic" early piano fugue of thirty-eight bars in C (29,801, f. 158)* and the late experimental

* First published in *The Musical Times*, February, 1955.

quintet, misnumbered Op. 137!) The first fugues to be noticed are the FINALES of the sonatas OP. 106 and 110. We may consider the latter first, since it is simpler. It may be heard in three stages—

(i) A balanced fughetta of eighty-nine bars, in which the counter-subject is mainly a sonorous support to the symmetrical subject, but appears also up a twelfth, a thirteenth, twelfth and fourteenth.

(ii) Return of the previous "Arioso," as a revealing episode.

(iii) A second fughetta, beginning with the inverted subject in a remote key, using the (normal) augmented subject casually in still distant keys, and the diminished subject for counter-subject in the transition (*meno allegro*) to a blunt restatement.

The whole movement shows the perceptible passage of a theme from fugal subject to ground-bass (in changing key) and finally to a melodic appeal. The middle preponderance of G tonality in this A flat movement lends special impact to the recovery of theme later. The lame descent of the inverted subject is at once taken in hand, in a bracing answer (**s r, f d** in D) and relaxed extra entry. Nothing is left to the caprice of the scale at such slippery turns. Fugue reaches here a point of mainly acoustic contrast (bass and transcendent soprano), but it has served its turn in securing concentration and pertinent detail.

The FINALE OF OP. 106 IN B FLAT is also broadly a three-voice fugue, twice the size of its successor. It may be heard in two stages—

(i) Exposition and development of an extended and explosive subject (with abandoned rectitude s_1 **t d^1** is answered **d . fe^{1}s^1**).

(ii) Free exposition of a second subject, which combines with the first, leads to a clear recovery and coda.

The distinctive elements may be summarized as follows—

(i) The subject is pronounced and symmetrical, and it has enough inner character to silence questions about the exact text of its reappearances. But, as it is so overpowering, there is an early shifting of ground: the first middle entries are at once on the flat side (D flat, etc.) and in different cross-accentuations. They are followed by a vast and immeasurable interlude, beginning from a stray arpeggio phrase but haunted by the "rocket" element of the subject, discharging in slow motion in the tonic minor at one point. A fresh subject, descending an octave (s^l–s) at leisure, strays across in B minor. The main subject returns in D (bass). It is answered by the inversion (at zero)* in G, D and, by a nice twist of sequence, E flat, but D is recovered.

(ii) At this point of exhausted humour, rather than of argument, comes one of those accessions of simple polyphony, too steep to be merely vocal, of which Beethoven was master. He here reverses Bach's invariable order in double-fugue by reaching a serene mood from a subversive one. The plain phrase is absorbed in a soft harmonic texture, only to be dragged out to combine with the main subject (A.B.) in B flat. This double-fugue, however, is no more than a piece of "free-wheeling" before further ascent. The subject reappears inverted, with its normal self in instant canon (B.A., S.B.). The descending trill of the former proves again a useful stimulus for connecting sequences. From these emerge two simpler entries (the second combining the subject with a fresh inversion at the third) and further cross-accentuations and canonic by-play. The subject is then absorbed in oscillating sonorities, retaining its still dynamic leap. The blunt, de-trilled return of this leap (answer version taken from the subdominant—f t^l d^l) contrives to concentrate in one decisive moment the fancies that have broken through two fugues by means of the subject, in a rich environment of pertinent incident. In this tremendous finale of an already monumental sonata, fugal procedure is by turns invoked, discarded and invoked in an increasingly impressionist context. The texture is elusive. Yet the main design is fugal, not polythematic. There is no question of any second subject superseding the first in a buoyant sonata form, as in the "fugue" of the finales of the quartet op. 59, No. 3, or of Mozart's quartet in G, K. 387.

These fugues in the last sonatas alternate with the variation-sets of Op. 109 and 111. Beethoven came to regard either of these historical genres as a likely base of fulfilment for his sonata-experience at the time. Two of the five latest and rarest string

* Cf. p. 177.

quartets employ fugue at the start or finish. The QUARTET IN C
SHARP MINOR (op. 131) opens with a MOVEMENT which, without
being quite a fugue, is fugued and monothematic throughout.
Fresh accentuation and melting key serve to convey a sense of
dissolution midway, which accounts for a subsequent assertion of
primal key, unusual in fugue. After this, the original subdominant
answer is passable, but is noticeably, yet inevitably, replaced by
an entry moving to the tonic, reinforced by the bass at half-speed.
The former answer returns, but it, too, is harmonized as a cadence
in the tonic. Thus unconventionally but pertinently does this
master-work begin with one single *Affekt*, in place of the usual
complexity of mood and motive. The answer trend (D major)
persists later.

In the quartet Op. 130 the last movement was planned to be a
fugue. Beethoven's last complete piece of creative work was to
replace the fugue, most questionably, with a more conventional
finale. But the "tantôt libre, tantôt recherché" movement thus
sequestered as GROSSE FUGE (op. 133) must have been abandoned
with a struggle, and must be considered in the context of op. 130,
that is, after the absorption of the Cavatina. This more than
accounts for the opening transitional statement, which makes a
virtue of an expedient introduction. After this prelude, announc-
ing a cogent theme (*a*) in symmetrical groups of semitones
(**d–de ta–l, de–r t–d¹**) in varying tempi, the music settles down
to four distinct movements—

   (i) Double-fugue at once on *a* and *b* in B flat.
   (ii) Double-fugue on *a* and *c* in G flat.
   (iii) Prelude and double-fugue on *a* and *d* in A flat, recalling (ii)
in order to deliver with full pressure—
   (iv) Prelude (*da capo*) and recovery of the initial combination
in a less taut rhythm, in B flat.

The pronounced curve of *a* renders it perpetually recognizable,
and at the same time the penetrating cut of *b* across the *tessitura*,
the decorative nuances of *c*, and the formal but joyous urge of *d*
make any confusion or sense of monotony impossible. In the
coda double-fugue is replaced at first by a harmonic advance at
dizzy heights, conveying immense space, before the original

combination "sails forth" in a fresh rhythm. Here, then, is Beethoven's "triple" fugue: there is no intention of combining *b*, *c* and *d* except horizontally. The fugues are much more independent than in any Bach triple fugue. In compensation, they sweep the listener to a wonderful variety of measure, which audiences for the five earlier movements of op. 130 are already conditioned to grasp, apart from the new *Leitmotiv*. The maintenance of this variety of subject and texture is a strain on a quartet of players, but this is no ground for giving the fugue with orchestral strings. Rather than submit to this vernacular touch it is better to wait for the next quartet. The composer arranged the movement for piano duet (op. 134), a desperate expedient, not to be taken seriously.

Last and not least, Beethoven could not fail to invoke fugue at some stage of his choral adventures. The fugue for ET VITAM in the MASS IN C is incredibly perfunctory and square-phrased; a reminder of the pedantic tone of Beethoven's approach to fugue, under prevailing influences, at the height of his second maturity. For the MASS IN D he went into special training. In the "Gloria," after a preludial and unusually choral "Quoniam tu solus," IN GLORIA DEI PATRIS develops into a vigorous fugue in D, the main key, for choral and solo voices and orchestra, the latter policing the polyphony from the start. (We might here recall the transparent vocalism of Bach's fugal openings.) There is a declamatory counter-subject, and the subject is good for a counterpoint of texture at any time, in which the flow of half-beats matters more than the precise melodic curve or (bars 40 *et seq.*) degree. After moving about comfortably (apart from twisting vocal contours) in various keys, the subject, suitably clipped, is recovered in D in close canon by soloists and, after a sweeping brief circle of modulations, chorus, in a context of broadening suspense (organ pedal and drum-roll). It is continued at half-speed in B.A.S. (with a beat extra or short to induce cross-rhythm), with fragments of the normal subject as counterpoint. This, the most thrilling and acutely set dominant pedal in all musical experience (sublimation of all anticipations in the fifth symphony and elsewhere) quickens the sense of "divine grace dancing" to a brisker tempo.

A new subject, part-inversion and the personal advocacy of solo voices swiftly raise the pitch of interest after an abrupt renunciation of the general momentum. As in Mozart's "Amen" in K. 427, the subject, increasingly melodic, absorbs this fresh development in an intense unison, but with characteristic and conclusive extensions which touch C *major* with vivid ecstasy and prompt soloists and chorus to release "Amen" phrases in D. At this crowning point the original (and canonic) theme of the "Gloria" bursts in, *presto*, and, after a broad promotion of intense differences of key, hurls the "Amen" cadence of the centuries to a moment beyond time, to repetitions of the fundamental, vernacular "Gloria," not the ritual "Amen." (Alternatively, a final *rallentando* for "security" brings the ascent of spirit with a bump down to an awareness of Maestro and middle age and the cleanliness that is worlds from godliness.) None the less, fugue has determined the manner of choral incidence, right up to the closing *presto*, which is still contrapuntal in the main.

The "Credo" motive of the third part of the Creed similarly intensifies from serial imitation to a broad and sweeping choral unison. In the aftermath of suspense after this commanding ascent, a fresh movement begins quietly for ET VITAM VENTURI, in B flat, the main key. It shapes in two stretches of fugue—

(i) A flowing double-fugue reveals singularly vocal terms (not texture) except for the ruthless heights that the soprani, at more than average personal risk, have to hold. The main and descending subject is sufficiently formal to stand the stimulus of inversion. Inverted at the second, it tilts subdominantwards (| s¹ | m¹d¹ta | | l f¹ r¹ | t s becoming | s | t r¹ m¹ | f¹ l d¹ | m¹s¹) and is so harmonized in A flat and D flat (B.S.); the counter-subject, now falling phrases in rising sequence (A.), supports this flatward turn. But the alto entry (E flat minor) irons out the subject to a plain ascending sequence of split triads and thus revealingly recovers B flat for two entries, ideally, of serene confidence (S.B.).

(ii) An inevitable jerk out of this harmonic groove prompts a fresh momentum in the orchestra, with signs of the halved beats which crystallize in the double-fugue that follows. The three-beat subject of four bars is now unevenly compressed to two bars in breathless chase. After a series of entries in dense counterpoint, the music broadens out to a supremely expectant phrase, from which the original subject emerges, again ironed out into falling triads in ascending sequence (S.), and now countered by the diminished subject (T.), with a pronounced cadence. The rever- beration of all this, with the subject in choral and its diminution in orchestral unison, in fundamental counterpoint of unsurpassed

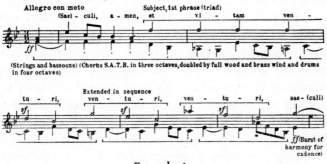

Example 60

abandon, reaches a stage of meditative harmony, which shapes into a final *Grave*. In that solemn contemplation of the life beyond this, soloists and chorus answer each other with trembling, exultant phrases, in which the bare pulse of the subject is still present. The final and more melodic return of the subject through the last chord is assigned to the traditional mystical group, the trombones, and the "advanced" unison effect is a final testimony to the Ricercar quality of the subject. Bach's tremendous con- clusion to his Credo moves from close, disciplined choral fugue to an *adagio* and a refrain movement in which the chorus has to snatch any space for the briefest fugue. It is Beethoven who maintains fugue almost to the end. This resort to its automatic reverberations of theme on the part of a master-symphonist reaching to the depths of his experience is sure evidence of his genuine need. His reduction of the subject to its rhythmic essence is a vivid response to a "strange, testing emergency."

Beethoven made his style of fugue necessary, ultimately by his passionate concern for detail. How elementary were current ideas on fugue, can be observed in the church music of SCHUBERT. In the "Gloria" of the MASS-music IN A FLAT, completed at the same time as Beethoven in D, a dramatic "Quoniam" leads to a fugal CUM SANCTO SPIRITU on a lively subject, incidentally the third setting for the occasion. But the subject is a square eight-bar period, and so it remains, with some development of component phrases. The movement is nearer a Ground with episodes than a fugue. In the MASS-music IN E FLAT, which so casually succeeded the great C major symphony, CUM SANCTO SPIRITU is set to a ten-bar fugal subject, treating sequentially the curve of Bach's W.K.ii, E. Close canon, partly avoiding and partly echoing Bach (bars 86, 119, 153), recurs, with stimulating touches of chromatic harmony. The total impact is technical and perfunctory after the compelling quality of "Domine Deus", where a recurring bass is heard, as in Bach's "Crucifixus," in the right place. ET VITAM VENTURI is a fugue on a plain and compact subject, which calls for counter-phrases in supporting sequences. Yet this long procession of elementary chromatic polyphony and sequence is not matter enough either for chorus or for symphony orchestra. Manifestly Schubert was satisfied here with social convention at a level he had long left behind in opera and symphony. He shows neither sympathy for the "heavenly impersonal" of fugal ritual nor Beethoven's keen ear for orchestral essentials. The fugue in E minor (organ or piano, or piano duet) is a sturdy exercise.

In Mendelssohn and Schumann, both Leipzig composers at one period of their careers, Bach had two avowed admirers. MENDELSSOHN'S ORGAN FUGUES, however, are more melodious than contrapuntal. At the last pedal entry in the fugue in G, for example, the hands simply replace the hockets of Bach's earliest C minor fugue by smooth harmony, echoing the bland prelude. The fugue in D minor—a longer original was sent with "modest" disclaimers to Vincent Novello (14,396)—suggests (bar 80) close *stretto* (S.T.A.) on its formal subject, but mainly over a dominant pedal, which seems to gurgle over the rough and inaudible attempts at "litigation." The well-known FUGUE IN E MINOR (1827) FOR PIANO, to which the too song-like prelude was added

much later, is a much more interesting composition. It begins
with genuine fugue on a fine sensitive subject (recalling W.K.ii,
D sharp minor), with extra entries in the dominant to brace the
tonality against the relaxations of the major key and of entries of
the inverted subject. But from bar 34 onwards the underlying
texture is increasingly harmonic, in massive or broken chords.
As a final confession of contrapuntal defeat, a major "chorale"
("Ein feste Burg" lowered to match Biedermeierstrasse?) is invoked, not as a picturesque episode but as a crowning theme. In
this pious mood the subject returns in an unctuous (tonic) major,
and through the (musically) smug, intrusive Medley a ghostly voice
cries, *Et tu, Felix*! By way of contrast, the troubled fugal overture
to "Elijah" finds a just issue in the choral outburst that succeeds.

Schumann's fugues and canons are said to have been suggested
by lessons with the Dresden organist, J. G. SCHNEIDER, whose
straightforward fugue in the FANTASIA AND FUGUE IN D MINOR
for organ achieves a plodding eight-bar subject, which inverts, a
chatty counter-subject, a close *stretto* at the octave and resourceful
organic episodes on bars 7–8, but is misjudged as "masterly" in
Grove's Dictionary (searchers of the past are usually reluctant to
admit that they have dug up an old bone, and not buried treasure!).
However, Schumann's constant interest in fugue is well-attested,
not only in the eighteen-odd complete movements published but
in the voluminous fugal matter in the note-books, including
nearly seventy "fugues," an unfinished manual after Marpurg
and Cherubini, and many themes which began as *fugue manquée*.*
But all these earnest attempts will not conceal from the general
listener a sense of wayward detail and general struggle in the published fugues. The latter do not provide an important clue to
Schumann's development; they either confirm an innate restlessness, inimical alike to fugue and concentrated song, or betray
an outmoded routine for which the subject is not fitted.

SCHUMANN'S SIX FUGUES ON B–A–C–H (op. 60) are "for organ
or pedal-piano." They are more suited to the organ, though they
derived from the composer's *naif* excitement over the pedal-
attachment he had hired at Dresden, as a bridge to Bach and a

* See Note 4 on page 250.

"unique" discovery of texture (however socially exclusive). The recurring pitch-curve was a typically romantic choice, based more on the delight in an open-secret symbol of the senior German muse of the time, than on any consideration of fugal suitability. It seems doubtful if Schumann knew the b–a–c–h (and e–f–d–s) of A.F. 14 or Albrechtsberger's op. 3 in G minor. Essentially transitional (to C sharp) in Bach's D minor fugue, the artificially "absolute" letter-sounds here make *b* (B flat) the main key-note, varied by mediant and subdominant (Nos. 3, 5). Each entry is committed to a sharpening of these notes at *h* (B). Except in Nos. 3 and 5 this becomes a strain; the perpetual stretch to the supertonic of the moment (chord and implied key) is at once characteristic (as in A.F. 4 *med.*) and tiresome in repetition.

Bach would never have accepted this twist for a whole gaggle of fugues. But let each subject bear its burden! This is just what Schumann does not contrive. In the solemn–lively No. 1, the subject shifts its accent after two entries, and, after a modicum of brooding entry and organic (but awkwardly corrective) episode, the restless suggestion of a diminished subject overlaps the subject with gathering speed. The original mood is abandoned, and precise details waived, without the secure sweep of Beethoven, op. 106. In sprightly-demure No. 2, a similar "censorship" occurs in the opposite direction. The subject, extensive, rapid and "North German," gains full exposition (seventy-three bars) with some defaulting in bass entries. But after that a bare hint of the augmented subject supplies interlude, recovery and coda, in which again the recollection of articulate detail has no place. No. 3 is a neutral-tinted transcription of vocal texture, without being true five-part fugue, and again with fudged pedal entries. No. 4, scarcely a genuine five-voice fugue, is enigmatic in another way: 116 bars on a two-bar b–a–c–h in fresh formation, with perpetual half-beat movement and as counter-subject a gradually perceived h–c a–b curve, for what relevance it may be worth and as fatally cadential as expected. The net gain is a turn to the subdominant, which scarcely needs restatement.

No. 5, an extended but reasonably quick-witted piece in F, has a shapely four-bar subject and is the most satisfactory whole.

The pedal entry defaults all but once. In the first restatement an augmented b–a–c–h motive appears as counter-subject. The inversion of the subject at the fifth paves the way to a gradual evaporation of counterpoint in favour of free sequence and primary bass (as in Aston's Hornpipe, 1525), leaving h–c–a–b melodically in possession. Fugue dissolves, but eloquently enough (perhaps) to give no time for discovery. No. 6 is a deliberate-hurrying double-fugue! The accelerator does not prevent the first fugue from slipping into "tram-lines" of triplet rhythm, or the second (manuals only, spoilt by a pedal warning-note at the end) from doing the same. After which, the combination reaches jaded ears, adding a gratuitous augmented sixth (bar 101) to the inevitable progression to the chord of the supertonic (cf. No. 1, bar 42; 2, 68; 6, 54), but little else, and the pompous coda,

Second subject in pedal

Example 61

harmonically striking at first, is forty bars long instead of ten. Of the exploitation of b–a–c–h as a *fugal* catalyst, like the motto of A.F., there is little in this series. The steady aim is rather to *lose* the clue in rhythmic variation, as Miss A–s–c–h buries herself in the mind's carnival. The constant contrapuntal floundering, whether discerned as such or not, confuses the cumulative variety of the set. If the fugues were more consistent, they would make a stronger suite. But there is no steady argument from the chosen variant; rather an escape from premises. Evidently Schumann was led (possibly by Schneider) to suppose that experienced fugue

meant the use of thematic devices. The still common acceptance
of this assumption by our modern Sophists, with a consequently
uncritical admiration for this set, has prompted the present re-
examination. If this is the romanticist's "Art of Fugue," it
replaces mastery by a choice of theme and treatment seldom happy
or genuinely cumulative.

The FOUR FUGUES FOR PIANO (op. 72), originally called character-fugues, are more compact, consistent and uneventful.
Indeed, they err on the side of monotony, partly from a lack of
episode. The "combination" in No. 1 (augmented and normal)
does not release the music sufficiently. The subject of No. 2
(echoing W.K.i, B flat minor in initial curve) is didactic and
insistent, *recte* or inverted, but the last entries are canon and
augmentation fudged, and betray an impatient hand, for the
resultant trite II–V–I progressions are not worth adapting the
subject for. The subject of No. 3 in F minor, uniquely subdominant (p. 134), reinforces its deep melancholy by a fresh counter-
subject for restatement (bar 32), and finally by chromatic contexts
for its now melodic state. The texture is vocal, apart from
range. Schumann sent the fugue to a Dutch friend for a collection. No. 4 is sheer *Home Chat a 4 voci*, such as figures often,
indeed, in the Diaries. The composer had cold feet about the
SEVEN FUGHETTAS (op. 126)*. They are short and monotonous,
and hover between fugue and variation. No. 6 is a true keyboard
fugue, with laboured humour at the end. (Contrast the directness
of the exhilarating finish of the fifth French Suite.) The doctrine
of Albrechtsberger and Cherubini died hard. There is something
ridiculous, or at least in the nature of an unfruitful exercise, in
these late excursions *antico modo*, with a fugue-manual solemnly
brandished in the background. Schumann was misled by Bach
into thinking that any fugue might be worth while. We must
turn to the impromptu double-fughetta which begins the epilogue
of the quintet (op. 44) for an example of live fugal writing.

The mystical (or hocus-pocus) appeal of b–a–c–h went on, in
spite of the Schumann set. No. 3 of the twenty-four FUGHETTAS
of Joseph RHEINBERGER (d. 1901), op. 123a and b, employs a *bach*

* See Note 5 on page 250.

motive in C major, changing the initial degree in bar 27. The use of the falling semitones in rising sequence improves on Schumann's falling tones in op. 60, No. 1. Yet the fugue is derivative. It lacks the thematic strength that Grace notes in most of the sonata-fugues. This charge cannot be laid against the trenchant texture of the last work of S. KARG-ELERT (d. 1933), "Passacaglia, Variations and FUGUE ON B–A–C–H" (op. 150). The fugue is a short double-fugue in three stages: a fughetta on an original subject (*a*, including a veiled allusion to b–a–c–h, inverted), a free acrobatic interlude, and the combination of *a* with the b–a–c–h motive which has already been established in the Ground of the Passacaglia. The chromatic texture is so rich as to be indigestible, but the placing of the accepted formula (with *b* as tonic) is well-calculated. The work probably owes something to Reger's fugues on this and other subjects in his resourceful but eclectic style (op. 46, organ; op. 86, two pianos).

In the ten canons and FUGUE ON "VATER UNSER" by WILHELM MIDDELSCHULTE (Leipzig, 1904),* the fugue consists in turn of a sizeable four-part fugue in D minor on a subject derived from the chorale by the theorist B. Ziehn, its total inversion at the fifth in the key of G major, with both inner and outer parts exchanged, and a summary finish in D major and minor (chorale). Pairs of entries in the tonic and mediant major (tonic and submediant minor, inverted) avoid the lameness of a normal inverted answer; inversion begins at the sixth entry, doubling at the seventh, and the canonic and inversionary temptations of the opening **s ma d** are not to be resisted. But these simple contrapuntal variants on the common chord are set in a violently chromatic context. The Bach of A.F. 12–13 is out-Bached; total inversion is rationalized by a change of key and mode, removing all sense of wayward repetition and contrast. This must be said before adding: But where's music, the dickens? I find it specious pedantry. Middelschulte then wrote a canonic fantasia on *bach*, and a fugue in D minor on four Bach-motives—*bach* and the principals of the Musical Offering, "Confiteor" (second subject) and the fugue in the violin solo-sonata in G minor (arranged by Bach for organ in

* See Note 6 on page 250.

D minor)—which coagulate at the end. Once more, Browning
has said it. There is no magic in a Bach theme, and still less in his
name. Nor can Tovey's own pair of invertible fugues for
A.F. 15 avoid the same challenge, whatever their educational
usefulness as an exposure of the problem Bach is likely to have
set himself. To "realize" two themes which with two chosen
outlines (the motto and b–a–c–h again) can embody the quadruple-
invertible is mental work of supreme gymnastic skill but not, under
such limitations, of creative thought. A cause has become a case.
However, B–A–C–H will go on haunting the minds of organist-
composers, a perennial invocation to ancestral introspection.

BRAHMS holds a modest but honourable place in the expiration
of fugue as a general structure. His twenty-five VARIATIONS FOR
PIANO (op. 24) on a theme already varied by Handel eventually
break into an extended "fugue" on a subject derived from the
opening bars. It is a measure of Brahms's acquired spontaneity
that one can be on performing terms with the finale for some time
before becoming aware of its spare economy of basic material.
However, there it is: early doubling and inversion, which reach
a point of concentration in the final period of restatement (as in
W.K.ii, B flat minor), augmentation that is not only good harmonic coin for entries but pays episodic dividends, a flow of false
entries at odd moments and to maintain penultimate suspense,
and sweeping grand-piano chords over a sequential pretence of
subject; all nicely disposed by a liberal key-system. Meanwhile
the subject has never been absorbed in any true polyphony, and
functions increasingly as a sonata-motive, as a summary of
Handel's theme. The "order of entry" is the chief contact with
fugue! The rest is accomplished rhetoric in a fugal frame. Of the
organ fugues, the A minor and A flat minor are more consistently
fugal than the "North German" but later Parryish G minor.

In the fugue which ends the SIXTH CHORUS in the GERMAN
REQUIEM, the subject is used with ample resource per immediate
counter-subject, selective handling of the descending and ascending curves of the subject, secondary subject (bar 83), abstruse
key, and augmentation. The treatment is both polyphonic and
symphonic, with the orchestra for more than security. This

includes refreshingly eloquent tonic and dominant drones. And
the end of the THIRD CHORUS is an accomplished double-fugue on
an everlasting tonic bass, token of a transcendent assurance for
genuine saints. In all these, Brahms's subject retains its integrity.
So with the two fugues in Bruckner's Mass in F minor. In the
PLENI SUNT COELI and LIBERA ME, DOMINE of VERDI'S REQUIEM,
on the other hand, fugue is just a fresh start, soon absorbed in
further declamation or *cantabile*. The same occurs at the end of
"Falstaff," and in Liszt's piano sonata and "Faust" symphony. In
the ballet-finale of "Švanda," fugue achieves a turgid climax.

Poetic justice demands that we end our survey of the wander-
ings of fugue in the country where the first music made to the
rule of imitation can be traced. In spite of all temptations to be
an Englishman and therefore to sprinkle his choral work with
fugue, PARRY kept away from it in "Prometheus," "Job,"
"Voces clamantium" and the rest, and he was content with free
imitational writing over a sustained dominant bass to match the
aspiring conclusion of "Blest pair of sirens." In the "WANDERER"
TOCCATA AND FUGUE IN G FOR ORGAN, published posthumously,
Parry displayed a mild interest in the art he had so penetratingly
admired in Bach for its characteristic features (not for its ingenuity). The "subject" is chiefly a theme treated polyphonically.
A plain contrast of key develops the seventh entry into an interlude, and an early change of degree (up a third) supplies the subject
with stronger terminal points, and also evokes homely tonic and
later dominant drones (echoes of Aston), against which the subject
can move youthfully in bundles of sonority, establishing harmonic
texture in grand organ style for the rest of the fugue. Perhaps the
once Oxford Professor was set against Ricercar by the mountainous fugues of Degree Exercises. Certainly he thinks in expanding phrases, usually in top or bass, not in the limits of a fugal
subject. This is true, too, of his more resourceful contemporary,
Stanford, who shows little sympathy for a sturdy imitational
style. As with Parry's celestial consort, the promise of a double-
fugue in the final "heavenly" chorus (Act I) of "Eden" soon loses
its contrapuntal urge over a dominant pedal, leading to a recovery
of earlier motives. When Stanford needed an echo of traditional

counterpoint to formulate his thought, his impulse was to go back to the sixteenth century. The last stronghold of fugue, scholastic, applied and whatever, seems to have been France.*

ELGAR, master of trenchant "double-fugue" for the proud outlaws of "Gerontius," wrote a witty fugue as interlude in his INTRODUCTION AND ALLEGRO, to reinforce the appeal of *soli-tutti* antiphony, bowing bravura and simple *cantabile*. His nervous temperament was inimical to a settled subject—from the exquisitely slippery turns of "Enigma" onwards—and his choral style was contrapuntal, if at all, for a kaleidoscopic sequence or other impromptu extensions, not for the establishment of a recurrent combination. Unlike Schumann, he realized that fugue for him could only be an affected style for special occasions.

VAUGHAN WILLIAMS wrote an agile RICERCAR in his INTRODUCTION AND FUGUE FOR TWO PIANOS, and a more characteristic fugue in the PRELUDE AND FUGUE IN C MINOR FOR ORGAN, later scored for orchestra (so showing less signs of deterioration, perhaps, than Samuel Wesley's arrangement of W.K.i, D, for (i) organ, (ii) full orchestra, for an organ concerto). In the organ fugue, there is a characteristic **d¹ ta s d¹** plainsongy start, and the minor third is that of the Aeolian mode; at the same time, middle entries occupy the Aeolian minor of A, F sharp and (by false entry) E flat. These having taken the subject for a ride, a

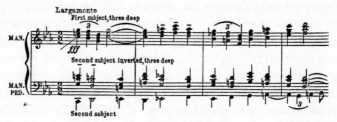

(*Copyright* 1930 *by the Oxford University Press, and reprinted by kind permission*)

Example 62

second subject develops, and after being steadily ignored by the first subject in favour of revolving sonorities (bars 98–130) is at last admitted, in full pedal pomp and inverted, three deep, in the

* See Note 7 on page 250.

left hand, as the pedestal of the subject, also three deep. After which, it is no surprise to discover that Vaughan Williams has confined serious fugue to interludes: the start of the finale of the piano concerto—a break with the rondo tradition—and of the epilogue of the fourth Symphony, and the start and odd moments of the scherzo of the sixth Symphony. His satiric comment on the reprise of the last, in his note for the first performance (April, 1948), must be taken with the text *litigat immo iocatur*, but it is revealing. "When the episode is over, the wood-wind experiment as to how the subject will sound upside down, but the brass are angry and insist on playing it the right way up, so for a bit the two go on together and to the delight of every one including the composer the two versions fit, so there is nothing to do now but continue. . . . Then once more we hear the subject softly upside down." The double-barrelled wit is aimed first, of course, at the painstaking attempts of Programme Notes to prepare audiences for a new work, but the reader will perceive the composer's serious implication (in spite of a rooted belief in fugue as an "essential" training*) that fugue is a useful but definitely archaic, self-conscious procedure, when it comes to the use of those devices which continue to afford some examiners so much simple delight. (Fugue was finally grounded in Toch's piece for four-fold declamation, to geographical nonsense on one pitch.) So with the jingling themes of Holst's "Fugal Overture."

The same resort to fugue as a method of thematic development marks the "double-fugue" of RAWSTHORNE'S CORTÈGES (1945), in which the Rawsthorne Tone (C–D flat- F–E–C) replaces BACH, and the fugue on a subject which combines with Purcell's theme in Britten's variations for orchestra. The RICERCAR of BERNARD STEVENS for string orchestra is more consistently fugal; but the quadruple plunge, *once* only, is a multiplication of rhythms which remains too solitary to be accepted as apex of the main pattern. RACINE FRICKER'S FOUR FUGHETTAS for two pianos (op. 2) are "character-fugues" of studied brevity (26–46–16–90 bars), pedantic and pompous, wayward, brooding and Puckish in turn. The craft includes chromatic subjects, strict answers, a pronounced

* This statement was personally verified in April, 1954.

polyphony whose harmonic progressions sound obstinate and
sometimes perverse, but a dominant pedal to show Dr. Strabismus
the door. The listener is left guessing the composer's intention,
as with Mozart. No doubt, the TWELVE FUGUES of HINDEMITH'S
LUDUS TONALIS for piano have had their influence, though only
the eighth and the canonic eleventh there are as brief. But one
would like to know whether Fricker (and others) extemporize in
this style, as one can imagine Bach improvising the Chromatic
Fugue in general counterpoint and stabilized harmony. (The
legend of the fugue written by a composer (D. Scarlatti) and his
cat dies hard, and much may be expected of an Orlando.) The
sustained argument is there, but the phrases slip about like words
in Ogden Nash's poems. The praise of Bach as "less intellectual"
than the Marpurgs and Rameaus, but so much the more moving,*
comes quaintly from the composer of "Ludus Tonalis," besides
being an unfortunate use of "intellectual," as if the developed art
of J. S. Bach could spring from anything but the most concentrated thinking in sound.

The FINALE OF TIPPETT'S SYMPHONY No. 1, much more consistently contrapuntal than Walton's symphony, follows the
tracks of a fugue which exhibits in turn (reversing Bach's order
of mood) a crisp two-voice theme, a pondering, symmetrical,
syncopated curve, and their very loose combination in uniform
harmony at various pitches. The first theme is countered or
overlapped by the second half-way and then at once re-enters as
counterpoint to the *same entry* of the second "subject," which,
thus taking tail and then head of the first in its stride, sounds
increasingly as an independent Ground. The so-far ponderous
movement marks a challenging innovation in structure—as once
(in the "Eroica") Variations on a bass made a novel finale—and
it claims full discussion in its context in any survey of symphony.
As fugue, it has its strong points of sonorous litigation, the final
ruminant echoes of which resolve compulsively on a tonal centre,
E (Mixolydian). The primary falling sevenths of the second theme
give the listener a feeling that he has been here before, especially after
the tenser sevenths in the finale of Bliss's "Colour" Symphony.

* *Johann Sebastian Bach*, a commemorative speech, 1950.

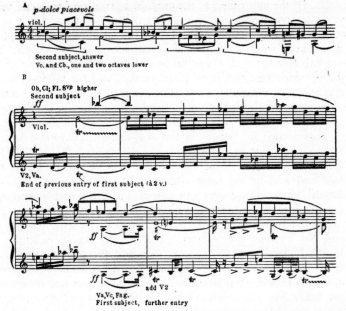

Second subject, answer
Vc. and Cb., one and two octaves lower

Ob, Cl; Fl. 8ve higher
Second subject

End of previous entry of first subject (à 2 v.)

add V2
Va, Vc, Fag.
First subject, further entry

(By kind permission of Schott & Co., Ltd.)

The brackets are in the score, as well as the bowing-marks

Example 63

NOTES

1 (*Page* 220) Cf. "People who are under the impression that they can make works of art by applying rules of procedure are merely trying to pass off a frame-work as a living organism." (Parry, *J. S. Bach*, p. 159.) (Cf. G. Tolhurst, *Ruth*.)

2 (*Page* 223) F. W. Marpurg (1718–95), a musical amateur of Berlin, produced without any real precedent his *Abhandlung der Fuge* (*Treatise on Fugue*) in 1753–54, in obvious continuation of his crusading preface to "The Art of Fugue." A few of the short illustrations of answer, inversion, etc., there are taken from Bach, Handel and Eberlin (fugues 5 and 6), but most are "hand-made." A supplementary collection of complete fugal examples stopped at Part I, a set of four vocal fugues and one longer example (C. P. E. Bach in D minor) for keyboard, without the projected analysis. Marpurg also ground an axe about bass-mindedness in a *Handbuch*, expounding Rameau (whom he met in Paris) in advance of its time. Like many self-appointed instructors, Marpurg tried to teach what he could not do. The fugue in D minor altogether fails to animate its cautious subject (see Ex. 59D,

p. 229). Of the nine others in the published "Fughe e Capricci," op. 1 (1777), the "vigorous" nine-bar subject of the two-voice No. 7 in D soon becomes merely voluble, and the more vocal subject of No. 8 in E flat makes a weak conclusion of its half-entries in close canon. Yet this combative figure deserves this much mention for showing an insight of which Emanuel Bach gives no sign, and for briefing, in his crusty reactionary manner, a lost cause and craft which by every test of *galanterie* seemed obsolete and misplaced. See, however, D. Plamenac in *The Musical Quarterly* (October, 1949) for evidence that Emanuel later championed his father—in the well-known *Comparison between Bach and Handel* sent anonymously to the *Allgemeine d. Bibl.*, LXXXI,1.

Emanuel himself developed double fugue in the glowing *Sicut erat* (*Magnificat*) and in the tense chorus cited, which succeeds unison "chorale" phrases heard over a processional motive—man passing, yet not passing, by the Cross (*Passion Cantata*). These deserve revival. The six keyboard fugues (*all* for Marpurg?) rely more on sequence than on fugue, No. 2 reducing its subject to declamatory octaves or tenths.

In W. F. Bach's organ fugue in G minor the subject suffers odd fixation in the pedal. Of the Eight Keyboard Fugues (1778) the best, No. 4 in D minor, gains from its pronounced subject and terse treatment, while No. 5 in E flat rambles on, florid and sequential. No. 8, the one that Mozart served up with prelude (string trio), affects a chromatic brooding it cannot sustain over 200 bars. In J. C. F. Bach the *galant* style is in possession (e.g. in the six quartets op. 1).

3 (*Page* 230) Curwen publish C. S. Lang's organ arrangements (of unspecified identity and source) of the fugues in B flat, C minor and G minor, op. 1. The divergences from the original edition include depriving Albrechtsberger of a German augmented sixth, inverted, by altering D flat quaver to A flat in the penultimate bar of the second fugue. For specimens of Beethoven-Albrechtsberger fugue, see *The Musical Times*, February, 1955.

4 (*Page* 239) See Wolfgang Boetticher, *Robert Schumann: Einführung in Persönlichkeit und Werk* (p. 572), quoted by Prof. Gerald Abraham in his symposium, *Schumann* (p. 261), with more approval than I should give. In 1837 Schumann was copying out "The Art of Fugue."

5 (*Page* 242) See a letter to the publisher quoted by Miss Dale in her essay in *Schumann* (ed. G. Abraham).

6 (*Page* 243) A kind of fulfilment of the 40 pioneer variations of J. U. Steigleder (1627), eloquent of sturdy contrapuntalism.

7 (*Page* 246) See the examples of "college" fugue at the end of A. Gédalge, *Traité de la Fugue*. But Ghislanzoni (*Arte e tecn. della F.*) invokes Fuga Bitonale and Dalla Piccola!

Chapter XIX

FUGUE IN MUSICAL EXPERIENCE

IT is part of the perfection of music as an art that certain patterns have proved almost as durable as the natural inflexions of voice and acquired instrument. The eight-note scale, modifiable in detail but gathered round tonic, dominant and subdominant, has remained the chief term of melodic reference up to 1890. Imitation is a deep impulse in human nature, and its musical counterpart, repeating intonations of words in the first instance, has long been established, choosing between intervals as determined by conjunct voices or by conjunct degrees, with similar variants of the initial "step" by quickening or retarding, and more abstrusely by inversion of theme or even of the whole consort of parts. In the pursuit of these variants, fugue has been the focus of resourceful imitation for its own sake, based on a rhythmic and melodic period which does not too easily detach itself from the polyphony, but yet catches the ear sufficiently to make the apprehension of a pattern developed on and around it not only audible but characteristic. Thus the convergence of an almost national economy of theme, organ and keyboard rhapsody, and the "resolution" of modal differences in the major and minor scales, met the genius of J. S. Bach and crystallized a historic period of composition by fugue, most persistently for keyboard, but also making evocative many choruses of the Gospel Pieces and other affirmations of life-experience in music for the Communion Service. Simultaneously an almost rabid contrapuntal movement, of which Fux's "Gradus ad Parnassum" is the pretentious progenitor, started an artificial continuation of fugue which, in brief, only Mozart, Beethoven and Brahms could make creative. They *used* fugue, where Bach had *thought* in fugue. The Albrechtsbergers and other frank imitators went on thinking in fugue without Bach's concern for musical issues. More critical composers of later decades could only treat fugue as a nucleus of imitation by rule; they could not follow in Brahms's special track up the mountain. As a creative stimulus, fugue is now dead, just as the sonnet is dead, as Arthur Waley maintained recently. The old patterns of rhyme and rhythm cannot be repeated. The realization of this technical certainty may cause despondency at first, not least to teachers who have pinned much faith on fugal grounding, but it may also save wasted energy over journeys to the moon, just as a blunt recognition of human breathing-powers and the like may put a stop to idle fantasy about actual lunar travel. The final stages of the Bach era show the wearing out of the time-honoured vehicle, and the exceptional and always qualified fugal achievements of Beethoven and after confirm beyond doubt an impression of exhaustion and emergency. The symbolism of music must proceed on other lines. But the comparatively short history of fugue has been an often fascinating and revealing experience. This composition "by rule" is finished, but its creations continue to warm the musician's hands and spirit, as a model for future types of thought and evolution. Rule is dead. Long life to it!

Appendix

A NOTE ON "THE LONDON AUTOGRAPH"

It is interesting to observe, in the respective autographs of the Forty-eight, Book Two—defined below—Bach's laborious efforts to fit each of the longer preludes and fugues into a sheet of four seven-line pages. The fugues in E minor, F, F sharp minor, G sharp minor, B flat, B flat minor, B, end on lines ruled below what are musically pages 1–2, 3–4 or both. The prelude in G minor begins on p. 2, and the fugue finishes in the *normal* top lines of p. 1, with the end of the prelude below. The G sharp minor fugue begins at the bottom of p. 2, besides spilling over later. Both it and the B flat minor fugue are cramped into eight-line pages. All this suggests that these are copies of music already composed and measured out, for general circulation.

The twenty-one pieces now assembled to form one of the British Museum's most treasured possessions (35,021) were once folded sheets with pp. 1–2 inside and pp. 3–4 at the back of this (a double sheet for P. and F. 17 similarly disposes pp. 1–3 and 4–6), thus giving one convenient turn between prelude and fugue, apart from fugues that spill over into pp. 1–2, but making ordinary binding impossible. These copies must thus have always been separate. The copies of Nos. 4, 5 and 12 of the collection are missing; at one stage or another they became detached from the rest and were never recovered.

Ownership of the set can be traced as far as Clementi (1752–1832), whose fugal essays are discussed in Chapter XVIII. Clementi quotes Fugues 1 and 4 "from an original MS.," in Part 2 of his *Introduction to the Art of playing on the Piano Forte* (*c.* 1820). The reprint of No. 1 agrees with 35,021 "in every significant detail." That of No. 4 is therefore likely to have done so, even if it does not quite agree with the Kirnberger MS. or the very early Broderip-Wilkinson edition (B.M.) and others. (At bar 15 Clementi reads, solitarily, A natural in the tenor, at 32 F *double* sharp and, less credibly, at 54 top-space E sharp (written as F natural) as the eighth treble note.) The collection passed into the hands of J. G. Emett, a London organist, who acquired it in all innocence, with a MS. copy of the Pachelbel "Magnificat" fugues discussed in Chapter XVII, in a pile of "various" music sold with Clementi's effects. When Sarah Emett played to her father (who was blind by 1832) Fugue No. 1 from her copy of the Clementi book (now in B.M.), he noticed a difference from the Wesley-Horn edition at the first conspicuous variant bar (66), and confirmation in the MS. copy he had acquired (and which he appears meanwhile to have given to Sarah's lifelong friend Eliza, the daughter of Samuel Wesley, but now received back) awoke fresh interest in the latter. With young W. S. Rockstro, who carried the precious MS., he·called on Mendelssohn, then a resident in London. Mendelssohn "recognized the handwriting instantly, with as little hesitation as if it had been his own" (Rockstro), and supported his assertion in writing later. That was in 1842, but, as his first glimpse of Mendelssohn, the brief encounter was vividly recalled by Rockstro forty years later. Around 1855, Sterndale Bennett examined the MS. and accepted it as Bach's (*Grove's Dictionary*, 1st Edn., IV, 483). When Emett died in 1847, however, he left his music, etc., to his young son by a second marriage. Ignorant or impecunious, this person sold it publicly in 1861-2, but the Bach MS. was bought back by his sister, Mrs. Edward Clarke. Fortunately there were no American speculators around as yet. In 1879 Sarah (evidently in bitter desperation) bought the MS. from her step-sister for £8. Her receipt specifies, honestly enough, copies of *twenty* "Fugues." Nos. 4, 5 and 12 were now missing, as Eliza Wesley recalls—she would have noticed this if it had been so when she had the MS.—also Mendelssohn's letter, which she testifies to have seen during Emett's lifetime; and—the humorous side of which will appear in a moment—Mrs. Clarke had stipulated to keep one piece, No. 9, probably because Mendelssohn had played it to the Emetts. Sarah bequeathed her set (she did not sell it, as Prout stated later) to Eliza Wesley, who, knowing that it was Sarah's wish as well as her own, placed it in the British Museum. In 1896, a year after Eliza's death, Mrs. Clarke sold No. 9 to the Museum.

In this truly English manner one of the world's manuscripts, acquired privately and almost accidentally, was preserved for all time and for all nations, first by the idealism of a musician who was determined to place it in hands that respected it, ultimately at severe cost to herself—eight sovereigns then was a great deal of money to save up—and secondly by the more complex but ultimately homogeneous aims of her half-sister. The chief correspondence can be seen in 35,022, in which Eliza Wesley's express confirmation of Sarah Emett's statements and handwriting appears. Thus the twenty-one pieces of the "London autograph" of W.K.ii can be traced romantically to Clementi, a likely enough owner and the pioneer of piano technique, with a strong avowal of its authenticity from Mendelssohn, in speech confirmed by Sarah and Rockstro; in writing, by Eliza.

But we can be far more positive about the essential integrity of seventeen of the scripts as autographs, and of the alien but scarcely less trustworthy hand of the other four. In a revealing article on the history and composition of the London autograph (*Music and Letters*,

April, 1953), to which the previous account is indebted for sundry documentary facts and comparisons of text, Mr. Walter Emery, after explaining that 35,021 is in fact twenty-one separate scripts, clears up the whole textual position afresh by means of a series of convincing analyses of the musical script in the seventeen works mentioned, in the other four, and in parallel samples of either writing. These script tests include a concern for—

(i) the formation of the C-clefs (used for R.H. in nineteen pieces and elsewhere), and of the C and 4 of time-signatures, as determined in Bach's writings after about 1725, with specific but not primary variants around 1735, and as reproduced in most works here but definitely replaced in certain scripts by another and more squat C-clef, a notably less elliptical C for $\frac{4}{4}$, and a perceptibly less curvilinear 4 (as exhibited in and outside the Book);

(ii) the correct down-stemming of minims (to show the true polyphony) in an identical majority of scripts, pointing to its patent neglect in the others (93/93 right in No. 23, 6/96 in No. 9);

(iii) the usually cramped character of the writing, with its equally pointed and consistent exceptions.

By *each* of these separate tests all the scripts except Nos. 2, 6, 9, 15 (and a page of No. 11) stand together, as agreeing with the autograph of No. 17 in the Berlin State Library, whose authority has never been questioned; No. 17 (London) being patently in the same hand (or its expert forgery). By each of the same tests Nos. 2, 6, 9, 15 and the first page of No. 11 stand together and apart from the previous group.

Let us call the two writers B and M, and rashly suppose them to be of conveniently opposite sex.

(i) It is just conceivable, Emery suggests, that in some pieces M, who obviously collaborated with B in the compilation of this fair copy, wrote (in advance) *only* the clefs at the beginning of the lines; but it is improbable that she did so in the pieces (P. 2, F. 2, 6, 15) which do not, after all, occupy all their staves; and she could not possibly have done so in the D minor prelude, where in lines 5-6 bass clefs are corrected to C-clefs (in M style) *ad hoc*. The natural inference is that she wrote out the entire music of the M group, with clefs as required.

(ii) It is just conceivable that the "odd" page of No. 11 was written by B in much earlier days, or when he was for other reasons careless about stemming, and not thinking of a fair copy; but to posit this throughout all the other four cases and exclusively, without the slightest ground, is too much to swallow as a temperamental but consistent variant of a confirmed custom.

(iii) It is conceivable that B wrote a page of No. 11 with a broad fist and then, remembering the long fugue to come, hastily set about saving space; scarcely that he economized in Nos. 1, 7, 8, 10, 12-14, as he did throughout the script of the B minor Mass score, but let his hand go in Nos. 2, 6, 9, 15. (See Frontispiece: 49/70 bars firmly packed into p. 3.)

(iv) It is inexplicable that B was tidy over the writing of dotted-quaver-semiquaver figures (illustrated by Emery *in situ*) in seventeen pieces, and untidy in the rest; equally, I may add, that in the M pieces semiquavers in fours tend to be parallel, while the rest tend to converge and curve with the melodic slope—unless there are two fists involved.

The sum of these inconceivables and improbables, each leaving a cumulative burden of disproof to the modern palaeographer, is as certain as anything can be with the manual signs of practised writers of music: B's scripts agree with, and show every cause (No. 17 beyond the shadow of a doubt) for being in the hand of the J. S. Bach of the Berlin autograph of No. 17 and many other undisputed autographs; M's do not, and must on the contrary be identified with the "Note-book" (1725) and other equally attested writings of Magdalena Bach, which correspond on all points. (Thus No. 9 was after all not in the composer's hand, Mrs. Clarke.) Marginal additions may be left out of account here. Short and inconclusive, their identity cannot affect the general argument. The upshot is that 35,021 shows abundant evidence of being in the composer's mature and coherent hand in $16\frac{3}{4}$ pieces, and in the remaining $4\frac{1}{4}$ the hand of his second wife, writing very probably under his supervision, since his hand always follows hers after one work, and in any case a trustworthy copyist. There is therefore not the slightest need to take any notice of the careless and impudent statements of Mr. F. Rothschild in *The Lost Tradition in Music* (pp. 194, note, and 250–52), in which he questions the authority and therefore alters the time-signature of No. 7 in the London autograph, alters and by implication questions Nos. 8, 9, 14 and 17 (London or Berlin!) on the same point, and by implication rejects the authority of the whole set, merely because these signatures disprove or modify his provocative notational hypothesis (see the case of the "Mass" choruses mentioned in Chapter XV here). The pretence of formed "tradition" is in fact most insecurely based on the score of certain documentary statements or a mere *I say*. Regrettably, some Bach editors have treated Rothschild's aspersion as if it were established criticism. For such reasons, and owing to the exceptional publicity which the Rothschild book has gained, partly owing to the unqualified advance support of Mr. Ernest Newman (on the dust-cover), it has been necessary to give this full account of the London manuscript now so satisfactorily clarified in its dual script of master and mate. If Emery's detective work is neat and well-knit, his cause is also noble and urgent.

Here, at least, London and Berlin are well met.

BIBLIOGRAPHY

[In view of the fashion for impressively extensive lists of books, I may inform the reader that, while I may not have read through every item enumerated below, it has at least "passed through my hands" except in one or two cases. With these exceptions, no entry represents a mere transference from another bibliographical list. I have tried to keep within practicable limits the selections from the vast material available under the first two headings.]

I. MUSIC BEFORE BACH

ANGLÈS, H., *La Música en la corte de Carlos V* (de Henestrosa) (Barcelona, 1944).

APEL, W., *Masters of the Keyboard* (complete illustrations) (Cambridge, Mass., 1947).

BEDBROOK, G. S., *Keyboard music from the Middle Ages to the Beginnings of the Baroque* (London, 1949).
"The Buxheim Organ Book," *Music Review*, **14**, 4 (November, 1953).
"The genius of Giovanni Gabrieli (1557–1612)," Ibid., **8**, 2 (May, 1947).

BORREN, C. VAN DEN, *The Sources of Keyboard Music in England* (London, 1914; original French edition, Brussels, 1912).

BUKOFZER, M., *Music in the Baroque Era* (London, 1948).

DICKINSON, A. E. F. "John Bull's fugal style," *Monthly Musical Record*, **84**, 961 (November, 1954).
"English virginal music," *Music Review*, **16**, 1 (February, 1955).

FROTSCHER, G., *Geschichte des Orgelspiels* (a most thorough survey). Two volumes (Berlin, 1935–36).

GHISLANZONI, A., *Storia della Fuga* (Milan, 1952).

HANDSCHIN, J., "Das Pedalklavier," *Zeitschrift für Musik*, **17**, 418.

JEPPESEN, K., *Die italienische Orgelmusik am Anfang des Cinquecento* (Copenhagen, 1943).

KASTNER, S., *Contribución al estudio de la música española y portuguesa* (Lisbon, 1941).

KINKELDEY, O., *Orgel und Klavier in der Musik des 16. Jahrhunderts* (Leipzig, 1910).

LANG, P. H., *Music in Western Civilization* (London, 1942, New York, 1941).

LOWINSKY, E. E., "English organ music of the Renaissance," *Musical Quarterly*, **39,** 3 and 4 (July and October, 1953).
Review of *Monumenta Musicae Belgicae*, Ibid., **40,** 4 (October, 1954).

MELLERS, W. H., "John Bull and English keyboard music," Ibid., **40,** 3 and 4 (July and October, 1954).

MEYER, B. VAN DEN SIGTENHORST, *Jan P. Sweelinck en zijn instrumentale muziek.* Two volumes (The Hague, 1934; 2nd edition, 1946-8).

MEYER, E., *English Chamber Music* (London, 1946).

MÜLLER-BLATTAU, J., *Grundzüge einer Geschichte der Fuge* (Königsberg, 1923; new edition, Cassel, 1931). (Organum to Pachelbel.)

NAGEL, W., *Geschichte der Musik in England.* Two volumes (Strassburg, 1894-7).

PLAMENAC, D., "The keyboard music of the 14th century in Codex Faenza 117," *Journal of the American Musicological Society*, **4,** 3 (1951).
"New light on Codex Faenza 117" (Utrecht, 1952).

POLS, A. M., *Uit Vlaanderen's Musikaal Verleden* (Louvain, 1936).

REDLICH, H. F., "Girolamo Frescobaldi," *Music Review*, **14,** 4 (November, 1953).

REESE, G., *Music in the Middle Ages* (London, 1941).

RITTER, A. G., *Zur Geschichte des Orgelspiels, vornehmlich des deutschen, im 14. bis zum Anfange des 18. Jahrhunderts.* Two volumes (Second volume: illustrations in modern notation. A pioneer survey) (Leipzig, 1884).

ROKSETH, Y., *La musique d'orgue au XVe siècle et au début du XVIe* (Paris, 1930).

SCHRADE, L., *Die handschriftliche Überlieferung der ältesten Instrumental-musik* (Lahr, 1931).

SEIFFERT, M., *Geschichte der Klaviermusik*, Band 1 (No more published) (A most thorough survey of the pre-Bach period) (Leipzig, 1899).

SHEDLOCK, J. S., "The evolution of fugue," *Proc. Mus. Ass.* **24** (1898).

STEVENS, D., *The Mulliner Book: a Commentary* (London, 1952).

SUTHERLAND, G., "The Ricercari of Jacques Buus," *Musical Quarterly*, **31,** 4 (October, 1945).

WALKER, E., *A History of Music in England.* (Oxford, 1907. Second edition, London, 1924. Revised and enlarged by J. A. Westrup, Oxford, 1952).
"An Oxford book of Fancies," *The Musical Antiquary* (January, 1912).

WASIELEWSKI, J. W. VON, *Geschichte der Instrumentalmusik im 16. Jahrhundert* (Berlin, 1878).

WINTERFELD, J., *Johannes Gabrieli und sein Zeitalter.* Three volumes (Berlin, 1834).

WOLF, J., "Zur Geschichte der Orgelmusik im vierzehnten Jahrhundert," *Kirchenmusikalisches Jahrbuch*, 14, (1899).

II. BACH

BRUYCK, C. D. VAN, *Technische u. aesthetische Analyse des W.K.* (Leipzig, 1867).

BUKOFZER, M., Op. cit.

DICKINSON, A. E. F., *The Art of J. S. Bach* (London, 1936. Revised edition, 1950).

GÉDALGE, A., *Traité de la fugue* (Illustrated profusely from Bach) (Paris, 1900).

GRACE, H., *The Organ Works of Bach* (London, 1922).

HAUPTMANN, M., *Erläuterungen zu J. S. Bachs "Kunst der Fuge"* (Leipzig, 1841).

HIGGS, J., "Bach's 'Art of Fugue'," *Proc. Mus. Ass.*, 3 (1877).

KNORR, I., *Die Fugen des "Wohltemperierten Klaviers" von J. S. B. in bildlicher Darstellung* (with E. and F. text). An appendix and supplement to the writer's *Lehrbuch der Fugen Komposition* (Thematic Analysis) (Leipzig, 1912).

MARTIN, B., *Untersuchungen zur Struktur der "Kunst der Fuge" J. S. Bachs* (Ratisbon, 1940).

NEUMANN, W., *J. S. Bachs Chorfuge: ein Beitrag zur Kompositionstechnik Bachs* (Leipzig, 1938).

PARRY, C. H. H., *J. S. Bach: The Story of the Development of a Great Personality* (The most illuminating study in print of Bach the musician, and of his fugal art in particular) (London, 1909. Revised by Emily Daymond, 1934).

PROUT, E., *Double Counterpoint* (Examples mainly from J. S. Bach) (London, 1891).
  Fugue (Examples mainly from J. S. Bach) (London, 1891).

SCHWEBSCH, E., *J. S. Bach und die "Kunst der Fuge"* (Scantily illustrated in proportion to its size) (Stuttgart, 1931).

SCHWEITZER, A., *J. S. Bach, le musicien-poète* (A study of Bach's art as the product and sign of religious conviction, by association with literary images) (Leipzig, 1905. English translation, two volumes, London, 1911).

SPITTA, P., J. S. Bach (The pioneer exposition of Bach's whole output and of its sources). Two volumes (Leipzig, 1873–80. English translation, three volumes, 1883–5).

THIELE, E., *Die Chorfugen J. S. Bachs* (Berne and Leipzig, 1936).

TOVEY, D. F., *A Companion to "The Art of Fugue"* (London, 1931).

III. MUSIC AFTER BACH

ALBRECHTSBERGER, J. G., *Gründliche Anweisung zur Composition*, Ed. von Seyfried, I.C. (Vienna, 1790. English translation, *Guide to Composition*, London, 1855).

BOETTICHER, W., *Robert Schumann: Einführung in Persönlichkeit und Werk* (This immense volume includes a study of the fugal origins of certain works in the light of a fresh survey of Schumann's sketches and notebooks, with quotations, in an appendix, from his projected text-book on fugue—along with a formidable biography in terms of the writer's acceptance of Nazi doctrine) (Berlin, 1941).

CHERUBINI, M. L. C. Z. S., *Cours de contrepoint et de la fugue* (Described as "largely the work of Halévy" in the article on the writer in *Grove's Dictionary of Music and Musicians*, 5th edition) (Paris, 1835).

DALE, K., Essay on the composer's piano music in *Schumann*, a symposium edited by Gerald Abraham (London, 1952).

DICKINSON, A. E. F., *Beethoven* (London, 1941).

"Beethoven's early fugal style" (with the first publication of the all but complete keyboard fugue in C, as found in the collection of Beethoven's sketches, B.M. ADD. MS. 29,801, and with two quotations from his studies with Albrechtsberger), *The Musical Times*, **96**, 1344 (February, 1955).

Essay on the composer's choral music in *Schubert*, a symposium edited by Gerald Abraham (London, 1946). (Cf. *Das Musikleben*, November, 1955.)

FROTSCHER, G., Op. cit.

GATSCHER, E., *Die Fugentechnik Max Regers in ihrer Entwicklung* (Stuttgart, 1925).

GÉDALGE, A., Op. cit.

GHISLANZONI, A., Op. cit. *Arte e tecnica della fuga* (Rome, 1953).

GRACE, H., *The Organ Works of Rheinberger* (London, 1925).

KNORR, I., *Lehrbuch der Fugen-Komposition* (Leipzig, 1911).

KURTH, E., *Grundlagen des linearen Kontrapunkts: Einführung in Stil und Technik von Bachs melodischer Polyphonie* (Berne, 1917).

LACH, R., *W. A. Mozart als Theoritiker* (With quotations from Mozart's fugal exercises, with facsimiles) (Vienna, 1918).

MARPURG, F. W., *Abhandlung von der Fuge* (A remarkably early commentary, quoting Bach, Berardi and Eberlin for examples) (Berlin, 1753–4. French edition, Berlin, 1756). As a supplement, and in order to provide examples of whole fugue, Marpurg produced the first part of a *Fugen-Sammlung* (Berlin, 1758), taken from works by C. P. E. Bach, Kirnberger and Graun. No further volume appeared. Previous to his treatise on fugue, Marpurg had produced, at the Leipzig Fair, a second issue (1752) of *The Art of Fugue* with a combative preface by himself. (English translation in *The Bach Reader*, ed. H. T. David and A. Mendel, London, 1946). He there forecasts the needed exegesis of fugue *per se* which he proposes to undertake.

NOTTEBOHM, G., *Beethoven's Studien*, Erster Band: *Beethoven's Unterricht bei J. Haydn, Albrechtsberger und Salieri* (This contains numerous and complete examples of Beethoven's studies in fugue in 2–4 parts, choral and double fugue, double counterpoint at the octave, 10th and 12th, and canon) (Leipzig and Winterthur, 1873). No further volume published.

OPPEL, R., "Albrechtsberger als Bindeglied zwischen Bach und Beethoven," *Neue Zeitschrift für Musik*, **78**.

PISTON, W., *Counterpoint* (London, 1949; New York, 1947).

RICHTER, E. F. E., *Lehre von der Fuge* (Leipzig, 1859. English translation, London, 1878).

SHEDLOCK, J. S., Op. cit.

VAUGHAN WILLIAMS, R., Article on Fugue in *Grove's Dictionary of Music and Musicians*, 5th edition (London, 1954).

GLOSSARY

ANSWER: the second delivery of a subject announced; hence, the melodic form which that delivery takes, sometimes apart from key; the "natural" answer being, more often than not, an inexact imitation.

REAL ANSWER: exact imitation of melodic curve.

TONAL ANSWER: a freer imitation, based on context.

ARPEGGIO: harmonic figures of melody, in *arpa* style.

AUGMENTATION: delivery at half normal speed, i.e. in notes of double-length, preserving some shape, but losing compactness.

BASS, FIGURED: an accompaniment on a given bass with harmony improvised from interval-signs underneath the bass, usually setting up a distinct harmonic rhythm and sonority.

CADENCE: a point of punctuation marked by the *fall* of the music, either melodically in the bass (or top) or by a decline of rhythmic energy, to a point of rest.

CANON: composition by rule; imitation by one "voice" of a phrase announced by another. Hence, a piece written entirely on this principle, usually with a change of lead from top to bottom (or vice versa). The leading voice is often called *dux;* the following, *comes.* The melodic interval at which the imitation takes place is measured *upwards* from the pitch of the operative *dux,* at whatever octave this occurs. Canons are usually at a primary harmonic interval of a fifth or a fourth, or on the next degree (second or seventh), but can be found at the other intervals.

CLOSE CANON (*stretto*): imitation close enough to produce cross-rhythm, fresh harmony and usually a rival key interest.

CODA: see EPISODE.

COMES: see CANON.

COUNTER-EXPOSITION: a second set of entries, preserving the fundamental tonality.

COUNTERPOINT: a line in disagreement, melodic or rhythmic, with a Point or phrase heard at the same time.

COUNTER-SUBJECT: an integral accompaniment of the subject, introduced in the answer or as a later development.

DEGREES OF THE SCALE are named: (i) *tonic* defining the Tone or basic note, *dominant* controlling the tonic, and *mediant* between them, with *subdominant* and *submediant* for similar intervals downwards; (ii) *supertonic* but (unlike the French *sous-tonique*) *leading-note* (moving to tonic). The exact sound implied depends on whether major or minor scale, or a modification of either, is intended. The sound-relation of these seven degrees is given below for the key of C major and minor, with common semitonal additions and variants.

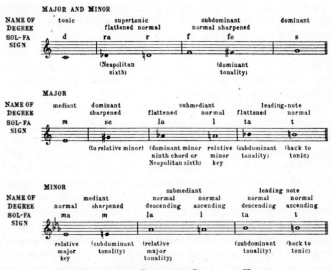

STEPS IN THE CIRCULAR CHAIN OF KEYS

(With normal or "diatonic" pitch-detail as indicated by key-signature, with sharpened sixth and seventh notes in the minor keys in certain contexts, chiefly **s l t d¹, d¹ t d¹**. The *dominant* of each key is the nearest to the right; *subdominant*, the left.)

Example 64

DIMINUTION: delivery in notes of half length (or less).

DOUBLE-FUGUE: a fugue on two subjects announced (i) separately (sometimes called *full* double-fugue here); (ii) together from the start (uncommon in Bach).

DUX: see CANON.

ENTRY: a recognizable delivery of the subject.

FALSE ENTRY: a partial delivery, abandoning the subject after one phrase or less, or, more subtly, repeating the first phrase in sequence and thus giving the illusion of completeness.

EPISODE: a more or less characteristic passage between entries. An episode which follows the last entry forms a *coda*.

INVERSION: (i) where not otherwise stated, *melodic* inversion by reversing the direction of a subject or (rarely) part, exchanging ascent and descent but preserving the original shape in variant detail. The inversion is usually at the fifth (i.e. degrees 1–8 become 12–5), but other exchanges are sometimes workable. The process is confined by Bach to very formal or decorative subjects, except in A.F.11 and after. In *Canon by inversion* the *comes* inverts *dux*, whatever the resultant relation to the subject.

(ii) *contrapuntal*, changing round the voices in the delivery of two or more lines. Inversions of phrase are normally *at the octave* (up or down) but may be *at the tenth*, *twelfth*, etc., thus changing the basic harmony more vitally.

KEY: Changes of key are commonly expressed, as they should be heard, in terms of the original tonic, whether recent or remote in recollection. *In the dominant* thus means, in the key of the dominant. Changes may be made in two main directions, sharpward and flatward, typified by the dominant and the subdominant or inverted dominant. Recoveries of key will naturally be flatward and sharpward. This constant veering of experience, or aid to experience of other contrasts, may be summarized in the major in a few token chords, the differences for minor keys being shown in brackets. The

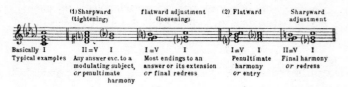

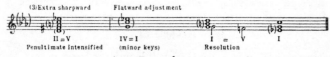

Example 65

change from major to minor, or vice versa, is more subtle, but modulations to the minor tend to be stimulating, while modulations from minor to major are in the nature of a relaxation. References have often been made vaguely to changes from a major key "to the minor," or the reverse, indicating a difference of effect to which the degree (in either sense) is not pertinent. In a major key the *relative minor* is strictly the submediant, and in a minor key the *relative major* is the mediant. The *primary* keys are the tonic and dominant, and later also frequently the subdominant.

When a fresh key is truly established, it tends to put up its own flags of tonality, and in many contexts "the dominant" has meant "the dominant of the moment," and other references accordingly, because this is how the music sounds. I have tried to be clear on this point, but the reader must be prepared to gauge by context whether a new key or the original key is the basis.

Chords are named in this contextual sense. The *dominant seventh* is in the first place the major chord of *the* dominant with the seventh above it, the *dominant ninth* adds the ninth in the same sense, each promoting the tonic chord and key, but either chord may be used *mutatis mutandis* on a new bass or root, promoting or confirming a new key. Based on the supertonic, for example, either chord promotes the *key* of the dominant (of the main key). The *diminished seventh* which marks the extremities of the dominant ninth when the bottom note is omitted—no longer a dominant chord but having a similar tonic-controlling effect—may likewise be used to promote either the main key or a fresh one; as a broadly symmetrical four-pointed chord, any one example can actually be used to point in one of four particular directions, by making each note the bottom of the seventh in turn, and reconstruing the chord accordingly. For example, in the *adagio* setting of "Et expecto" (B minor Mass), bars 18–19, the same general sounds make first D sharp and then B sharp the pivotal note of two diminished sevenths. This disintegrating and independent chord is thus a refreshing challenge to the settled harmony of the diatonic or eight-note scale. It bounces into fugue from opera with a Mephisophelean "What is your will?" It is also a trenchant penultimate chord in cadences, as a plain pro-dominant sonority.

The *augmented sixth* marks the extremities of the combination of submediant, tonic and sharpened subdominant in a minor key (**la dⁱ feⁱ**), leading strongly to the dominant chord. It is thus a striking pre-dominant chord in cadences, either in the Italian version given above, or, by adding supertonic or mediant, in the French or German variety. It is used by Bach in any key (e.g. the submediant minor in O., F). The chord of the flattened supertonic (*Neapolitan sixth* when the third is in the bass) is another pre-dominant chord used rarely but as freely. There are other such chords, contrived by "sliding" semitones and ornamental diversions, but as they were not the product of national or municipal style in opera they have not acquired names, and no one has so far bothered to improve on a technical definition.

MODE: a scale tabulation of the melodic basis of a musical setting in reference to the final or central note, originally made for or from the psalm-chants. The modes here concerned, which borrow their names (no more) from the tribal terms of ancient Greek theory, may now be conveniently distinguished as white-note scales on the piano, as follows: Dorian, D to D; Phrygian, E to E; Lydian, F to F; Mixo-lydian, G to G; Aeolian, A to A. "Rationalization" of the modes consisted of conflating the first, second and fifth of these in the ascending and descending minor scale, and the third and fourth in the major scale. This went on for at least two centuries (1500–1700), and even in Bach's time the modal chorales and idiom were not obsolete, "modern" only in the cadences.

NEAPOLITAN SIXTH: see under KEY (*fin.*).

RESTATEMENT: a final (or midway) assertion of the subject in or around the main key, in a set of two or more entries.

SEQUENCE: the extension of a phrase in one part by repeating, often serially, some feature of it a step (or more) higher or lower; i.e. development horizontally, where imitation is always vertical.

SUBJECT: that part of the initial phrase which preserves its identity in later entries, sometimes shortened, inverted or otherwise altered later. A second or third subject may be announced separately, but usually proves subsidiary. "There can be only one subject to a fugue" (R. V. W. in *Grove*).

TONALITY: key-tendency or key-definition.

TRIAD: the *three* of a note with the third and fifth above.

TRIPLE-FUGUE: an extension of double-fugue in either sense.

VOICES: a term used in instrumental fugue to convey an analogy with the vocal consort and for convenient reference. It is not ever clear which "voice" enters first, but it transpires later that it was top, bottom or inner voice, which it is useful to distinguish by a vocal name.

INDEX TO MUSIC

Main references are printed in bold type where necessary. The first page only of such references will be given, except where an allusion begins at the foot of a page and does not mention the index-heading until later. In general, a citation of consecutive pages will indicate a series of isolated references. I have not presumed to inform the reader when there are two references to a heading on one page.

Keys are major where not otherwise stated.

In some instances the specification of title, etc., is ampler here than in the main text, or is in the original language, where an English equivalent has been used in the text. This is in order better to define a written source, where this may be desirable for discriminating readers, but would burden the main commentary. I have not employed the Bach catalogue, however, of Wolfgang Schmieder, on the assumption that few of the working musicians for whom the book is intended will be able easily to consult it. The point only concerns a handful of stray and mostly early keyboard works, of whose existence few are aware. The mature but isolated keyboard works, and the more numerous organ pieces worth considering, are all sufficiently characteristic in one way and another that there can be no serious doubt which work is intended, after reading a line or two of comment. In the doubtful cases, I have fallen back on the Bach Geschellschaft edition, since this is at present the most authoritative statement of the musical text available in each case, and assembles all the "uncollected" pieces in two or three volumes.

In some cases the reader may turn up a reference, only to find the music considered scarcely worthy of comment, as fugue or as art. But if my judgment holds, that is not my fault. I should be much more to blame if I made a "song and dance" of a trifle, or a historical achievement of a pipe-dream.

I. BACH

(A) Keyboard Fugues, Fugal Movements, and Canons

[1] *Bach Geschellschaft* edition, vol. 42
[3] Ib., vol. 36.

[2] Ib., vol. 3.
[4] Ib., vol. 45.

(B) ORGAN FUGUES, FUGAL MOVEMENTS, AND MISCELLANEOUS PIECES

[1] Prelude/Fantasia with Fugue by traditional association, rather than by decisive evidence.

[1] Now judged *not* to be in Bach's hand. (*Music and Letters*, July, 1955.)

II. BEFORE BACH
(Keyboard, below, may mean clavier or organ)

[1] See an article by Thurston Dart in *Music and Letters*, January, 1955, on the possible identity of family.

---

[1] A brief survey of relevant matter is in time for publication. A full account of the collection as a whole is in hand.

III. AFTER OR CONTEMPORARY WITH BACH

[1] Also contemplated for string orchestra, it seems, for the possible autograph of B.M. Add. MS. 28,966—following a copy of K. 426 in another hand—shows a division of the violoncello part into violoncelli and contrabassi in bars 110–15. (See, however, p. 277.)

ADDITIONAL NOTE ON MOZART'S ADAGIO AND FUGUE, K.546

With all respect to Dr. H. Redlich (Eulenburg edition, 1953), the evidence of Mozart's intentions is anything but positive—

1. The script of the Adagio, the more crucial movement, is "missing." The only script of the fugue (B.M.), so far from being a clear autograph, exhibits four kinds of ink: (*a*) pp. 1–18, upper half: the score of K.426 (plus barring for K.546 below), in a hand not generally accepted as Mozart's; (*b*) pp. 1–11, lower half: the score of K.546, bars 1–75, written out very scrappily and hastily, not in a hand easily identifiable as Mozart's; (*c*) pp. 12–18, lower half: the remainder of K.546, with bass part divided as stated, all written normally and in a hand not typically Mozartean but rather resembling that of K.426; (*d*) (darker) "violoncelli" and "contrabassi" over these lines.

2. The early edition for string quartet (Hoffmeister, Vienna, *c.* 1791 by Redlich), since incorporated in the standard edition (XIV, 27, Breitkopf and Härtel), is not, therefore, necessarily discredited by so dubious and improvisatory a script, which looks like an adaptation and may well have been one. Mozart's own catalogue reference to a "short adagio for 2 violins, viola and bass" for the two-piano fugue implies a quartet, and every van Swieten precedent favours this. The transciprion is complete without the double-bass bars.

3. As music the fugue, being closely woven and transcribed keyboard stuff, can perhaps stand the rougher orchestral manifold and heavier bass. Beethoven had a go later. But the extended spacing of the adagio (e.g. bar 42) demands the rarer quality of a solo-quartet; and, while odd unisons of bass are common enough orchestrally, the initial bottom C, playable only at the unison on the double-bass, is a weak orchestral start, but a trenchant pitch-location on a violoncello. So, too, the blunt unison entry of bars 31–2. Material evidence, then, is not at all firmly in favour of the use of the string body, which seems to some present listeners, as to past editors, to be the surrender of individuality to the majesty of numbers, as in some renderings of Beethoven's Op. 133 but without the pretext of technique at unprecedented stretch. Will no quartet risk a trial performance of this admirable work?

TECHNICAL INDEX